W9-CED-620

CLEVE JONES
founder of the AIDS Memorial Quilt

with JEFF DAWSON

STITCHING A
REVOLUTION

The Making

of an Activist

STITCHING A
REVOLUTION

HarperSanFrancisco
A Division of HarperCollins*Publishers*

PHOTO CREDITS

Grateful acknowledgment is given to the following individuals and organizations for the photographs that appear in this book. Photos "Castro Street Rally," "Cleve Jones's Birthday," and "Birth of the Quilt" appear courtesy of Rink Foto. San Francisco City Hall, Stella crew, Joseph Durant sewing, Jack Caster in workshop, Gert McMullin with Rick Solomon, circle of volunteers, and Lily Tomlin photos all appear courtesy of Gert McMullin, from her private collection. Men grieving photo appears courtesy of Chris Hardy/*San Francisco Examiner*. Rosa Parks, Elizabeth Taylor, Quilt on the Washington Mall photos appear courtesy of the NAMES Project. Bill and Hillary Clinton photo appears courtesy of the White House. Helen Rupert Jones and Vera Davy Kirk (photographed by Elizabeth Jones Ettinger), Blythe Randolph Jones, Marion Jones dancing, young Cleve in Amsterdam (photographed by Scott Rempel), subpoena, Christopher Street cover, Jesse Jackson and Art Agnos, Cleve with family photos all from the author's private collection.

HarperSanFrancisco Publishers will donate a percentage of the net profits of this book to the NAMES Project Foundation.

Library of Congress Cataloging-in-Publication Data
Jones, Cleve.
ISBN 0-06-251641-8 (cloth)
ISBN 0-06-251642-6 (pbk.)
Stitching a revolution : the making of an activist - Cleve Jones, with Jeff Dawson.—1st ed.
1. Jones, Cleve. 2. AIDS activists—California—Biography.
3. AIDS (Disease)—Patients—California—Biography.
4. NAMES Project AIDS Memorial Quilt. I. Dawson, Jeff. II. Title.
RC607.A26 J6573 2000
362.1'96792'0092—dc21 99-052721
[B]

00 01 02 03 04 ❖RRD(H) 10 9 8 7 6 5 4 3 2

To my parents, Austin and Marion Jones;

my sister, Elizabeth Jones Ettinger;

and the memory of my friends who did not survive

CONTENTS

CONTENTS

INTRODUCTION

OCTOBER 7, 1989
THE ELLIPSE
WASHINGTON, D.C.

THOUSANDS OF PEOPLE stand on a grid of canvas walkways. Within the grid lie brightly colored panels of fabric, each bearing a name in cut-out cloth or paint or ribbon. Over a distant public-address system the names are read aloud. The reading is endless; some of the names are famous—politicians, movie stars, sports heroes—but most are unknown. Some say only "Joe," or "my brother," or "my darling daughter." The crowd of people is nearly silent, reverential. We hear only the litany of names and occasional sobs, whispered words.

And then the silence is shattered by the sound of an engine roaring to life on the White House lawn. The throbbing increases and lifts overhead above the trees: a helicopter whirls into the air above the White House. Thousands of figures turn their faces skyward, hands shielding their eyes from the noonday sun. And then a different sound begins, muted at first, but swelling furiously against the blast of the helicopter rotors; the thousands of people now are pointing at the sky, and their voices are thunderous: "Shame, shame, shame!"

That day, nearly a decade ago, when President George Bush so casually flew off to more important duties was on my mind one afternoon as I drove home from a meeting with the NAMES Project staff. We were planning the tenth-anniversary display, wondering if President Bill Clinton would recognize the Quilt, as Bush had not. As I sat there, among so many smart young people, I realized that forty-six of the original team members had died. Is that what age is, a whittling away? I'm only forty-four. I must unwhittle the block of memory that is me.

Six years ago I came to this house in Villa Grande, California, to die. Instead I have survived. Thanks to tiny diamond-shaped pills called Epivir, my health and vigor and a certain ambition revved back up. I found myself in a tomb and decided it looked more like a home. What to do? Travel, of course. I'd never given that up. It's how I make a living— traveling around the country giving speeches. And yet, as anyone will tell you who's made final preparations, a second chance is bittersweet. There is hesitancy after the initial euphoria. Why I'm here—drinking coffee, working at the computer—when so many are gone is unanswerable.

I did all those things that were, are, supposed to kill you quick: the baths; drinking, smoking; coming home at dawn, dazed and sated, head filled with music and clothes scented with someone's cologne. What was his name? I used to scoff at the HIV-negatives whipped by survivor's guilt onto a therapist's couch. Now I'm not so sure.

I am here now and alive. I don't often visit cemeteries and wouldn't trade places, but I can at least try to make sense of my own first chapter so that my second chance is both a tribute to lost friends and a foundation for what lies ahead.

I'm writing this in my study, a small room at the back of my house shaded by ancient redwoods and looking out onto a narrow lane. After these years of living in Villa Grande, a tiny village on the Russian River ninety miles north of San Francisco and a world away from Washington, D.C., I can usually pick out my neighbors by the sound of their footsteps. There's Mr. Greer tripping along after his whippets. And the slow-moving Brody, who comes by frequently, wanting to say hi or borrow a rake; he's never in a hurry. If I'm on the phone, he just nods and keeps on walking. Most days he finds an open door.

The film director Gus Van Sant called this morning. He's sending me the script, probably the twentieth version of Randy Shilts's *The Mayor of Castro Street*, a biography of the gay politician Harvey Milk. He wants to know facts from those early days in San Francisco, Harvey stories, impressions of an era now cloaked in legend. I've got stacks of material, date books, diaries. Notes from Harvey's campaigns for city supervisor, old speeches I gave in my twenties, not so old speeches I gave in my own mercifully brief campaign for supervisor. Love letters. I've kept too much, probably. The first Quilt designs are in my desk, near at hand. I always wanted the panels laid flat on the ground so people could touch them. The closets in my house are historic minefields. At least the photo of me shaking hands with a rather strained looking President Bush is positioned properly over the toilet. In all the political memoirs, he's called a "kind man," "extraordinarily sensitive," "approachable." I remember an icy dismissal. "Kinder and gentler" indeed. That was a strange day. I'll return to that.

What shall I tell Gus? I first met Harvey on the sidewalks of Castro Street, where so much began. He was passing out fliers and we got into a conversation. I think it was his second run for supervisor. He tried to pick me up, and I was kind of rude. Not my type, I said to myself, too old. Sorry, I smiled. And he laughed and changed the subject to politics, something north of his crotch and closer to his heart.

But that's a private memory with not enough fireworks for Gus, certainly not for his potential producer, Oliver Stone. I'm sure the scriptwriters will dismiss most of what I say, but I hope they will at least give the movie a sense of Harvey's humor. Later, after his third successful run for supervisor, when we'd become friends and allies, he would encourage me to wear tight, butt-cupping jeans to city hall. "Leave one of the buttons undone," Harvey would suggest, winking. "Danny boy will notice that." He was referring to Dan White, a fellow supervisor and his eventual murderer. It was funny at the time.

But who is Harvey Milk? A man from the '70s who led the gay movement and was assassinated because of it. I think he was a great man, complicated, one of those heroes who rise up like a force of nature and part the cultural tides. Do people remember him? Do the young people have a sense of how he changed the world, and will they remember the Quilt when—oh wonderful day—it's packed off to a museum?

I have been warned that writing is a different sort of animal than speaking. There's no barometer to gauge your success. Instead of an audience with changing facial clues telling you you're doing well, or worse, screeching chairs announcing departures, writing is solitary, and the only response you get is from the paper. But that doesn't concern me so much as does the intent to be truthful. Everyone's memories sort out differently over time. I can only hope that mine are credible and my readers patient as I weave present and past into my own remembered history. The present will intrude, not only because it's a trigger to memory but because it is the link to what's come before—the first bloom of gay liberation in the '70s, the rising panic that changed to the apathy and fury of the '80s, and now, when a cure, strange word, may make that journey from lab vial to front page and maybe—just maybe—even to the people who need it.

Where should I begin? Over my desk on the wall above the couch where I nap too often, there's a picture of my great-aunt Frankie, christened Francis, in an old oval frame. Nothing was ever said about Frankie. She was just this woman who used a man's name, who lived with Stella, another woman, for most of her life. But then everyone has a gay relative, if they think long enough; Frankie wouldn't provide sufficient spice for a curtain-raiser. And here's a picture of my friend the AIDS journalist Randy Shilts laughing beside his stuffed grizzly bear. What party was that? They're wearing matching pearls, double strands like Jackie O's. There's a Neiman Marcus bag in the bear's paw, a bottle of Calistoga water in Randy's. The image is telling, but too flip for my purposes. But then, Randy was never appropriate. Should I follow his lead?

Why do I now fix on Rosa Parks, a woman whose experience is a million miles away from my own? When she handed me the quilts she'd made for her neighbors, she wanted to relish only their lives, not the divisions—just memorialize her friends and what they'd meant to her. *You're doing a wonderful thing, young man,* she'd said. There were no tears in her eyes, just a message for me to continue. Did my fatigue show? Did she see that the death threats and potshots had taken their toll? *Dismiss them,* she seemed to say, *and grow old.* A challenge. I brighten and feel combative.

And there on the bookshelf, pushing rudely into view, is Larry Kramer's novel. *Faggots!* shouts the title, loud even in this quiet house.

Why do they stick in my mind, these polar opposites? One wearing a Sunday hat, the other shaved and combat-ready. Perhaps because Rosa Parks, like the Quilt, symbolizes the power of community—something I've always fought for, something stitched into every panel. Larry Kramer stands publicly for separatism, a self-defeating stance. I've had my share of leading angry crowds against police barricades and throwing myself against the hard blue line. And it was effective and necessary. But today's conflicts are not those of fifteen, ten, even five years ago. If I do get angry nowadays, my anger is directed at those who refuse to recognize that times have changed, that we have moved forward. Whenever Larry tells me he wants to burn the Quilt, I say fine, dear—but let's wrap you up in it before the first match is thrown. If given the choice, I choose the strategies less likely to end in blood on the streets. So much for Larry. He'll only laugh. And so I begin.

EARLY ONE AFTERNOON in February 1987, Joseph Durant and I went into my backyard and made the first two quilts. It had been months since my friend Marvin died, and I had not allowed myself to think about him and why I loved him so much, and why within moments of meeting we knew we'd be best friends for life. I thought about his family and his father's experience of liberating the Nazi death camp at Ohrdruf. And I knew that when he looked at his ravaged son lying in the hospital bed, he saw those gaunt faces and the bony fingers grasping the fences.

And I decided that everything that was Marvin, his drive and ambition, his personality, sense of humor, sarcasm, the way he moved on a stage and on the dance floor—that everything had to do with the fact that Marvin was a Jew and a homosexual: two classes of people that had been subject to genocide—as Marvin frequently pointed out. And in my lame attempt to communicate that, I cut out triangle stencils, some blue and some pink, overlapped to form the Star of David. I lettered his name in capitals then stepped back and thought, Well, this is a piece of shit, Marvin would hate this. He'd want something that could hang in Bloomingdale's if not in the Museum of Modern Art, thank you very much.

I looked over at Joseph's quilt. He'd been painting furiously without speaking for some time. There was a stormy red sunset sky and flowing script in the center spelling out "Ed Mock." Ed was a very tall, handsome black man from Oakland, a member of the Black Panthers who'd become a choreographer and dancer. Joseph opened a can of gold paint, took off his shoes and socks, dipped his feet in the paint, and danced across the fabric, leaving golden footprints on the stormy sky. It was beautiful.

Months later, when we brought the Quilt to Washington, D.C., for its first display in 1987, we thought these handmade testimonials would put a face on statistics and change the world. I thought of the Quilt as evidence. So many had died, and there'd been no memorial. Parents would come in and take the ashes, the furniture, leaving nothing behind. If there was an obituary, and often there was not, it would describe the cause of death as cancer. The slate was wiped clean, as if this person had never been. Close friends were erased; lovers were never identified. Every one of us, whether friend or family, felt the empty echo of loss and grief and saw no way to express it. We were on the wrong side of a cultural canyon. I wanted to change all that, and believed that when we unfolded thousands of quilts on the National Mall, the stony walls of Congress would come tumbling down and the nation would awaken— that our quilt, my quilt, would crash through the fear and indifference.

IN ALL THE years we've been traveling with the Quilt, there's been very little real trouble. I was picketed by the Ku Klux Klan in Fresno, California—six hoodlums, faces hidden in sheets, hollering from a pickup truck. There was a guy in Missouri who was going to sue us and "come after us" if we displayed the quilt his son's lover had made.

We used to see a lot of anger and desperation. The dead person's gay family would send us a quilt, and then soon after an indignant letter from the biological family would arrive saying angrily, "Do not display the quilt sent by our son's friends." "You don't have our permission! Take our son's name out!" Often, Mom and Dad don't have a clue that their son is sick, let alone gay, until that last final call when, all of a sudden, he's dying.

In time, many of these families made quilts, too. And when they attend a Quilt display, they've reached a sort of peace with memory, usually believing, at least outwardly, that gayness and the virtues of family are not enemies locked in a fight to the death. But at the confusing moment of receiving that last call, when a stranger's voice tells them that Bob or

Larry or John or Joan is in the hospital and would like to see them one last time, they often panic. They haven't seen their child in years. And then there's that uncomfortable flight away from home to New York or San Francisco or West Hollywood or D.C., and they find themselves in an unfamiliar America. Strangers, foreigners really, are taking care of their child. Washing his sores, emptying the bedpan, changing the pic line. The pills are separated and counted out according to hourly dosage. Mom and Dad stiffen when they notice the people around them—an earring, a limp wrist. The pictures on the bedside table show all these laughing people, none of whom they know. Their son's body is turned and washed. The telephone rings and someone goes to get groceries. "Don't forget the toothpaste." It's all so matter-of-fact, so intimate. And they feel replaced.

Who was this person, their child? Whose fault is this? With luck, all the surface differences fade in the urgency. The parents recognize what's really important: that these people are kind and their son is sick and hurting. Many times, the long-separated parents are just blown away by the drama of seeing their dying son. Especially the fathers. And you look at your friend's father, standing there, hands rammed in his pockets looking out to God knows where, and try to imagine what he's feeling. You fight back the urge to shake him, and then you take a deep breath and pray that this father will open his eyes and realize that the separating distance is just an arm's length. This one has come to his son's side; many don't. He has to wake up on his own, in his own time.

Usually, they do. The resentment and confusion are lessening as AIDS has spread to more recent, less secretive generations. People talk more now, and the Quilt has become so much a part of the American experience with the epidemic that we don't even have to recruit panels any longer. They just keep coming in.

WHETHER I'M SPEAKING to an audience in Kansas, California, or Massachusetts, the story most people come to hear is of how the Quilt began. Somehow hearing that story seems to give comfort and a continuance to what is beyond understanding. I tell it swiftly, in forty minutes, up there at the microphone in front of all those searching faces. I love telling that story. And usually it is enough, at least for the time being. That is what I do: travel the country and speak about the Quilt, then step aside and listen as they walk silently to the podium, pronounce their beloved's name, hand over a quilt, and step back into their worlds.

I say that the Quilt really began when I'd reached rock bottom. By the mid–80s, friends were dying daily, I'd been attacked and stabbed for being gay, and then I myself was diagnosed with the virus. My own suffering was not untypical of that of thousands of other gay men and women, but the AIDS epidemic was ignored, compartmentalized as a small localized tragedy, like a serial killer whose victims were expendable, and relegated to the back pages of the American psyche.

There were, though, pockets of outrage, people who would not go gently into the night. I was standing with just such a crowd of protesters on a wet and foggy San Francisco evening in November 1985. We'd covered the walls of San Francisco's old Federal Building with cardboard posters bearing the names of people who had died of AIDS. It was such a startling image. The wind and rain tore some of the cardboard loose, but people stood there for hours reading the names. At near midnight I was telling myself, *Go home, Cleve. It's been a good night, get some rest.* But something held me there, something to do with an inexpressible wish, a sorrow unarticulated. I couldn't leave. It's my habit to wander through crowds and listen to what they're saying, and so I did that for perhaps the fifth time, until I realized something was happening. In all the pain these names conjured up, there was release, a sort of exhalation of our tight-held emotion. My eyes scanned the wall one last time and then stopped. It reminded me of a quilt, like the one made for me by my great-grandmother back in Bee Ridge, Indiana. A warm, comforting blanket, a patchwork of family history, a treasured keepsake each generation of my family passed on to the next. And then it was as if a slide had dropped into place, and in an eerily prescient scenario, I saw my future. There, spread out in perfect panorama, was a single quilt made of thousands of quilts connected as one and rolling over the Mall in Washington, D.C., and up to the steps of the Capitol. All the silence and fear and faith and love, every emotion of knowing and losing a loved one, was collected in one great memorial and laid out at the nation's door, symbol to symbol. In that moment, I knew we needed a monument, our own memorial to those we'd lost. And I knew deep inside exactly how it would one day appear.

Within a year and a half, three events propelled my vision into reality: grief at losing my best friend, Marvin; fear at finding out that I, too, was positive; and rage at the heterosexual world because two boys, skinheads, had stabbed me and run away laughing as I lay bleeding in the gutter. Of course these points weren't clearly marked signposts or burning bushes. But one thing I've always known is that you play the hand you've been dealt. And that you act. It's a question of survival. These three moments, together, changed my life.

CHAPTER ONE

EARLY YEARS

N OT UNUSUALLY, I had a happy childhood, full of encouraging relatives and the sort of peace and stability that are said to be necessary for rearing well-adjusted children. I have no memories of my parents ever fighting, not once. They loved my sister, Elizabeth, and me, and we knew we were loved. Perhaps equally important, my parents planted within us a strong sense of family, the idea that we were part of a chain running back through generations of Joneses and Kirks and all their accomplishments, both small and large.

But contrary to logic, which would have said, "You will be loved for yourself whether you are as smart as your father the college professor or as strong and successful as your grandfather," I knew from an early age that I must hide my true self. I lived, as did most every gay boy or lesbian girl, a paradox. Outwardly normal, we were, we felt, inwardly flawed. Irrevocably so. It took me many years to resolve that conflict and in the resolution find the seeds of activism.

I was born right in the middle of the century in the middle of the country—in 1954 in Indiana—to a farming family that had, like so much of the country, left the farm during the Great Depression and found itself working in the city and living in suburbia.

My parents were teachers, and we had an itinerant life, moving from college to college, from Rochester, New York, to Pittsburgh, Pennsylvania, and finally to Phoenix, Arizona. But in all our traveling there was the anchor of family: Thanksgiving and Christmas along with all those long endless summers of childhood that always began with our thrice yearly migration by car to my grandfather's house on Southfield Road in Birmingham, Michigan.

I have wonderful memories of his high old place, bounded by a victory garden in the back and rows of iris and lilies on one side and green lawn rolling to the street in front. The house itself was three stories and made of stone painted white. I remember it as a kind of palace with echoing halls and high ceilings and lots of rooms—some secret, like my grandfather's library with its smell of pipe smoke and leather and pictures on the walls of Papa, as I called him, and his friends standing stiffly side by side in the formal style of those days. Later I discovered that many of the men in the photographs were politicians he had known— mayors, state officials—and that the one with the big belly crossed by a watch fob was a senator. What they were celebrating I never knew exactly, but even as a child I understood that we Joneses had a connection to government and politics. It seemed a natural thing to be involved, an honorable pursuit, worth a frame on the wall.

Along with his vast-seeming house there were other grand aspects of Grandfather, testaments to his power. Where I was just Cleve, or Cleve Edward Jones when I'd done wrong, he had many names. I called him Papa, but when Grandma or his old friends addressed him it was as Casey, as in Casey Jones, the mythic train engineer. Also, I'd seen that the name on his strongbox and on his driver's license was Blythe Randolph Jones. Unlike everyone else, he needed many different names, further proof of his power and mystery.

He was a big man with huge hands and a square-jawed, handsome face, and was always formally dressed. He traveled a lot in his work, and whenever he went to Hong Kong he came back with a new silk suit—

handmade, he said, by Mr. Chu, a wonderful little man. He'd put his hand just a few inches over my head . . . *Almost your size, Cleve.*

His word was law. When I was very young, my great-aunt Katherine brought her fiancé to dinner and fled in tears when Papa slammed his fist on the table and told the man, from Virginia, to "leave my house this instant." Katherine's fiancé had used the word *nigger,* a cardinal sin that not even the mantle of family would excuse.

Sometimes his harshness was, at least in retrospect, troubling. One day my grandmother lost her keys and asked me, conspiratorially, to find them. *If you do,* she whispered, *I'll give you twenty dollars*—a fortune in those days. I promptly found them, and as I reached out for the promised twenty, eyes aglow, she said, holding tight to the reward, "Swear you'll never tell Papa I lost the keys." I swore. We had secrets, she and I.

If there was one defining activity for Papa, it was when he sat in state at the head of his long table overseeing twenty relatives, more if extra settings were squeezed into the corners. He loved to eat; it wasn't unusual for him to eat two steaks at one sitting. But I think he took an equal enjoyment from watching his clan dig into the heavily laden platters and hearing the talk, always loud and boisterous, as we feasted. *Feast* is the right word. When one dish was empty, magically there was Grandma in an apron, carrying in another platter heaped with yet more of her famous barbecued chicken or the honeyed applesauce she made out of fruit from the trees in back. Very often there were surprises: sweets from the Far East, rich liquors from Mexico. One Thanksgiving Papa had lobsters flown in all the way from Maine. I remember walking into the kitchen and watching horrified as Grandma tossed them live into boiling water, and later refusing stubbornly to join in as the rest of the family cracked their stiff red carcasses with pliers.

And those enormous meals always seemed to end with generational stories—old people reminding each other of conversations told by old people when they were young. Papa and his sisters, Great-Aunt Katherine and Great-Aunt Frankie, would push their chairs back from the table and top each other's tales of the days when ancestral Joneses lived in log cabins and hoisted deer meat on ropes up into the trees so bears wouldn't steal it, of when the Model T Ford had to be pulled out of the mud by mules and of how precious writing paper was and of how rough life was in the old days but how work, that sacred work ethic, always pulled them through.

As Aunt Frankie died before I was ten, she is something of a mystery to me and I suppose to the entire family. In photographs she appears as a stern woman with short hair and trousers, standing not beside her brother, my grandfather, but off to the side of everyone else; with us, yet alone. But she wasn't alone. She lived for twenty-seven years with a woman named Stella, whom she invariably addressed as Miss Kerr and who always called her Miss Jones. Stella, it is said, wore dresses and had soft curling hair and a sweet smile. Were they lovers? Certainly they fit the rigid coding of the time, femme and butch. But when I ask my father about Frankie, he says we have no evidence that she and Stella were actually having sex. So, in deference to my father, I must say that we have no proof, no family photographs, just those twenty-seven years.

Though Stella was absent, at least in my memory and in reticent family lore, most all the other relatives came to those holiday dinners. My grandfather Arthur Kirk had died when I was four, but his wife, my grandmother—or Nana, as we called her—was always there. They had emigrated from England before the Second World War, and though she was about chest high to Papa and not nearly so intimidating, Nana stood her ground with grace and a tart English wit. She also had many names: Vera Marion Alexis Spearing Davy Kirk. And when she felt that the Jones history had been adequately glorified by tales of farming and pioneering in the Midwest, Nana would start telling her own stories of the life she and Grandpa Kirk, a silversmith, had lived in the artistic bohemia of London in the '20s. Those were fabled days, of skipping dinners to save money in order to buy art supplies or tickets to a performance by Isadora Duncan. Nana felt, I think, a strong impulse to represent the artistic Kirk side of the family against the rationality of the Jones heritage. There must have been a certain rivalry there, not only of whose legends were more vivid, but of which ones would most impress my young, eager ears.

"The nights during the war," she would say in her clipped British accent, ". . . the nights were most horrid." Her soft, almost translucent hand would reach out to mine. "This was when I was about your age, Cleve, living in London. . . . I'll never forget one hot summer night in 1917. We heard explosions and leapt from our beds out onto the balcony, and there by the light of flares we saw a German zeppelin looming into view, like a dark flying whale as big as the British Museum. And then it trembled and a little flame shot out from the side, and then as if in slow motion it listed downward, wounded. And then another explosion and it jerked upward in flames. Everyone cheered to see we had won and shouted as the Germans fell from the sky, their bodies burning in the wreckage falling slowly onto our streets. . . ." Then she'd shake her head, sit up ramrod straight, and say, "But that was nothing to what your great-uncle Algernon lived through in the trenches. So much more death there, so much filth." Then Nana would straighten the starched napkin in her lap and take a sip of wine, and a small, sad smile would cross her face as she stared off into the distance, leaving me spellbound not only at the picture of a burning London but also at the image of the mysterious Algernon crippled by a cruel world.

Were the stories about Algernon and the bohemian days in London intended specially for me, an allusion to my own growing estrangement and isolation? I doubt it. Nana was first of all talking for her own enjoyment, not as educator. Surely memory has overlapped here and my identification with outsiders must not have begun so early, not until I began waking up to the sleeping certainty of my own differentness.

Whatever she meant me to understand, Nana did hold me in special regard. During her last years, living with my parents in Phoenix, she'd often single out my father and sister as targets of ridicule. I was never abused, never used as a whipping post for the bitterness of a solitary woman who'd outlived her contemporaries and recognized less and less of what she had once so passionately loved. I must add that my father always put up with her outbursts exceedingly well, patiently leaving his own house until the tempest passed and never forgetting to make a toast to her homeland at Christmas dinner: "God save the queen. Amen."

In her middle eighties, despite the isolation of her widowhood and the cataracts that clouded her eyes and left her almost blind, Nana retained perfect hearing. Somehow, even while listening to the BBC re-broadcast on NPR in her room, she could hear every conversation in the house. I remember once humming "Stairway to Heaven" in the kitchen and then hearing, seconds later, from the far side of the house, the sounds of Nana pounding out an ornate Edwardian version of the rock ballad on the piano. No secret was safe from her sharp ears.

One Sunday night in 1985 she called my mother, who was working late at the university, to say I was being interviewed by Mike Wallace for a *60 Minutes* program called "Life and Death in San Francisco." I'd told my mother I would be on the show, but we hadn't anticipated Nana watching it. Up until this time I'd never discussed my personal life with her. That was at my parents' request, and I had agreed. Nana was too old to understand, a remnant of the Edwardian age, after all. She wasn't fooled by our subterfuge, though, as we found out that night when she telephoned my mother, saying excitedly, "Marion, Cleve's on the telly!" After a pause, Mother cautiously asked, "What's he talking about?" Nana said, "Well, you know I can't hear a word he's saying, but he looks marvelous. Must ring off now, he's back on, so handsome. See you soon, dear."

Later that year, I was home for the holidays. In the middle of the night I heard a tap at my door and there was Nana, all of four feet tall, hunched over her walker. She looked up at me with a sly smile and a twinkle in her eyes. "I've finally figured out why you're still a bachelor,"

she said. I was speechless and cautiously asked, "Why is that, Nana?" "Oh, the Davy men have never married. You know, when I was a little girl, my father left my mother to work on the railroad and I was raised in my grandfather's house by my three uncles. They were bachelors, never married."

"Cleve, these men were marvelous, delightful. You would have liked them. They loved art and gardening, and they were very good with animals and children, and they kept a beautiful house." Just before leaving, she told me of her grandfather and how he'd always worn a little gold ring on his pinkie. "I want you to have it," she said. I really felt that without saying the word *homosexual* or *gay,* Nana had, in a few minutes of storytelling, communicated that she considered homosexuality genetic and that I'd inherited it from her side of the family. The ring, now almost paper-thin, fit perfectly.

WHEN I SAY that I am normal and suburban to my bones, I'm not being quite accurate. For although my parents raised us within safe, orderly neighborhoods with neatly trimmed lawns and two-car families, they were not as compliant as that environment implies. They both had degrees, she in dance and he in psychology, and they were college professors during the '60s, and hence lefties.

Although they fit the stereotype of activist academics, they were not agitating for a socialist upheaval as were their louder, famously revolutionary counterparts Angela Davis and the Berrigan brothers. Instead, they worked against the Vietnam War and for civil rights through more conventional methods. I remember Dad bringing home petitions for my mother to sign and her reading them very carefully and him getting impatient as she mulled over whether or not she'd sign. . . . *But, Marion . . . Yes, Austin, I know.* And she'd lay down the paper and busy herself about

something in the yard or go for a walk, and sometimes she'd sign and sometimes she wouldn't. Once I remember her looking up from a petition and saying, *Always be careful of what you sign, Cleve.*

Perhaps the first time I became aware of Mother's more studied views was the day I came home from school and told her that some of the kids were saying that I was going to go to hell because I'd never been baptized. We were, as I well knew, the only family in the neighborhood that didn't go to church or synagogue. Was it true? I asked her. Could I go to hell? Instead of a simple no, she answered me quite typically with a broader truth, tied characteristically to family. "My father," she said, "your Grandfather Kirk, did not believe in going to church. When he wanted to be close to God he would go for a walk in the forest and listen to the trees." She would tell me that story, but she would caution me about repeating it. When I pressed her further, worried as always about being singled out from my classmates, she would say only, "Well, a lot of people just have to have someone to hate. They like to hate people that are different. Your father and I will let you make your own decisions."

My parents were not sloughing off God or religion or family values. And they weren't disinterested in my moral well-being. They simply trusted me and felt that I would gain day-to-day guidance by their own example and that spiritual needs were met best through individual paths. I knew that "making my own decision" was a challenge and responsibility to sort things out myself and not blindly accept the assumptions of any large institution, whether religious or governmental.

Both my mother and father had been deeply influenced by the depression and World War II, but like a rather small and hardy bunch of intellectuals in the '50s, they had been scalded by the McCarthy witch-hunts and forever after viewed individual freedoms as the root principle of political life. This was especially so for Mother. Not only had she an English reserve, she had lived her twenties in Greenwich Village during the McCarthy trials and seen many of her friends—writers and artists—

blacklisted because they'd joined the Communist Party. Where my father, eight years younger than Mom, would plunge headlong into organizing the university faculty to support the antiwar effort, Mother was less sure that such actions wouldn't one day disrupt our lives in unforeseen, disastrous ways. And yet she was proud, and rightfully so, of my father's increasing pacifism, reminding us pointedly on the many evenings he was away that what he was doing was important, "perhaps especially for you, Cleve." She was looking forward, as always. Indeed, it was my mother who would eventually introduce me to the Quakers and the potential of becoming a conscientious objector to the war in Vietnam.

PEOPLE SAY THAT the baby boom generation is spoiled and looks upon the good life as an entitlement. Perhaps that is true. But our soft, cradled lives were the first to be rocked by the possibility of nuclear annihilation—a sinister lullaby that I don't think has the same force for the later generations, at least not the ones I know. Certainly the fragility of things penetrated my world, most especially through the evening news, Huntley-Brinkley in our house. Evenings at six we gathered and listened to what seemed a never-ending drumbeat of troubles: the Cuban missile crisis, race riots, the Kennedy assassinations. I remember bicycling from home over to a nearby street to see tanks rolling toward the inner city the night of Martin Luther King Jr.'s assassination and realizing that there was a connection between that fire and those sirens and the next night's meeting at our house of somber academics and bearded grad students talking intensely of Selma and the Freedom March.

Still, as in most suburban homes, we children were safe from the struggles tearing at the campuses and inner cities. For a time my parents' strategy worked. We were sheltered from the worst of those years. There were the trips to Michigan to visit my grandparents. And later, when my parents bought a summer house in Omena on Lake Michigan, troubles seemed far away indeed. Those were idyllic days, full of endless hours roaming the beachfront or swimming out to the floating dock and lazily letting the day drift by until dinnertime, when my mother would come to the porch and sing out, "Cle-eeeeve. Cle-eeeeve." We'd play card games in the evening, and there was always so much laughter. Dad would walk us out onto the lawn, pointing to the constellations in the night sky. And mother would be especially spontaneous those summer days at the lake house. I'd wake to her singing silly faux opera lyrics: "Toreador-a, don't spit on the floor-a, use the cuspidor-a, that's what it's for-a." And she had a fascination with Katharine Hepburn and Spencer Tracy. She'd puzzle over the tantalizing ambiguity of their adulterous affair and then pull back. "He's still married," she'd say, approvingly.

Though my mother was light and funny and mischievous, my father was more ponderous. He could tell stories like all the Jones men, but invariably there was a point to his tales, usually something serious or instructive. I went to movies with my father. Or rather, he accompanied me dutifully to what seemed to him the worst kind of fluff. We saw the Beatles in *A Hard Day's Night* and *Yellow Submarine,* and big epics like *Zulu* and *The Bridge on the River Kwai.* And I was allowed to watch some television: *That Was the Week That Was, The Man from U.N.C.L.E., Laugh-In.*

Most often, though, these indulgences were balanced by more substantial pleasures that would, so my father hoped, engender the constructive purpose of leading me toward a career in science. Here's a typical scene from those days: I am in my bedroom, reading Hesse or Tolkien, happily adrift in imaginings of far-away centuries. I hear my father's car come up the drive and the dream is suspended. Book on my chest, I listen. If the front door slams within a short time, I'll be spared. If it takes him a while to come inside, that means he's wrestling a package out of the backseat and will soon be presenting me with one of his gifts—mazes with hamsters and complicated charts. Or sets of fuses and wires, and diagrams on how to put them together. Utter boredom. But, trying to please him, I would time the hamsters as they waddled through the maze or match colored wires and attempt to fathom the enigma of a fuse box. Fortunately, my father's expectations did not include sports or military service. I always knew that my parents loved me, as I do with much more appreciation today.

- -

CHAPTER TWO

COMING OUT

WAS THERE ONE incident that marks the end of my carefree childhood, when things started falling apart? I don't remember any cataclysms. Just a series of episodes beginning in junior high that forced me, inch by inch, into brooding sullenness and eventually onto the highway to San Francisco.

One summer, when I was twelve or thirteen, I went camping in the woods with a bunch of the neighborhood boys. We did this fairly frequently, the woods being only a mile or so from our block. If we were lucky, we'd steal beer and *Playboy* magazines, and the Brozgal boys would tell us about their older brother's girlfriend who let him do it to her, and we'd pass around the *Playboy* and drink beer and jack off and afterward have pissing contests into the creek.

One night we were camping out and somebody said, "Let's jack off," and I was thinking, *Yeah, let's.* Then somebody said, "No, we can't do that anymore, we're too old. If you keep doing it that means you're queer." I remember, as if it were yesterday, feeling a terrible chill, a clenching in my gut, my throat tightening. *That's it,* I realized with dread. *I am one of those. That's the problem. I'm a queer.*

For the next several years my main preoccupation was how to get out of gym class. I was afraid I would get aroused, yes; but mostly I feared that if I was naked in the showers, other boys would see me and somehow know I was a queer. I developed all sorts of excuses—coughs, shortness of breath—none of which the doctors my mother took me to see could diagnose. But each, for a short blessed time, got me a pardon so I did not have to strip in front of my peers. Whether I was clothed or not, though, everyone seemed to know I was different, and had known it long before I myself knew.

I'm sure you've met Rob. Big for his age, surrounded by a small army of followers, he was the Hitler of my junior high. He'd swagger down the halls, knocking over anyone foolish enough to be in his way. He was a bully and I was his favorite punching bag. I gave him loads of pleasure the first day of eighth grade. He was there on the steps of the main entrance with his gang. I was running late. There was no way around him; I had to go through the same doors. I looked down and aside as I passed. It didn't matter. He shoved me, yelled, "Faggot," kicked me down, and laughed when my brand-new books skidded down the stairs. All my classmates saw my humiliation. It's an old story, just another sissy boy getting the boot.

One evening after school my father asked me his habitual day's-end question: "What did you learn about today?" I told him we'd learned about the domino theory and that America had to stop the Communists because if they kept going, they'd take over. I showed him the map in *Time* magazine (to which he'd just given me my own subscription) with Vietnam, Cambodia, and Far East Asia all crosshatched in red to signify their vulnerability. Then I asked him how far it was from Vietnam to Hawaii and from Hawaii to California and on to Mount Lebanon, the Pittsburgh suburb we were living in.

"Not everything they teach in school is true," he said. Well, that was really big news. And there was more: "Not all of us believe that we have to fight Communism with guns. We have to look beneath the surface and really understand what is motivating people." He went on explaining about the influence of economics and sociological history—but I don't recall much beyond my utter surprise that my teachers could be telling lies. He hadn't said the word *lies*, of course, but in my mind if a truth wasn't true, what else was it but a lie? This was not, I must add, my father's intention. He was trying to get me to question, sort objectively through every assumption, but the result was radically simpler: I had no use for liars, and to this day I can only recall the names of a very few teachers I've had.

Distanced from my peers, suspicious of my teachers, and painfully aware that even my family would reject me if they knew the truth, I found refuge in a growing fascination with the counterculture, long-haired hippies, rebels—anything that questioned and snubbed authority. I would go to the Shady Side neighborhood, an area that had been seedy and was now becoming hip. My favorite destination was a head shop called Bag End, a reference to *The Hobbit*, the book that fueled my favorite fantasy world of those days. I'd often come home with psychedelic posters, with which I plastered my bedroom. I wanted to escape—from school, from Rob, from a world that was filled with the hate of race riots and burning campuses and something called the Tet Offensive and a war in which thousands of people were being killed by "carpet bombing."

Just after the Democratic convention in Chicago, which played out on the television screen with Mayor Daley's police beating protesters bloody on the nightly news, Mom and Dad packed us up in a car and we drove cross-country to Phoenix, where they'd both got jobs at Arizona State University. I, who was used to the heavy green woods of Pennsylvania, saw nothing outside the car window but an endless sandscape punctuated by sinister-looking saguaro cactuses. It was 112 degrees the day we arrived at our new home in what had been an orange grove and was now called, with absolutely no irony, the Arcadia district. There were still a few weeks before school began, and although I'd been miserable in Mount Lebanon, I wasn't prepared for the incredible loneliness of this sterile neighborhood in this strange, furnacelike city.

Things seemed to come full circle when, on the first day of school, I was once again a target. This time my tormentor's name was Brad—Rob reborn in the desert.

After my sophomore year, hoping for a miracle, my parents pulled me out of public school and enrolled me at Phoenix Country Day, a private school with smaller classes and "nicer" students. I hated it. But it wasn't so bad when I was on acid and inhabiting another planet while my classmates were prepping for college. We were comfortably off, but not rich. Certainly I didn't have a 'vette or a BMW. When the other kids would go for lunch breaks to their cars, I'd go to my locker and get out my beach gear. I had an umbrella, sunglasses, and a lawn chair. While they were blasting their radios and smoking cigarettes, I settled in for a nice day on the asphalt beach, finally agreeing that, yes, I was the school weirdo, and fuck you all.

One scene describes my banner years at Phoenix Country Day: I arrive in class and head to the back row, overhearing a group of students talking about President Nixon's just-announced bombing of Cambodia. "The president is a liar and a murderer," I say, loudly. Bobbi-Joe Laurentzin, a cheerleader, turns around in her seat and yells, "Don't you ever talk about the president that way again!" "The president is a liar and a murderer," I reply. She slaps my face and I repeat, "The president is a liar and a murderer." Slap! This probably would have gone on all afternoon if the teacher hadn't walked in. I was not a popular kid.

By senior year I'd developed a survival strategy: withdraw, shun team sports, leave school as soon as possible. And sneer. I'd like to say my family was spared the sulkiness of those days, but it wasn't. In 1972 I saw my first issue of the *Advocate* and came across a cartoon by Gerard Donnelen that perfectly captured my teenage mood. There's a gay activist being interviewed: "... My first involvement in the movement was when I detonated a small nuclear family in southern Arizona. . . ." I loved that; that was me.

My first boyfriend was Karl. He had black curly hair and blue eyes, smelled of patchouli oil, and wore the same frayed bell-bottom jeans for weeks on end. How do you describe your first lover without gushing? I dreamed and fantasized about him for a full year, seizing every opportunity to brush against him. And when it finally happened, I was shaking so much I couldn't stand up. We saw each other for three years. We had plans, of course, lots of plans for the future, when we'd move to a commune in British Columbia and live off the land.

I met Karl at a Quaker meeting. Though I was only fourteen, the draft seemed near enough that my mother had decided to introduce me to the Quakers and explore the possibility of my becoming a conscientious objector. The Quakers' monthly meeting of Friends took place in an old building set on the edge of the desert and looking out toward the mountains. It was a very plain building, no ornamentation or stained glass, with wood walls, wood floors, and a large window opening onto the desert. During meetings there were about sixty people facing each other in folding chairs; no clergy, just this deep silence.

Mom and I sat there and maybe half an hour passed and then an old woman stood and spoke about her decision to send money for medicine to North Vietnam. And another Quaker got up and talked about spending World War II in prison because he'd refused to join the army. These were brave words and actions here in the middle of Goldwater country. And that was all. No benediction, no recessional pomp. No sermon. No preacher.

Afterward we had tea and cookies, and no one asked us anything about our beliefs or mentioned Jesus Christ, and there was no Bible reading or preaching or threats of hell. This was much more to my style, more real—"authentic," as we said then.

Karl was a Quaker, too, and we began to meet at the Quaker building on Saturdays to clean it for the next gathering. All the sweeping and mopping took hours, or so our parents thought. Actually we'd be done in minutes, free to spend the rest of our time getting stoned and wandering out into the desert or making love. One day we were caught, not in the act but just after. We were sweaty and flushed and naked. I don't remember hearing the door open, only the sight of an old Quaker man staring at us expressionlessly and then turning away.

Weeks passed. Nothing happened. It was torture. Finally, after meeting one Saturday, an elder asked me to go for a walk in the garden. She was a plain-style Quaker woman in a gray dress, and she used the plain speech. I remember thinking as I followed her that the older Quakers didn't swing their arms when they walked as most people do, they just sort of floated along. Then she turned and touched my arm. Using the plain speech, which is reserved for intimate situations, she said, "Friend, as long as thee loves, it matters not how or who thee loves . . . but perhaps it matters where."

I felt the most exhilarating sense of relief when she said that. That sentence is one of the most important ever said to me. Though some of my ancestors were Quakers, I was not born into the faith; I chose to join it because Quakers seemed to be people who lived their lives the way they said they believed. They were self-effacing, letting actions speak for themselves. They didn't recruit or proselytize or foist their views on anyone. Action, choices, living a contemplative, purposeful life—that was their ideology. Not words. To this day their humble searching seems to me the most valid, courageous way of making sense of life.

My relationship with Karl went on in fits and starts after our discovery. Finally, frightened by my increasing openness about being gay, Karl refused to see me. Now he's married and raising a family.

Mel was wonderful. He was my second romance. He was older, mid-twenties, an associate sociology professor at Utah State. We met at Ghost Ranch in northern New Mexico for the Inter-mountain Friends Fellowship, an annual gathering of Quakers from Colorado, New Mexico,

Utah, and Arizona. When the gathering ended he invited me to join him in Colorado and then drive on to San Francisco for the Pacific yearly Quaker meeting. Although by then I was staying in Omena, Michigan, spending the summer with my family, I somehow persuaded my parents to allow me to leave with Mel. On the second day of driving, Mel said, "There's something I want to tell you about myself. I'm bisexual." I thought about that for a little while and then said, "I am, too." Then there was a pause, and then he said, "Actually, I'm gay." And I said, "So am I."

Looking back, it's hard to imagine that just saying those words would make my body shake and sweat—I'd feared this moment for so long. It was even more significant because that last night with my parents in Omena, I'd walked down to the beach where I'd played as a kid and felt so desperately alone. Shortly before, I'd come out to Karl, and he'd said, "I'm not gay, you're gay. I'm going to get married and have kids." I felt so crushed and remember thinking that if I couldn't find others like myself, I would . . . I don't think I allowed myself to use the word *suicide,* but I just saw the future as desperately bleak.

When Mel and I arrived in San Francisco and found our way to the Quaker conference, I saw a bulletin board with postings for the various meetings. One was an index card for a meeting of gay and lesbian Friends. I was paralyzed. I didn't want anyone seeing me looking at the message board, even if that particular notice was only one of hundreds. I couldn't find Mel, and though Karl was at the same meeting, he was avoiding me. So I walked around and around until I finally screwed up the courage to get within sight of the meeting room. I kept telling myself, *You have to do this, you have to do this.* I was trembling.

Finally I grabbed the doorknob and burst into the room, and every single head swiveled to look at me. They were all my favorite people, and they were smiling. "We were wondering if you'd show up," said one woman. With a bravado I didn't feel, I said, "Well, I'm here!"

The last night there was a meeting of all the Quakers, several hundred, and we all stood in silence for a long time, then sang "Amazing

Grace," and I remember being in that large circle, and on both sides of me were Friends who'd been at that gay meeting. Mel was there; I'll never forget his wonderful smile across the circle. He must have known that although I was sure we'd be life partners, a seventeen-year-old's pledge of eternal love is, by the rules of youth, changeable. He was there for me but not clinging when I inevitably moved on. Our affair was short, but opened up an incredible vista of adulthood—freedom to be who I was, and to be loved for it.

THOUGH I'D MARCHED in antiwar and civil rights demonstrations in high school, there was no outlet for activism I felt a more personal stake in until my freshman year at Arizona State University, where I was accepted despite terrible grades, with the help of my father, head of the psychology department. Within about an hour of walking onto campus, I gravitated to the sole gay and lesbian group and became a member of GLAD, Gay Liberation Arizona Desert, in the two seconds it took to sign my name.

It was a curious group, very typical of the times: more concerned with '60s idealism and self-expression than hard-edged rights advocacy. There's a picture of us in *Life* magazine standing in the desert, all of us (sans me) smiling in our long hair and bell-bottoms and beads, real Aquarians. Of course, we wanted to change the world. Recently organized and recognized by the university, our organization made it our first order of business to put on a conference of gay and lesbian speakers. We thought of inviting Merle Miller, the Harry S. Truman biographer who'd come out on the Dick Cavett show, or Jim Foster, the first out gay man to address the Democratic National Convention. But they were blackballed as "too elitist"—the first time I'd heard the term. Then I suggested Del Martin and Phyllis Lyon, founders of the Daughters of Bilitis, the first lesbian organization in America. They turned out to be the two big draws. Though I went to the auditorium hours early to help with the setup, there was already a line from the ticket office out to the parking lot. Once you got inside, there was an incredible sense of anticipation and camaraderie. And the place fairly vibrated with sisterhood. There were some men in the audience, but the overwhelming majority were lesbian women who'd driven to Phoenix from all over the Southwest. It was an extraordinary tribute.

Del and Phyllis were the classic butch/femme couple. Del had the guy's name and was butch, and Phyllis looked an awful lot like my mom. Their theme was how threatening they were as lesbians to men, and so during the Q&A, smart-ass Cleve raised his hand and said, "It's funny to hear you talk about yourselves as so threatening; because, Ms. Lyon, you look just like my mother." There were a few snickers in the audience, and as Phyllis teased out a long and increasingly embarrassing pause, I began to blush. Who the hell was this little queen to stand up in a sea of dykes insulting one of the founders of lesbian activism? Finally, Phyllis smiled sweetly, flipped me the bird, and said "Fuck you, kid. I'm not your mother." That brought down the house; everyone loved it. It was the beginning of a friendship that continues today.

As one of the first gay and lesbian groups at a major university, GLAD was frequently asked to send a representative to various gatherings. Though I'd never considered it before, Del and Phyllis's example was the push I needed to sign up as a speaker. I felt no sense of moment as I wrote out my name, no recognition of what I'd done. But when I was asked by one of my father's colleagues in the psychology department to talk about gay life as I knew it, a little warning bell went off. Academia is a very small world. By agreeing to speak, I'd be outing myself to my father. I'd thoughtlessly set in motion the inevitable collision. One evening as my father and I drove home, I decided I had to tell him. Better to hear it from me than from a co-worker, I thought. Not saying anything would be squirrelly. Noble words. All my resolve, all the confidence I'd felt when signing up to speak for GLAD, was gone. Strangely enough, it was my birthday that day.

"Dad, there's something I have to tell you."

"Yes?"

"I'm going to speak at Professor Marx's class next Thursday."

"Oh really. What will you talk about?"

"I'm going to talk about the gay liberation movement." Here it was, like a train coming through the tunnel. There was no escape.

Silence. My father is very self-controlled. He didn't slam on the brakes or pull off the road.

"What are you telling me?"

"I'm gay."

"Why are you telling me?"

"I thought you should know. It's important . . ."

"Fine, tell me about it. What do you like best, getting it in the ass or what!"

Even if I'd been able to respond, what could I have said? Guilt, anger, fear—every painful emotion whipped me raw and left me red-faced and dead silent. When we got home, I ran to my mother and told her what had happened. "Oh Cleve," she laughed nervously. "Don't be silly." It wasn't a joke at all, it was my life, the revelation of something I'd hidden for years, knowing that it would—as it has done—separate me irrevocably from those I loved most and make me a stranger in my own home. That smile on my mother's face was terrifying. It hid the intense fear she felt for her son. She was a dancer and had many gay friends and knew what the world could do. My dad's response was guilt. He'd fallen for all the neo-Freudian bullshit.

I remember checking the mirror and seeing nothing changed, except a pair of frightened eyes grown too large and worried. Was I so different than I was yesterday? I didn't belong anymore; I was related to those furtive men at the bus station, an outsider, a pariah. Something shattered that day, a trust that would take years to rebuild.

Everything was altered overnight. Neither my grandmother nor my sister was told. Things were just frozen in the house. We couldn't talk about anything without stumbling into silence over the unspoken impasse we had reached. What did my parents think of their son at seventeen? *Obedient* was not a word they would have used to describe their proto-hippie child. *Gay* was not in their vocabulary, either. Though they fought for civil rights and revered Martin Luther King Jr., gay lib was irrelevant or worse. I hear my father's angry voice, his disbelieving rage that I could equate something as trivial as gay liberation with civil rights: "What do you know?"

All I knew was that I wanted out, and when a friend said he was going to San Francisco, I told him I'd go, too. I left a note for my family on the kitchen table. I remember feeling frightened and feeling also that, all right, I'm ready for the road; bring it on.

CHAPTER THREE

SAN FRANCISCO, 1972-1976

END OF SUMMER, 1972. Fog hangs like a tent over San Francisco; the taxi honks echo. I'd hitchhiked cross-country from Phoenix to the corner of Sixth and Mission Streets. I was eighteen years old and on my own, not because of abuse or poverty or because my parents kicked me out. In fact, they'd urged me to stay and finish school, but with the proviso that I try to become heterosexual. They might as well have asked me to change the color of my eyes.

Like so many other gay men and women of the '70s, I took the chance and made the choice to be myself in a town that had a reputation for tolerance. It was about freedom, simple as that. I started walking and came upon a printing company that had a hand-lettered sign in the window advertising for a bicycle messenger. I walked in and asked about the job. The man behind the counter asked me how well I knew the city and I told him I grew up here. Fine, he said, there's a stack of stuff to deliver. I went to a gas station about two blocks away and, when no one was looking, stole a street map.

The other messengers were back long before I dragged in at the end of the day. One of them was named Joey, a Filipino with long hair, very queeny. He looked me over, tossed his hair back à la Farrah Fawcett, and said, "You gay?" "Yes." "Got a place to stay?" "No." He took me to the Leland Hotel on Polk Street, an area known suitably as the Tenderloin. A few hours before, a transsexual had attempted suicide and there was blood splattered along the walls winding down the hall to where about seven of us slept in old blankets and sleeping bags. That night, staring at the ceiling, I remember thinking, *Oh shit, there's blood on the walls*. But there was no crying myself to sleep, no mourning over the path I'd chosen. I had assumed things would be different, and I remember feeling a naive fearlessness about this new life, whatever it was to hold. It was just my first day on this new journey.

Next day, we went to work: coffee for breakfast, no lunch. That night, we went to Bob's Burgers and on the corner of Polk and Sacramento Streets my friends bought me dinner—a ritual in our group. Whoever had money would buy the others dinner, often the only meal of the day. We were a gang and did anything we could to survive, from panhandling to selling dope and hustling. I was coached on how to question customers to make sure they weren't cops and how to cadge money from older men. Sometimes we slept on rooftops, sometimes in doorways. This went on for about two years.

ALTHOUGH MY TIME in the Tenderloin was pathetic, something out of a Dickens novel, with all the exaggerated cruelty and pornography, it was followed by a rather tender stretch in the Haight-Ashbury. By the mid-'70s the Haight's glory years were over and the last vestiges of the flower children had degenerated into violence and decay. Many of the storefronts were burned out and boarded up, plywood sheets scrawled over with revolutionary slogans.

The Black Panthers had an office on the street with tough-looking guys standing guard, and to walk the sidewalks required a sort of zigzag dance around the panhandlers, musicians, and just plain zonked-out characters.

But following the neon-lit desperation of the Tenderloin, it was a relief, especially after I moved into a gloriously roomy Victorian on the corner of Central and Page. Rent was ridiculously cheap, something like two hundred dollars for an entire six-bedroom house. I had five roommates, more or less, depending on the month. People would come and go, moving out for a lover or on to another, more happening town. It was all very loose. Among the tenants I remember was Patrick, who had a huge red Afro and was the first person I knew to use cocaine. Silas Narland was a handsome guy who'd been a teacher until he'd come out of the closet and been fired. He worked at the Ritch Street bathhouse. And there was Shoki, and Rhoda Dendron (we made up new names to match our new lives). Living on the top floor was a placid queen named Dora who had a moon face and long, straight brown hair. He chose his bedroom because of its shape—a perfect twelve-by-twelve cube, which he painted bright yellow. The floors, ceilings, and walls—everything was a bright yellow. And there was absolutely no furniture except a bed in the exact center, and in the closet he had milk crates painted yellow, in which he kept his two pair of pants, three T-shirts, one sweatshirt, and one jacket. I can't remember what Dora's real name was, but I heard years later that he became a monk, which seems right.

Another friend of this time was Bobby Kent. He was a brilliant pianist and accompanist for the singers Sylvester and Martha Wash, whom we called "the white boy with a gospel voice." Bobby built a Victorian tree house, with gingerbread trim and stained-glass windows, high in a gnarled eucalyptus tree in the middle of Buena Vista Park, for many years a cruisy hippie park in the Haight. A group of us would camouflage the house with fallen eucalyptus branches, and inside we kept a large leather-bound book of blank pages that we filled with poems and love letters and messages among the close-knit club who knew about the tree house. Eventually, the police discovered it and burned it. I heard that Bobby went to Germany when we lost the tree house; we all lost touch with him after that.

Looking back, all of us resembled caricatures living out a comic-book version of life. But it seemed real enough at the time, and all its kookiness mirrored the era. If we wanted some reassurance that our lives were not unusually bizarre, we needed only to look at the papers, which were full of the Patty Hearst kidnapping—an extravaganza rivaling the O.J. trial of some two decades later in all its fascination and weirdness.

Our household on Page Street was particularly interested in the Patty Hearst drama, since we knew one of the main characters—Cecil Williams, the firebrand minister at Glide Memorial Church. Glide was a refuge in the Tenderloin where we'd all gone at one time or another for medical referrals or a free dinner. Cecil was then and remains today the good shepherd of the city's dispossessed. Appropriately enough, he acted as liaison between the Hearsts and the Symbionese Liberation Army during negotiations. We were all rooting for the SLA and credited Cecil when a deal with the Hearst family was worked out: if the Hearsts would give a couple of million dollars' worth of food to the poor, Patty would be released. The relief scheme was called PIN, People in Need. Trucks were to fan out over the city into designated neighborhoods and hand out staples to the masses. The Haight qualified, of course, and scheduled drop-offs were listed in the paper and on fliers—like party invitations, we joked. It was a windfall we weren't about to miss, and so when the truck rolled up Haight Street we lined up, dressed for the occasion in costumes from Goodwill. We got frozen turkeys—four, I think—along with as many boxes of Rice-A-Roni as we could carry. Years later I ran into Patty Hearst's cousin Will, the publisher of the *San Francisco Examiner,* and told him about that strange summer. He wasn't much impressed. It wasn't terrifically tasteful of me, but I always thought it was funny, seeing the SLA's snake-head logo printed on all those boxes of Rice-A-Roni—"The San Francisco Treat."

Although this was the beginning of the sexual revolution, it was one revolution I was slow to join. It wasn't for lack of desire; I just wasn't considered a hot number. I had hair to my ass, was too thin, too something. So I went out dancing. In the Haight there was a cavelike little gay bar called Gus's Pub where you could go and have a cheap beer in a greasy glass. And even if you were underage, which I was, you could get in the backdoor of Hamburger Mary's, the Stud, and sometimes the Mindshaft on Market Street.

The greatest bar in those days, and for my money the best bar ever, was the Stud. To this day if I meet someone who says, "I used to hang out at the old Stud, before it moved, before the epidemic," I feel a sense of kinship with them. Sort of the original gay hippie bar, it had none of the strict leather or western dress codes, no door policy against blacks or Hispanics common to gay bars at the time. There were even a few women in the mix. It was a fabulous place, wild and unpredictable. The music was a rich mixture of soul, disco, and funk put together by D.J. Larue with such skill and flair that even if we weren't familiar with a tune we'd stay on the dance floor and most often find that, with a few new moves, we'd be in the groove. Every so often they'd lock the doors for an after-hours party, and at one time they had "religious services" starting at 2 A.M., so the bar stayed open later than anywhere else. Though it was small and the ceilings were low, they had great live shows. Etta James and Sylvester performed there, along with the Angels of Light, and Pearl, the extraordinary Janis Joplin impersonator who appeared later in the Bette Midler movie *The Rose*. My great pal on many of those nights was Shondel. He always said he was inspired by the David Bowie's androgynous hero Lady Stardust, and felt that the lyrics summed up his view of life on the beautiful margin: "Lady Stardust sang a song of darkness and disgrace. And it was all right. . . ." Another dancing buddy was Tedde Matthews, who went on to become a famous drag queen/performance artist/activist and is featured in the film *Word Is Out*. He's dead now, of AIDS, but we had great times.

I went to the Stud at least three time a week, but never on Tuesdays, because that was two-for-one buddy night at the Club Baths at Eighth and Townsend. When people talk about the baths nowadays it's always in the context of disease. That's misguided. For a short period in the middle and late '70s, the baths were simply another extension of our freedom, part of this grand new experiment in gay liberation. If that freedom went against every religious stricture, so much the better. Why pure sensual pleasure is so wrong and frightening to so many people is beyond me. Later, of course, we realized we were playing Russian roulette, and most of us stopped. But in those days it seemed romantic and innocent—strange words to today's ears, yet true. It was a dream world. Many of us, myself included, had been programmed to be afraid of our bodies and our desires. I was petrified of gym class all through school; it was where I was beat up more often than not, humiliated, and powerless against fears real and imagined. And now to walk around in just a towel or less with delight and anticipation was a great release, a second coming out.

That's not to say I didn't see the bad side of the baths. Some were filthy, others were racist, and there could be a very cruel pecking order built solely on physical attributes. But, as best we could, we worked to change those things with boycotts and picket lines. That really is the historical point: that when we knew something was wrong, we tried to change it.

And somehow, this idea that everything around you was on an upward, harmonic rise extended even to geographical boundaries. Change was in the air—literally, in the case of the postcards flown to me from around the world by my friend Scott Remple. He was one of a circle of friends who coalesced in the Haight-Ashbury days and then dispersed to other cities, other countries. For most of 1974 and into the spring of 1975, I would get seductive cards at monthly intervals from the globetrotting Scotty. The postmarks were exotic and mysterious—one from Bangkok, another from Greece, and a cluster from New Delhi and Bombay. "Come see the world" said a postcard from Kabul, Afghanistan. "You must get out of America and see the rest of the world. It's much better." The offer was attractive and slightly dangerous, an enticing combination I rarely resisted in those days. With the extravagant confidence of youth, I began planning. I could save a few hundred dollars, which seemed a lot in those days. My expenses were always low. I ate practically nothing, and all the clothes I would need fit in a backpack. Once there (wherever that turned out to be), I was sure to find a job. . . . Could I just go? Yes, I could, and did. In our next communication Scotty gave the date. Meet me in Amsterdam, he said, at the American Express office on Damrak, on or about the fifteenth at noon. If I'm not there come back each day at the same time. He couldn't be exactly sure of the date since he was hitchhiking from Turkey. I must say it was intoxicating to toss around these end-of-the-earth destinations so casually. Surely my parents or family had never contemplated life on such a whimsical map. I would be the first, and it seemed easy.

So, on April Fool's Day 1975 I stuffed a couple of pairs of jeans, some T-shirts, and a few socks into a duffel bag and stuck out my thumb. I hitchhiked north to Vancouver and east across Canada. At Montreal I got a student ticket to London and from there a ride from a Dutch trucker to Amsterdam. Scotty was late, by almost a week. But one day, exhausted and more than a little scared, not only of this foreign world but of a fever that had me shaking one minute and sweating the next, I turned the corner, looked up at the regal columns of the American Express facade, and there he was, camped out on the marble steps in a tie-dyed shirt, floppy hat cocked over his eyes. I ran to him and collapsed. Scotty, always composed, held me up and we went to a nearby café. He ordered us strong brandylike drinks called, I think, *genevers,* and then turned to me. Very nonchalantly, as if my trip around the world had been a small thing, he said, "So, slowpoke, it's about time you got here."

He was astonishingly at ease, and I drew strength from that. A little sleep, a few hot meals, and I was fine. We moved on to Munich, where I found work in the Hotel Bayerscherhof as a dishwasher. I was surrounded by a babel of languages spoken by my co-workers. There were dark, unshaven Turks, rough red-handed Yugoslavs, and sad-eyed World War II veterans who stood at their tasks with stoic grimness and wore their stumps like badges of honor. If anyone was antagonistic, I didn't feel it. As long as I showed up on time, Herr Wilsh seemed grimly pleased. I didn't think much in those days about delving into the lives of others: why they had left their countries, why they would occasionally rage at one another. Equally, they didn't weigh me in any moral balance or social context, but just thought of me as *der Amerikaner.* If this long-haired, comparatively fey kid was odd, it was only because I'd left a country where everyone was supposed to be rich. And when I'd finished my shift, laying out my tools in perfect Teutonic order, I'd return Herr Wilsh's brisk bow with a deep flourish of my own and stride out to whichever coffee shop Scotty and my new friends Rosemarie and Rico had agreed to meet at. When I felt the tug of home, I'd hop a plane and return to San Francisco, work for a while, and then go back, to Munich, Greece, Egypt—wherever fancy beckoned. It was all a sort of vivid parade I'd joined; it was simply life, new and unconstrained.

------- ------- ------- ------- ------- ------- -------

CHAPTER FOUR

POLITICS

MEETING HARVEY

B Y THE SPRING of 1975 I was a twenty-one-year-old
kid on top of the world. I'd just moved "over the hill"
from the Haight to the Castro, enrolled in film courses at San Francisco
City College, had friends, the bars, the baths; every few months I'd go
to Europe. Politics, any sense of activism, existed only on the periphery
of my thinking back then. It still seemed something far beyond my talents, whatever they were.

I'd looked up Phyllis Lyon and Del Martin and gone to a few meetings of BAGL (Bay Area Gay Liberation), only to be bored silly by endless discussions of how Marxism-Leninism applied to homosexuals in
'70s America. My only involvement was a little anarchy that John
Canali, Joseph Durant, and I would occasionally let loose on San Francisco. We called ourselves Sissies in Crime. About once a month we'd
make statement art about societal wrongs and place them conspicu-
ously in high-traffic areas around town. One of our first works illustrated

passages from Jean Genet's play *Our Lady of the Flowers* and another was a sort of multiple shrine to Divine, the outrageously voluptuous drag queen and star of many John Waters movies such as *Pink Flamingos* and *Female Trouble*. Each piece was set in large, clear plastic bags and affixed to walls in frames of colored tape.

We always made up about thirty of these things and would place them wherever they'd be most unwelcome and jarringly out of context: in a line leading to the main branch of Bank of America or in the financial district subway station at eye level for the pinstriped morning commuters. They were sensationally ugly and sometimes rather dangerous. One series protesting police brutality was titled *Blood Blisters*. The plastic bags were swelled with red dye and cracked glass, and a tiny black baton swam menacingly in the muck. However crude our art was and difficult to explain, Sissies in Crime did have an impact. The *San Francisco Chronicle* took note of our work and called us "conceptual terrorists."

In the summer of '76, I was on another of my trips to Europe with a German boyfriend named Wolf Kern. My goal, as quite often in those years, was to be wherever the action was, and right then, just after Generalissimo Franco had died, Spain seemed the place to be, a country in the tumultuous transition from fascism to democracy. Certainly I'd read reports of the various parties vying for power and been fascinated, but I was mainly drawn to what I saw as an exciting ferment of people shattering old molds and searching for something new. And yet, one hot afternoon on that trip to Barcelona, I felt, if not the twinge of fate, at least the glimmering of direction signs that seemed to say, This is what you want to do.

The first thing I noticed when we got to Barcelona was a tremendous excitement in the air. The streets were crowded and lively, and as we got to the center of town—to Las Rambles, the main boulevard—everywhere you looked there were hundreds of people queuing up. I didn't know if it was a festival or holiday, but as I got closer I realized

streets, waving banners and shouting "Liberation," things collapsed and everybody started piling into one another. I peered ahead over the jumbled crowd and saw, to my terror, a wall of the Guardia Civil, Franco's security guards. Hundreds of them, in black uniform and wearing glinting black helmets like Darth Vadar's, had formed a cordon barring the avenue, with guns pointed at us. Everybody stopped, confused, and then, incredibly, hesitation exploded into righteous anger. People began gesturing and shouting insults and throwing things at the guards. And then, with no warning, the guards began to fire. The first volley ripped the scalp of a drag queen next to me, took the skin and wig right off. I'll never forget the terrible piercing scream she let out. The next volley came and everyone scrambled, crying out, *"Assasino! Assasino!"* They were using rubber bullets, like super balls that would ricochet off the ground, off the walls, off bodies. In seconds it was a horribly bloody melee: the report of gunfire mixed with screaming and windows breaking and the wounded moaning. Routed, the crowd retreated and then coalesced into a running group, storming into a nearby plaza and ripping up tables and piling up chairs, newsstands—anything to build a barricade. It was brutal urban warfare, with the crowd melting into buildings and side streets, only to regroup in smaller numbers throughout the night. From my room that evening, I could see flashes of the fires they lit and hear the echoes of their calls in the night: *"El pueblo unido jamas sere vencino"* (The people united will never be defeated).

Scared, unsettled, yet whole, when I got back to my hotel room I wrote a letter describing the riot to Howard Wallace, one of the pioneers of the gay movement in San Francisco. Something clicked for me then as I wrote of what I saw, and later, when the letter was published in the San Francisco weekly newspaper the *Sentinel*, I felt that my wanderings, my jumping from job to job, may have led me to something worthwhile. Exactly what that was I didn't know. Without a degree, I had only a remote possibility of being a reporter or filmmaker; I wasn't a novelist; and yet I wanted to communicate what I'd seen and been part of, what I believed was the beginning of a new movement that was going to transform the world.

When I got back to San Francisco, I began paying more attention to the papers, but conventional politics seemed a pallid thing next to the thrill of revolution. I have no idea why I stopped to talk with a long-faced Jewish guy with a New York accent named Harvey Milk. He was handing out flyers for his supervisorial campaign. I knew he was the first openly gay candidate to run for public office, but I just hadn't been in the city long enough for local affairs to mean much to me, let alone the campaign of a two-time loser running as a ponytailed gay shop-keeper.

Looking back, though, I presented exactly the sort of challenge that Harvey loved. When I told him, wide-eyed, about my experience in Barcelona, he must have seen the seeds of a convert. "What are you going to do about it?" he asked. I remember being thrown by that. I knew I liked politics and that writing the article had been satisfying and the piece itself well received, yet how did my inchoate Barcelona experience apply to life here in San Francisco?

But a smart-aleck, dance-crazed hippie boy with the thinnest revolutionary veneer was catnip to Harvey—attractive exactly because of my unlikeliness. I don't think he even asked me if I was old enough to vote. As I got to know and work with him, I recognized this quality often: he loved a challenge. In front of his natural constituency of gay men, Harvey could be dull and unfocused; even his syntax would come unglued. But faced with a dilettante kid like me or a distrustful blue-collar audience, he came alive with charisma, more often than not creating followers. That day on Castro Street, once we got beyond a half-hearted pass and on to politics, he piled on the charm and made another convert.

Since his camera store was just four doors down the street from my apartment, it was easy for me to stop in and talk. I knew something of the gay and lesbian movement from GLAD, but it was there in that store, or hanging out with him as he passed out fliers on the street, that I learned about crucial moments in the gay rights struggle, like the Stonewall riot in New York and the long battle with the American Psychiatric Association to overturn its designation of homosexuality as a disease.

Harvey made it all personal, and before long it seemed important, then crucial. I liked the seriousness of it, the passion. And despite his incredible fluency, he was a good listener. He made me feel as if I had something to say. That was intoxicating to a young man not yet sure of what he was doing or where he was going in life. As a part-time student at the University of California at San Francisco, I expected to eventually complete my degree in film studies and become a film director. But within a few months I'd changed my major to urban studies and was well on my way to becoming a political junkie. As Harvey pointed out, I had no talent for film.

We didn't only talk shop. He told me about his problems with lovers, each of whom, with the exception of his last lover, Doug Frank, was alcoholic or heavily into drugs or both. I never once saw Harvey Milk drink alcohol or smoke. He may have had a Champagne victory toast after winning an election, but even when a calming drink would have seemed most natural, he didn't want one, or need it. I remember coming home one night and seeing Harvey on the sidewalk in his bathrobe sweeping up broken pottery that Jack Lira, his lover at the time, had thrown out the window in a rage. He just smiled and shrugged.

As messy as his own personal life was, Harvey could give wonderfully clear and sympathetic advice. I remember a terrible heartbreak I had over a Greek god named Danton Grant. Danton was just as dumb as the heroic marble sculptures he resembled and about as capable of loyalty, but I was mad for him. Three months into our affair I found out he was cheating. Crushed, I went to Harvey and he said, "Get over it. . . . You're a gay man living in the twentieth century, and that means you are going to have many love affairs, many lovers, and relationships. Connections will change over time in ways that you can't predict. Just accept that you're not trapped in the heterosexual way of living, so you won't go from high school to college, to marriage, to career, to children, to grandchildren, to retirement, to death. We're separate," he said, "an experiment, a unique generation. Why do you think gay people of all ages, races, and backgrounds love telling their coming-out stories? The only the thing that unifies us is our common experience of coming out— that extraordinary liberating moment when you realize that you aren't a freak and that, my God, the world is full of queers, millions of them, and they're good-looking and they work hard and they're real people. This is the one great shared experience that gives us the power to create something new . . ."

I don't pretend to recollect Harvey's words exactly, but the gist of it is there—a refusal to be locked into the straitjacket of old assumptions about life and love, and a challenge to be and do what you felt was right no matter what anyone one else thought. It was a credo he followed in his own life. When he'd come to San Francisco, dead broke, with nothing but enthusiasm, he'd looked around and decided he'd like to become mayor. It didn't matter that he was a faggot in a straight world, that he was a hippie who liked listening to opera while the rest of us were deep into disco, or that he was twenty years older than most of the guys flocking to the Castro. He wanted to run this town and make it better. Hope was always his message, and sometimes his dreams came true. In his last relationship, with Doug, he found an equal, a peer who had his life together and made the abstract ideal of love real—just one of the bittersweet achievements that made his death so tragic.

CHAPTER FIVE

MISS AMERICA AND THE BRIGGS INITIATIVE

THE SUMMER OF 1976 marked a turning point for me and for the gay liberation movement. Without anyone's quite realizing the extent of it, the country was going through a backlash against homosexual rights that crystallized in Anita Bryant's insidiously named ballot initiative, Save Our Children. As a contestant in the 1959 Miss America pageant who'd built a show business career out of singing patriotic songs like "Battle Hymn of the Republic," she tapped into the fears of a society still reeling from Vietnam and the social changes of the '60s. America, in her view, was under siege. And worst of all, homosexuals were "recruiting" children, most especially in the schools. Her answer—and God's—was to raise a campaign to overturn the recently passed laws against discrimination in Dade County, Florida. As her initiative gained followers and the megapublicity guaranteed by that professional smile of hers on the cover of *Time* magazine, every gay man and lesbian woman was threatened.

In his perversely canny way, Harvey welcomed the fight. While most of us felt betrayed, indignant that once again we had been branded criminals and degenerates, he was energized by the attack and saw it as one more reason to come out of the closet and declare yourself. I'd sit on the couch in his camera store, a ratty old thing that was never cleaned, and listen as he tried to convince the doubters who dropped by to talk politics. Every movement needs something to push against, he would say. What better opponent than Miss America? (That she had only been second runner-up was a detail he thought only added to the irony of what he felt was her un-American stance.) He was right. Bryant's campaign was such a high-profile assault that a lot of Harvey's audience was energized to vote, often for the first time in their lives. Whether he spoke to them in the store or while drumming up support on the streets, Harvey harvested believers. Even conservative closeted queens and radical lesbian separatists seemed to set aside whatever personal antagonisms they felt and agreed that something had to be done for all of us. The idea of gay rights had taken root, and the thought of playing the victim, whether individually or collectively, was repellent, like returning to slavery after a taste of freedom and self-respect.

Along with welcoming the battle as cathartic for the community, Harvey saw it as an opportunity to politicize the electorate in ways that would, if played right, finally lift him into office. The strategy he worked out was very straightforward. First, there must be large demonstrations, both to energize the gay base and to show our numbers to the outside world. Second, someone had to organize fund-raisers; we needed money, not only to fight Bryant, but also to combat copycat measures cropping up in Kansas, Minnesota, Oklahoma, Oregon, and Texas. The trick was for Harvey to be active on both fronts but to finesse the harsher aspects of street marches and play up the more statesmanlike role more suitable to his eventual election as the first gay supervisor. He needed a front man, a radical who was political but not overly ambitious and ideally not weighted with the baggage of association with one of the many factions on the San Francisco scene. Oh yes, and a good speaker who was unafraid of being hauled in for civil disobedience. As we were building a profile, Harvey asked me if I'd ever been to jail. I said no, and asked him why. "Oh," he said airily, "they usually arrest whoever's leading the march." At the time it sounded romantic as hell.

As he spoke, he was looking at me with his Cheshire cat smile. I got the message. *Me?* I couldn't think of any reason not to do it. In fact, I was flattered as hell as I absorbed this crazy notion. Harvey became all business. "Here," he said, "take my bullhorn." And then I knew he was serious. It had been passed on to him by Allen Baird, the head of the Teamsters Union when Harvey had organized the gay bars to support the boycott of Coors beer during the truckers' strike—the first time organized labor and the gay movement had joined forces, resulting in the removal of Coors products from most gay bars and restaurants, a boycott that continues in lesser form today. That gift and the solidarity it symbolized had been a huge breakthrough, both in recognition of gay clout and in deeper human ways that meant more to Harvey than anything else.

I was more than happy with the arrangement. I loved the streets, the crowds and chaos and excitement. And I loved my new bullhorn— with a siren attached. Of course, I had no experience at it, but neither did anyone else. All of the earlier uprisings had been spontaneous and short-lived replies to local events such as raids or police brutality. Though there were political clubs, the largest in San Francisco being the Alice B. Toklas Memorial Democratic Club, there was no precedent for long-term protests, no structured organization that had experience leading marches week in and week out over the months running up to when Dade County would vote the initiative in or out.

It was all very casual. We had no offices or set hours, but we worked at organizing the demonstrations with a great intensity. Friends and activist allies like my roommates Eric Garber and Allen White and Gilbert Baker and I would meet at my place or at Dennis Peron's kitchen table for hours, planning and preparing for the next rally. We'd make up fliers with a press-type kit (those were precomputer days), then go down to a little print shop on Nineteenth Street and run off a couple of hundred, which we'd staple to phone poles and on corkboards in Castro bars and restaurants. The headlines were different, but there was one message that always stayed the same: "Come to the Castro!" And they did.

My career as a public speaker began at this time. In all but the last two of the twenty-five years I've lived in San Francisco, Castro and Market has been under construction. There was a big plywood box painted blue that covered the entrance to the subway they were building, and it became a semipermanent stage for street comedians like Ruby Rodriguez and Tom Ammiano (a future San Francisco supervisor). Sharon McNight (who went on to a Broadway hit in Mickey Rooney's *Sugar Babies*) sang there, and Harvey and I gave speeches on whatever regressive measures the far right, invigorated by Bryant, was pushing all over the country, from Dade County to St. Paul to Portland and Wichita. I'd stand up on the box, then take a big breath, hoist the bullhorn, and welcome everybody: "We're here tonight to talk and march against what is happening in Wichita, Kansas," I'd say. "They want to knock us back into the closet, slam the door, and destroy our civil rights. [*Crowd boos.*] And we're going to have to get to work! [*Crowd cheers.*]" I'd give the power salute, fist clenched, and exit, a little terrified, a little exhilarated.

Then we'd charge off in a strategy we called "March 'em till they drop"—a purposely exhausting trek down Market, up Van Ness to California, around Grace Cathedral and down to Union Square, which we'd fill. It was a demonstration of our numbers and our defiance, proof that the gay community was a real constituency that could no longer be ignored. We wouldn't break things or hurt anyone. There'd be more speeches, and then it was back up Market to Castro Street. Initially the crowds numbered a few hundred, but as the weeks went by they grew into the thousands.

We often benefited from the power of some very closeted figures. For example, C. K. McClatchy, the heir and owner of all the *Bee* newspapers up and down the Central Valley of California, was a gay man.

Consequently, when we were fighting John Briggs or John Dolittle or whoever, we could count on the editorial support of newspapers in the most conservative sections of the state: the *Modesto Bee,* the *Fresno Bee,* the *Sacramento Bee.* And then to complete our hold on the Central Valley media, there was also Ted Fritz, publisher of the *Bakersfield Californian,* who was also gay. And there were others, in high positions within the Democratic Party, who silently helped us and continue to help, behind the scenes.

On election day in Dade, over fifteen thousand angry queers stormed out of the Castro, carrying candles, blowing whistles, and chanting, "Gay rights now! Gay rights now!" It would have been impressive in daylight, but we did it at midnight, further dramatizing the event.

It was incredibly exciting, not only to be part of a mass outpouring of emotion and energy but to lead it. Whenever you're lucky enough to work at something you love and feel is important, it becomes consuming. I'd lie awake at night thinking of the next march and how to make it more effective. Every detail became fascinating for me, especially media coverage. I quickly came to understand what the newspapers and television reporters would and wouldn't cover and how to construct your remarks in interviews so they'd be quoted. This was before the term *sound bites* was coined, but that's what I tried for. For instance, we called Election Day in Dade Country "Orange Tuesday." And I was always thinking about the photographs, trying to help the cameramen get such a good shot that the newspaper would have to run it on the front page, above the fold. I'd tell them that for a really great angle here's the corner we'll be at or suggest they go to so-and-so's apartment or up on the roof of a particular building for a long shot of the crowd marching en masse down Market. We always had twenty-foot banners out front, and part of my job was to make sure nobody stood in front of them. I also injected touches of camp, surprises, things the media and the marchers loved, like arranging to have the Gay Freedom Day Marching Band hidden in an alley along the route and suddenly come bursting out into the parade playing "San Francisco, Here I Come."

I loved every part of it—the technical stuff, designing the flier with a bold headline to capture people's imagination, coming up with short programs so people could be inspired by the speeches and not get bored. I tried to be as disruptive and confrontational as possible without anyone getting hurt. We never got permits or registered our routes with city hall. I loved confusing the motorcycle cops along the march routes by telling them we were going to turn left on Bush Street when really we were going to turn right on Pine, or going up the wrong way on a one-way street. They'd sit astride their Harleys, very official and imposing. As we approached, they'd block off an intersection, indicating we were to go right or left according to the route they'd desired. Sometimes we'd comply and sometimes we'd march straight between their bikes and they'd just sit there scowling behind their visors. Very pissed off.

One of my favorite maneuvers, if I really wanted to shut down the city, was to stop the buses by disconnecting their electrical arms from the overhead wires. With just one yank, the buses would stall, snarling traffic and making life even more miserable for commuters and the cops. When we marched, everyone was part of the demonstration, whether they were with us or against us.

I'm often asked by young activists, "How can I be effective?" What I always tell them is that if you are doing this out of some sense of sacrifice, don't even try. If you don't enjoy it, if you're cynical or arrogant, that will come across and you'll step on the message; you'll end up preachy. Think of yourself as speaking not to the crowd but for it, like a conduit. And you have to be aware of group psychology, especially if the issue is explosive. When you've got ten, fifteen, twenty thousand angry people looking up at you, they want to hear their own feelings expressed in concise, satisfying terms. They don't want an endless harangue, they don't need a lecture; and if you get drunk on your own words, forgetting your role as a warm-up for the main event of the march, you'll lose them. You have to direct the anger in such a way that the crowd feels that their point of view is being reflected in the demonstration. If you are accurately communicating, then they really give you a lot of power. If you say we're turning left here, they'll go along with it. If you say we're not breaking these windows, we're not storming city hall or torching police cars, or beating the shit out of this Christian minister with the offensive sign, they won't.

D URING THAT SUMMER of '76 and well into the next year, I was getting a name as a street activist and Harvey was involved in an exhausting third run for supervisor, beginning with the Briggs Initiative fight. Harvey benefited from being only one among a fractious number of candidates, but he was by now the most recognized. It was to be a tumultuous election all around, resulting in the election of an African American, a Latino, an Asian, and a single mother, Carol Ruth Silver. But Harvey's was the sweetest victory of all and the most historical. He would now have his national stage. He received letters from all over the country, both adoring and hate-filled.

He loved it all, especially the diversity of the board. He and Gordon Lau had a set piece at community meetings: Lau would ask Harvey to redecorate his house and Harvey would say he'd bring his laundry. But as progressive as the board was, it also had a new member in Dan White, representing an area called the Outer Mission, an economically depressed pocket of blue-collar workers. White's campaign slogan was "Stop the Deviants."

Of all the fund-raisers over those months, one the most memorable was titled *Moon over Miami*, a revue with performers and speeches by local politicians held at the Castro Theatre, a grand old movie palace set in the heart of the Castro. The ending was a special treat. Armistead Maupin, whose weekly series, "Tales of the City," was at the height of its popularity, agreed to read from an early episode of his column— where Mouse writes home to his mother and father that he is gay. Home, of course, was Dade County.

Tickets sold like wildfire, but Harvey wanted to get maximum publicity and so organized a press conference to announce the event. He chose a church, and we had no doubt of making a splash. AP, UPI, and the local papers confirmed they'd show up, but about an hour before we were to go before the cameras and microphones we realized that the press would outnumber the audience. Harvey wanted a big crowd—and not just gay people. "Call Jim Jones," he said. "But be careful what you say. They tape everything." And then I relearned the old cliché that politics makes strange bedfellows. I called the People's Temple and asked if they could send some people over. They asked me how many I wanted. A couple of hundred. The guy on the other end of the line (not Jones) put me on hold, then came back and asked what time they should come. I might have been calling in for delivery of a few dozen roses.

I'd known the People's Temple mainly through their newspaper, which was at that time sent to every doorstep in the city. It was nothing but a propaganda sheet, with every paragraph praising the good Reverend Jones, but he'd become something of a local player by the sheer circulation of his paper. Also, in the months leading up to an election, he consistently endorsed the progressive candidates and was pro-gay, pro Harvey. We had no idea he would eventually become a mass murderer, killing a congressman and nine hundred others in Guyana. All we knew was that here was this strange, intense man with hundreds of followers at his beck and call. He was useful.

Five minutes before the press conference was to begin, three school buses pulled up in front of the church, and the People's Temple congregation marched into the hall. They were ordinary looking, mostly black, many older, and they walked in lockstep, eyes trained forward. Once inside, a black man in wraparound sunglasses stood up in the front, the conductor. When he clapped, they clapped. When he laughed they laughed. When he was silent they were silent. The whole thing was creepy as hell, but none of the reporters saw anything wrong, and in fact they remarked on the huge supporting crowds. Harvey later told me that they were weird, but excellent volunteers. "You take help where it comes from," he said. "But don't trust them."

WHEN THE SAVE Our Children initiative passed with a wide victory margin that November, it spawned similar initiatives around the country. And we lost all of them, preludes to the main event here in California. It was called the Briggs Initiative, named after State Senator John Briggs, from southern California (from the same district that was later represented by the reactionary homophobe Robert "B–1 Bob" Dornan).

I met Tom Ammiano during our work fighting the Briggs Initiative. He and Hank Wilson were among a handful of openly gay teachers working in the school system at incredible personal risk. I watched Tom care for his lover over many years as he died of AIDS. He's an extraordinary person who began his career as a teacher and then decided to become a stand-up comic but at the same time was so annoyed at school board policy that he ran for a seat on the board and got elected. Then he ran and won a seat on the San Francisco Board of Supervisors. And as of this writing, this utterly improbable, funny queen is president of the board.

In retrospect it's hard to imagine that we were as fearful of Briggs as we were. He had none of qualities that had made Bryant such a forceful opponent. He was small and balding, he wore ill-fitting suits that hung on him like hand-me-downs, and except for a holier-than-thou attitude, his command of Scripture was limited to repeating, over and over, "God created Adam and Eve, not Adam and Steve." When he got flustered, which was often, his lisp became exaggerated and his hands would flutter up like birds' wings. He was so effeminate that there were rumors he was gay. I remember watching him on television one night and turning to Harvey in surprise, amazed that this ogre was so fey. He smiled and said, "Our worst enemies are ourselves." That was one of Harvey's tenets: that if you didn't come out, the result was evil. It was the closet cases who ratted in military purges, the closeted preachers who became messianic persecutors. Negative energy when you stay in and positive when you leave. Briggs was an obvious example.

But as improbable as he was, he had ambitions. In addition to fashioning the antigay initiative Proposition 6 to ban gay teachers, Briggs further polished his archconservative credentials by proposing another law—one that would broaden the application of the death penalty: Proposition 7, to kill more criminals. If there were two hotter buttons in those days, I didn't know of them.

As the first polls came in, Briggs had the tide in his favor. Though there was some support for antidiscrimination laws, whenever you threw children into the mix the polls went south. And the Briggs initiative was focused specifically on "protecting children" by outlawing homosexual teachers in the public schools. Despite all the data and every study result refuting the invidious myth that gays preyed on children, most of us thought his initiative would win.

It was chilling to hear Briggs's speeches, read sympathetic interviews in the paper, and realize that this hate-spewing man was being taken seriously. But it was worse when you were seized by paranoia. You'd go out for a coffee, or around the corner to buy groceries, and every straight person you saw became a potential enemy. How would they pull the lever? We'd gotten used to being tolerated foreigners, but now we felt hunted.

Following the loss in Dade County and the lionization of Anita Bryant (there was talk of her running for Congress), it didn't take a genius to figure out that if Briggs won, more witch-hunts would follow, and so there was a spasm of organizing up and down the state. As a student at San Francisco State University, I organized the California Campus Conference on Gay and Lesbian Rights, which brought together students from twenty-two universities around the state. Still, for all our efforts, most of us thought Briggs would win. Students, gays, most teachers were on our side, but support beyond our base was extremely tenuous. Briggs always shaped the debate as a choice between people's children and sexual predators. Faced with that wild distortion, the average Californian didn't see much choice; 80 percent of Californians said they had never met a gay man or lesbian woman.

Among the anti-Briggs organizations, the only statewide association was the Socialist Workers Party, which at that time had a much larger membership than today. All up and down the state, members of the party worked to set up CABI groups (Californians Against the Briggs Initiative). They were good people and excellent organizers, but they were mostly nongay, leftist ideologues who couched their speeches in the party rhetoric of class warfare—not the sort of lingo that goes over well with the suburban moms and dads we needed to convince. Very quickly, Harvey and others became concerned that the SWP-dominated CABIs would mobilize the disenfranchised but alienate the largest bloc of voters.

By this time, 1978, Harvey had finally won his seat on the San Francisco Board of Supervisors, and along with using his office as a platform to blast the opposition in press conferences and public pronouncements, he began the development of an organized opposition. First he set up the United Campaign to Defeat the Briggs Initiative, which he hired me to run. It was a tiny operation by today's standards. I don't think we raised more than thirty-five thousand dollars from mail solicitations, and our headquarters was my ten-by-twelve-foot living room. But we achieved our objective, which was to pump money into every county in the state, especially rural districts. That was very important— that the defense come not just from San Francisco, but from communities all over California, especially within Briggs strongholds like Orange Country in the conservative south and Sacramento, the capital, in the north.

Harvey also helped organize San Franciscans Against Prop 6 and the statewide campaign hired Dan Bradley, a big gun Democratic Party political consultant, to run it. Neither of these creations sat well with the CABI ideologues, who, though genuine in their defense of gay rights, were far more interested in building a revolutionary movement. They hated the idea of a slick campaign, despising television and most radio as elitist. Finally all the grumbling came to a head when the CABI people demanded a public meeting. It was like a very uncomfortable wedding ceremony, with Harvey's forces on one side of the hall and the CABIs on the other. We all observed the proprieties, but there was an unmistakable chill in the air. Things got quite tense with the first question. A black gay activist named Claude Wynn stood up and asked Harvey, "Do you consider yourself a member of CABI or San Franciscans Against Prop 6?" Our side stiffened, theirs stiffened, and every eye was on Harvey, leaning casually on the lectern as if he didn't have a care in the world. After a few beats, he gave the crowd one of his trademark little smiles. "Of course I'm a member of CABI. Of course I'm a member of San Franciscans Against Prop 6. Everyone in this room is a member of both. Let's get to work." I must say the CABIs took it well and did not lessen their supporting activity.

Though muzzling the socialist agenda required a light touch, it wasn't only about practical politics. Harvey was never much interested in talking about social theory beyond his basic populist stance of being with the little guy against the big guy. He would speak in terms of justice and compassion, but his program wasn't based in any kind of political or economic philosophy at all. It was about individuals.

On October 11 of that year, a month before the vote, we had televised debates hosted by KQED, the PBS station for the San Francisco area, whose membership and audience are second only to those of WNET in New York. Each side was to field two representatives, and there was a lot of discussion as to who would join Harvey. He was leaning toward someone from CABI, as a sort of peace offering, sure that if they got off track he could cover for them and just take over. I told him that was foolish and that he couldn't shape the message for any motive but winning. We could do fence mending later, after we won. I suggested Sally Gearhart. First of all, she was a woman; and second, she was a credentialed, respected college professor.

Also, she was a lesbian. Harvey was a little resistant because he'd never met her, but when I pointed out that inviting her might go a long way toward mobilizing the lesbian volunteers and the women's vote, he began to listen. Sally, whom I'd met at UCSF, was sympathetic with the separatists and had many friends among them. Harvey knew as well as any of us that there was enormous division between the male and female activists. This was at the height of the lesbian separatist movement, and there were thousands of women who'd begun to totally rebuild their lives outside the male-dominated culture. Certainly they shunned any sign of male authority, eschewing shaved legs, makeup, and dresses, but they were most concerned about changing the fundamental precepts of society. They wanted, in short, a revolution. And the most effective method of mounting the revolt was politics, to which they were dedicated but cut off by their isolation.

So I set up a meeting between Harvey and Sally at a Castro Street café called Without Reservations, and they liked each other very much—so much so, in fact, that they would tease each other mercilessly. (The afternoon of the debate, Harvey telephoned Sally and with mock innocence asked if he could borrow a pair of earrings.)

Equally important to how well they got along was how they looked together. Neither one had anything in common with the monsters Briggs described. No pierced noses or Mohawks or leather jackets. Harvey had clipped his ponytail and quit wearing his earring during the campaign. They came across as slightly older, middle-class, Middle American people.

Though the poll numbers had evened out over the summer, thanks in part to declarations by ex-governor Ronald Reagan and President Jimmy Carter that they did not support Briggs and would vote against the measure, I think the KQED debate put us over the top locally. Harvey had his New York edge and Sally had a slight southern drawl, which made for a nice chemistry, and each was relaxed and enormously articulate. No matter how Briggs tried to bait them, they remained unruffled. Harvey, in particular, could match Briggs's inflammatory rhetoric phrase for phrase.

At the end of the debate, after yet another apocalyptic description by Briggs of homosexual teachers corrupting the moral fiber of America itself, "a greater danger than communism," Harvey rounded on Briggs himself, questioning his morality and motives in words that echoed the historic moment when Senator Joe McCarthy and the House Committee on Un-American Activities were finally called to account. "In your drive for personal power, how many careers are you willing to see destroyed? How many lives will you destroy in your lust for power? And when will you stop?"

Following the live broadcast, Harvey and Sally joined us at Mission High School, where we'd all gathered, and everyone went nuts with standing ovations. It felt like a joyous family reunion, wonderful and shattering. People were crying. We all felt immensely relieved and elated, believing that the emotional roller-coaster ride was nearly over and that we'd be vindicated. Afterward, we walked over to the Castro. Everyone seemed to have seen the debate, and if they weren't in the streets rushing up to shake Harvey's hand or pat him on the back, they were leaning from windows, yelling out, "We love you, Harvey." He was a king that night.

We ended up at his favorite bar, the Elephant Walk. And in the middle of it all, he pulled me over and hugged me and started singing: "Happy birthday to you, happy birthday . . ." The lights went dark and one of the bartenders brought out a doughnut with a candle stuck in it. Amid his triumph and all the hoopla, he'd remembered that it was my twenty-fourth birthday, October 11, 1978. I was so proud and touched. It was typical of Harvey to remember.

On November 4 we had our victory. The Briggs Initiative, Proposition 6, was voted down by a huge margin, with nearly 70 percent of Californians against it. As the head of the anti-Briggs forces, Harvey was credited with a stunning upset, further enhancing his reputation as the voice of gay politics both within the state and on the national stage. He was the hero of our movement, or the villain, depending on your point of view.

CHAPTER SIX

ASSASSINATION AND WHITE NIGHT

T HE MORNING OF November 27, 1978, began much like any other day in the eleven months Harvey Milk had been supervisor. I dropped by the office around nine and spoke briefly to Harvey's two aides, Dick Pabich and Anne Kronenberg. Dick was young, strikingly handsome—a born political operative who liked nothing better than to sit for hours plotting strategy. In fact, he was about to start his own campaign-consulting firm with Jim Rivaldo, called Rivaldo-Pabich, and I was slated to move into his position as administrative assistant when he left. Anne Kronenberg was a very hip young lesbian with an eye for detail and sharp political instincts. She also had a knack for keeping frenetic Harvey on schedule. We spoke briefly, and I left to get some notes at home, then was going to return to the city hall records department to do some small-scale opposition research. Though Harvey's core support was strong, no politician is ever truly secure, and since his term was for just two years, he'd begun campaigning almost immediately. We'd heard rumors that a few would-be adversaries had recently moved into the district in order to be eligible to run. I was to look up exactly when, or if, they'd fulfilled the residency requirement.

When I left my apartment, I walked over to the Bakery Café (now the Patio Café). The employees were picketing because the owner refused to allow them to unionize. The strike had turned into something of a cause célèbre, and I was there to listen and mediate on behalf of Supervisor Milk's office. (The Bakery Café eventually became the first gay restaurant to join Local 2, yet another landmark in the struggle for equal treatment under the law.) I was talking with the strikers when I heard a series of strangled remarks . . . *shot . . . the Mayor, shot and killed. What? Shooting . . . Is he dead?*

I grabbed a taxi and raced down to city hall. It was crawling with police, most of whom were rushing toward the mayor's office. The private entrance to the supervisors' offices is off the main hall. I opened the door and saw, down that corridor, a policeman in profile outside Dan White's offices. Looking inside, I saw a body on the floor. I knew immediately it was Harvey. I recognized the shoes, beat-up old wing tips, worn away in the soles. He was facedown in a pool of blood. I'd never seen a dead man before.

In memory everything seems dreamlike, in slow motion. Dick Pabich and Jim Rivaldo are watching from Harvey's office, directly across the hall. I am standing next to Dianne Feinstein, a colleague of Harvey's on the board of supervisors. She is stock-still, white as a ghost, just staring. As we look down at Harvey, a cop turns him, and his head flops over and blood and brain tissue seep out onto the floor.

Life changed forever that morning. What had begun as a bright day, at the end of a solid year of what looked like the beginning of a new era, was now over.

• • •

WHEN I THINK of Harvey now, I picture him at ease, wearing faded, torn blue jeans with a ripped knit sweater. He knew who he was and had gone through a lot to be comfortable in his own skin. It was as if he'd tried on a series of disguises over the years before finally, literally, coming out. From a young Republican stockbroker in New York, he'd transformed himself into a long-haired Haight-Ashbury-type hippie fag, which he again recast into a short-haired, business-suited Democratic wheeler-dealer politico. Three radically different incarnations in one abbreviated lifetime. I've often wondered what he was like on Wall Street, his most contrary incarnation. Did he have the same explosive laugh, that sadness in his eyes? Did the gentleness come after, or was it always there? He talked very little of his past.

Harvey did not have much in the way of ideology, which made him a very effective politician. He was for the grassroots, whatever that meant. He was for the little guy, a populist. He was genuinely empathetic and would go to great lengths to look everyone in the eye and really listen and be respectful and talk in real terms of everyday living, with grace and humor and hope. He was famous for the little touches: delivering flowers to the woman on Church Street who'd had a miscarriage, making friends at Douglas School with the children and their parents, remembering my birthday.

It was a thrill to go with him to the union hall for a meeting with crusty old labor guys. "Get a load of this fruit," I remember overhearing. "He ain't half bad." They liked him. Everybody liked him. And always, always, he was tossing out self-deprecating remarks to make someone else comfortable. He knew that he was an intimidating figure, and if wearing a clown suit to a fund-raiser or stepping in dog shit for the evening news cameras would make his point, he'd happily do it. It was a tradition at his birthday party that people would throw pies at him. He led the laughter against himself, to let out the contradictions and flaws—if, that is, he wanted to get through to a person. His flip side, if he was on the attack, could be coldly sarcastic and terse. He had no patience with socialists or gay conservatives, nor did they with his flamboyance. He called their brand of accommodation "sneaking fascism."

All the tragic consequences of homophobia were very real to him— the fear of disgrace, being hounded from jobs, from family. I think he suffered as a consequence, but out of the experience he crystallized what became the sum total of his message for gay people. *Come out* was his constant refrain. *Be yourself, we'll stand with you.*

And his power? He was a novelty. Harvey had no money. He was destitute when he died. What is the authority of the most exalted San Francisco supervisor? It's pretty small-time stuff, and he took the pomp and circumstance very lightly. He used city hall as a foil, as evidence that government can work, even for the poor and the disenfranchised, gay or straight. "What do you think of my theater?" he'd ask friends as he gave them a guided tour of the neoclassical splendor of city hall. "My stage!"

He always thought he'd be killed. "I'll get it from a closet queen," he'd say with an oracular tone. And I would tease him about his delusions of grandeur. You're not important enough to be assassinated, I'd tell him. You're not a Gandhi, or Dr. King or Malcolm X, just a gay shopkeeper. I was wrong. Harvey was my confidant, my mentor; he was about to become my employer. I was totally committed to him and a future in the open brand of honest politics he fought for. He was our first public martyr. And the power released by his murder is the proof that his mission was genuine. On the nameplates of the hundreds of memorials across the country, in the sea of candles we carry every year on November 27 and in the hearts of gays and lesbians the world over, Harvey's message survives: come out; there is hope; we can be ourselves. That's his legacy.

• • •

A S A TYPE, Harvey's murderer, Daniel James White, bears a startling resemblance to today's killers: a fresh-faced, seemingly normal son of a suburban family, who for incalculable reasons became utterly convinced of his righteousness and finally crossed the line into madness and murder—even as he remained convinced of the rectitude of his role as husband, father, and policeman. As a supervisor, White had been a failure. Rigid and dogmatic, he didn't know how to play politics, didn't know how to cut deals or negotiate—all essential tools on the board of supervisors. You compromise on everything, bargain, and form partnerships with other members. Everything was black and white to him. He couldn't do it. Harvey had tried to work with Dan, both in private and in public. While I and everyone in Harvey's office dismissed him as a hopeless puppet of the police and real-estate interests, Harvey saw a young guy scared stiff by hardball political pressures. Harvey thought that with a little time and encouragement, Dan would see that gays were not so horrible as his Irish Catholic preconceptions made us out to be. "He is educable," Harvey would say.

Along with his political failures, which were disastrous enough to deeply undercut even the strong support from his highly conservative, working-class constituency, Dan was a complainer. Shortly after taking office, he began whining that his salary was too low. It was a typically naive pitch for sympathy, one that puzzled the public and was treated as political poison by the other board members. All the silence just egged him on, and a few days before the murders he called a press conference and abruptly quit. Eight hundred dollars a month wasn't enough to support his family. He wouldn't be doing his duty as a father and provider if he remained. He was compelled to leave by his conscience. He might, he smilingly told reporters, go back to the police force, but for the time being he had to focus on squeezing an income from his fried-potato business on Fisherman's Wharf (which had been bought for him by his wealthy conservative backers).

From all accounts, White was immensely relieved to be an ex-supervisor. But his decision had the opposite effect on the powerful old-boy network that had spent so much money getting him elected. The police and fire departments had backed him as a favorite son who would deflect the pressure to modernize and integrate their forces. The downtown real-estate developers had subsidized his campaign and expected sympathetic treatment in return. But Dan had disappointed them, so they called him in for a little pep rally. We'll never know how much pressure was exerted on him at that meeting or precisely what was discussed, but it isn't hard to guess. It must have been something like: "Danny, you can't resign, you're our voice on the board. The mayor will appoint a liberal in your place and give that cocksucker Milk a majority. You're screwing up. . . ." He was told he had to go to Mayor Moscone, hat in hand, and get his job back. "We've invested money in you. Don't let them run you off the board, Danny, be a man."

Dan asked for his job back. The mayor, who hated confrontation, agreed, brushing off the incident as a young man's mistake. When Harvey got wind of Moscone's blunder he stormed over to his office and said, "George, don't be stupid. This is our chance to control the board. We've lost countless decisions by a five-to-six vote. Now we can reverse that and take control." To Harvey it was a golden chance, and he painted a vision of the city's future in the terms Moscone dreamed of and had won his campaign on. Moscone saw the light and reversed his decision. Harvey was jubilant, rushing into the office and telling us to write up a press release saying the mayor would not reappoint White.

Dan White learned about Moscone's reversal when reporters began calling his home that evening. Early that next morning, he strapped on his gun, went to city hall, and crawled in through a basement window in order to avoid the metal detector at the front door. The mayor's secretary, Cyr Copertini, let him into the mayor's office. Dan strode in and blew Moscone's brains out. He coolly reloaded and walked to the other side of city hall, where the supervisors' chambers are, called Harvey into his office, and shot him several times, including a coup de grâce to the head. He then met his wife in the chapel of Saint Mary's Cathedral, told her what he'd done, and turned himself in—to his best friend on the police force.

At 11:45 A.M., the acting mayor, Dianne Feinstein, announced: "Mayor Moscone and Supervisor Harvey Milk have been shot and killed. Supervisor Dan White is the suspect."

A S THE BODIES were wheeled out of city hall, Pabich, Kronenberg, and I were already facing the question of who would take Harvey's seat on the board. Grief-stricken as we were, it was what Harvey wanted. One year before, just two weeks after his election, Harvey had made a secret tape recording that outlined his wishes should he be killed: "This is Harvey Milk, speaking on Friday, November 18, 1977. This is to be played only in the event of my death by assassination." In the first section, he talked about what he'd tried do politically: "I stood for more than just a candidate. . . . I have always considered myself part of a movement, part of a candidacy. I've considered the movement the candidate. I think there's a distinction between those who use the movement and those who are part of the movement. I think I was always part of the movement. I wish that I had time to explain everything I did. Almost everything was done with an eye on the gay movement." After a blistering attack on those gay activists who he felt were in politics for personal, egotistical reasons, he named four people whom he believed in and trusted enough to carry on his work as supervisor: Bob Ross, Frank Robinson, Harry Britt, and Anne Kronenberg.

It was an extraordinary situation. Even beyond the grave, Harvey was urging us to pick up the pieces and continue the fight, orchestrating the future strategy of a movement he lived and died for. He had known how we'd feel—the confusion, the fear, the sense that everything was hanging in the balance. And he'd planned for it. At the end of the tape he reiterated something that was part of his stump speech, something that gave us all a sense of will and purpose to go on: "I ask for the movement to continue, for the movement to grow, because last week I got the phone call from Altoona, Pennsylvania, and my election gave somebody else, one more person, hope. And after all, that's what this is all about. It's not about personal gain, not about ego, not about power—it's about giving those young people out there in the Altoona, Pennsylvania, hope. You gotta give them hope."

Of the four acceptable replacements, two were complete wild cards. Bob Ross, publisher of the local gay weekly the *Bay Area Reporter,* was always a behind-the-scenes kind of guy whose views were considerably more conservative than those of most of Harvey's circle. Equally as puzzling was the choice of Frank Robinson, a friend of Harvey's who'd helped craft campaign speeches and co-written the best-selling novel from which the movie *The Towering Inferno* had been made. He was a wordsmith, and a sweet man, but not a politician. The last two recommendations seemed more logical. Harry Britt was a postman who'd worked on Harvey's campaigns and was now president of the San Francisco Gay Democratic Club (to be renamed the Harvey Milk Gay Democratic Club that night). And last—or rather first, by my standards—there was Anne Kronenberg, who'd been his aide.

All the political activists, including me, immediately backed Anne. Harry Britt was just too shy and reactive, as he himself admitted by declaring he wasn't ready for the job. Anne Kronenberg was smart, had keen political instincts, and was familiar with the job. In the tape Harvey admitted she was very young, only twenty-four, but said she represented a new generation. We all pledged to support her.

The only trouble was that Anne didn't live in the district. Walter Caplan, a lawyer, came up with the remedy: we'd move her into Harvey's apartment. So that night, before Harvey's body was yet cold, we got a truck and moved all her furniture into his apartment. The next day we printed Anne Kronenberg for Supervisor signs in the same colors and font that Harvey had used, only reversed to blue on white instead of white on blue.

At about 4:30 that afternoon I was back at my house, putting batteries in the bullhorn. We'd spread the word that there'd be a candlelight march for Harvey and George that evening. By the time the sun was down, Castro Street was filled with an immense and somber crowd whose number was estimated at forty thousand. We started out slowly marching in step, the single drum leading the way. We were mostly gay and lesbian, but mixed in were people of every background and race and age—young and old, black, Irish, and Chinese. But what I remember most is the extraordinary silence. Beyond a faint tramp of shoes on asphalt, there wasn't a sound to be heard. We got to city hall and Joan Baez sang "Swing Low, Sweet Chariot." There were a few speeches. I spoke, as did Harry Britt and Dianne Feinstein. None of us said anything memorable. It was anticlimactic. The silent march itself had been the most eloquent expression of our grief. When I returned to Castro and Eighteenth, I saw a haunting message scrawled out in graffiti: Who Killed Harvey Milk? It was a question that the straight world didn't understand.

AFTER HARVEY'S DEATH, everything went out of kilter, and that winter and spring seemed endless. The famous "gay bloc" that had seemed such a disciplined force during the Briggs and Bryant campaigns began splintering along various issues that each side thought crucially important. The most divisive argument was over who would replace Harvey as supervisor. Backed by the pledges of support for Anne by those in the inner circle, including Harry Britt, I naively lobbied the mayor's office to tilt things Anne's way. As it turned out, I was on a fool's errand, working for a candidate whose support had fractured even as I believed it was coalescing.

Just months before the murders, Dianne Feinstein had announced her retirement from politics in her own version of Nixon's "You won't have Nixon to kick around anymore" lament. "I always dreamed of becoming mayor" she said, "but that dream, I now know, will not happen." She considered herself a failure. She'd run for mayor and hadn't got anywhere with it, been outfoxed, and concluded that there was no place for a moderate in the polarized politics of the late '70s. As a Pacific Heights society woman, she found her bona fides doubted by the progressives, and the conservatives were dead set against her pro-choice position. And she was a woman.

And now this hybrid creature had found her dream, and with it came power as well as the choices. Whom would she appoint to Harvey's seat? As Feinstein wavered and waffled and made us all thoroughly nuts, bickering set in and ratcheted up until there were rumors that she might ignore Harvey's wishes and appoint someone else—maybe even someone straight. These were false rumors, but the degree of paranoia was just part of the heavy weather that set in after Harvey's murder—and a measure of how precious that seat, the first gay position of any importance, was, both symbolically and in a practical sense.

Eventually, twenty-four-year-old Anne Kronenberg was cut down to size and Harry Britt deemed the better choice. He was also one of those Harvey named on the tape; he was better known, less radical in appearance than Anne. He'd been a preacher, after all, had a country accent, and was more palatable to traditionalists. He didn't scare anyone by riding a motorcycle in full leather—which Anne did (and very sexily, I always thought). Pat Jackson, the firebrand Service Employees International Union activist, was one of the early agitators for the upset and drew support from the other unions. Surprisingly, she turned the trick with the remaining Kronenberg loyalists, and when Bill Kraus, Dick Pabich, and others in the "gay bloc" reneged on their pledges to Anne, the deal was nearly done. Harry tied the bow to the entire backroom package when he said, humbly, that he'd take the job. It was a disappointment to me personally, but a wash politically since Harry and I were in sync on most issues. Anne left town soon after, heartbroken, but Harry did remain true to his progressive principles.

In addition to the tension over the appointment that winter, the police, who had been restrained under Moscone, went back to all their bad ways. There were a lot more intimidating "tours" of the Castro by black-and-whites. Cops would park in front of the Elephant Walk or Twin Peaks, flip their lights on, and stroll through, knowing full well the anxiety their presence raised. I myself was shoved around one afternoon while sitting on the steps in front of my apartment. "Move on," the cop said, swinging his billy club. "But I live here." "Move on, faggot." I moved on. And they kept pushing, trying to see just how far they could go, which turned out to be pretty damn far. In December, a bunch of off-duty police officers burst into a lesbian bar called Peg's Place and beat up everybody, including the owner, Erlinda Simaco. Mayor Feinstein was shocked! *shocked!* at the mayhem, but the official response was only noise. The perpetrators got off with a slap on the wrist and were soon back on the beat.

Added to all this was the trial of Dan White, the darkest cloud over very cloudy times. All during the ordeal he sat stone-faced and never recanted his confession of the double murder. But—he had a defense: that afternoon he'd gorged on Twinkies. He and his lawyer and a parade of expert doctors claimed he was not himself, not responsible; the sugar rush had triggered the rampage. I will never understand how anyone on that team could face themselves in the mirror, then or now. Had there been the slightest shred of doubt, anything to raise even a moment's hesitation that he should not have been locked up for life, we could have at least looked on the trial and the legal system with a few molecules of respect. But Twinkies? It was humiliating.

When the closing arguments were read and the jury went into deliberation, the entire city held its breath. Some of us, myself included, had very little hope and believed the trial had been a sham from the start, when potential jurors were accepted or rejected depending on their answer to the question, Have you ever supported controversial causes, like homosexual rights? Affirmative answers guaranteed excusal. Would blacks have been asked the same question if the trial had been about racism? Of course not. It was just one more example of institutionalized homophobia.

The resentment and anger boiling just beneath the surface were palpable even before the verdict came in. Just two weeks earlier, there'd been a near riot when a cop tried to arrest a photographer friend of mine named Guy Corry for putting up posters on telephone poles. A crowd of us surrounded the cop and made him leave. He called for reinforcements and more police showed up, but people began to throw pennies and cigarette butts at them, and they withdrew.

Sure that this was just a preview of what was to come, I went, together with Priscilla Alexander from the National Organization for Women, to Captain Jeffries at the Mission Police Station; we told him that the atmosphere was so poisoned that we expected a violent reaction if Dan White got anything less than a life sentence. Jeffries was extremely condescending. He all but patted my head as he assured me, "You just march your people down Market Street like you always do, Cleve, and we'll just give you an escort." And I said, "I don't think you're listening. I'm predicting serious violence if Dan White gets off." Jeffries scoffed.

Late on the afternoon of May 21, 1979, I was at home with my roommate Eric Garber, one of the pioneer gay historians. We were making coffee and turned on the television for the five o'clock news when a bulletin flashed across the bottom of the screen: "A verdict has been reached in the Dan White trial. It will be announced shortly."

Within minutes the phone and doorbell started ringing as people began to come over in anticipation of the verdict. We were all fidgety and keyed up; my hands shook as I rolled a joint. And then a newsman broke into regular programming and announced that Dan White had been convicted of involuntary manslaughter for the killing of Mayor George Moscone and Supervisor Harvey Milk. His sentence was five years. The phone rang and a reporter asked what I thought. "This means that it's all right in America to kill faggots," I said. I became literally sick to my stomach, and when I got out of the bathroom, the house was filled with people, friends from the Castro, activists, neighbors, and many I'd never even seen before—all furious.

At some point I got word that there was a news team who wanted to talk. I went down to Castro and Market and met up with Del Martin and Phyllis Lyon at the Twin Peaks bar. The reporters knew I had a permit to close the Castro the next day for a celebration of Harvey Milk's birthday, and after a few questions on the verdict ("How would Harvey feel?"), I was asked if the response would come the next night. I looked straight into the camera and said, "No. The reaction will be tonight."

The reaction had already begun. We finished up the interview, and as I ran back to the apartment for Harvey's old bullhorn, crowds were forming. By the time I returned, thousands of people had already gathered, and more were pouring off buses and piling out of cars that they left parked every which way. It was eerie and frightening to see familiar faces so distorted by anger as to be nearly unrecognizable. Chris Perry, the president of the Harvey Milk Gay Democratic Club, was usually the mildest little guy, but his face was so twisted with rage that I hardly knew him. By the time we had organized enough to start marching down Market, the crowd had tripled in size. Everyone wanted blood, wanted revenge. I stood up and yelled into the bullhorn, "Today, Dan White was essentially patted on the back. He was convicted of manslaughter—what you get for hit-and-run. We all know this violence has touched all of us. It was not manslaughter. I was there that day at city hall. I saw what Dan White's bullets did. It was not manslaughter, it was murder."

There were lots of signs, many with much more violent slogans. Chris Perry's said, "Avenge Harvey Milk." As we began moving out of the Castro, I saw Captain Jeffries wading toward me through the crowd. "I hope you have my escort," I told him. "Yes, Mr. Jones," he said, with newfound respect. And then I began the chant: "Out of the bars and into the streets. Dan White was a cop! Dan White was a cop!"

As we headed for city hall, the mob grew in size and fervor and the chants became increasingly ugly, changing from "Dan White, Dan White, hit man for the New Right" to "Kill Dan White." At the corner of Van Ness and Market we could see that a gang had already arrived at city hall and was heckling speakers on the steps. As we got nearer we saw that the group on the steps were representatives of an organization called Lesbians and Gay Men Against the Death Penalty. Having assumed that the verdict would be the death penalty, they'd come to explain their position. It was the wrong classroom. The crowd was completely unsympathetic, and to make matters worse, the sound system broke down just as we arrived. Our numbers had spooked the cops, and as they rushed in to set up a defense line blocking the city hall doors, they'd inadvertently, or maybe intentionally, knocked over the generator.

Harry Britt, Carol Ruth Silver, and I got up on the stage and passed around the bullhorn, trying to calm things down, but it was like talking into gale-force winds: no one could hear anything above all the shouting. And as people filled the street and spilled over into surrounding areas, they began pushing up the stairs, climbing past the ornamental grillwork until they were nose to nose with the phalanx of cops standing guard at the city hall doors. And then a woman named Amber Hollibaugh grabbed the bullhorn and yelled out, "I don't know why we keep apologizing. I think we should do this more often!" The crowd roared. In all the turmoil, people started throwing things and Silver was hit in the face with a brick. I knew the situation was beyond hope of any control. Almost immediately a band of rioters engulfed the lone police car parked at the curb of city hall, smashing the windows and lighting it on fire. It exploded in a huge ball of flame that sent the crowd wild with excitement. Then a group of young lesbians kicked through the lower windows of city hall, crawled into the basement, and ran through the building setting fires with bits of paper.

Meanwhile, the police seemed confused and stood behind a couple of dozen police cars parked just across the street in front of the state building on McAllister Street. They were outnumbered a hundred to one, and the crowd, like a predator scenting quarry, turned on them and charged. They fell back and the crowd attacked the police cars. You could hear glass shattering and high-pitched wrenching noises as metal was torn loose and strange popping noises as the vinyl seats sizzled. When the gas tanks blew there were fireballs and deafening explosions, and the flames burst up thirty, forty feet. The heat was tremendous. Over all this was an unearthly howl, the combination of sirens and shouting and whistles shrieking.

Finally the police, in helmets and black vests and gloves, got organized. They formed a riot line and began advancing Roman-gladiator style, beating their shields with billy clubs and making deep militaristic grunts. The crowd panicked. The people in front started pushing and shoving to get away, but those in the back were still pressing forward and the crush of bodies was suffocating. Gradually people began to break away in waves, with the cops in pursuit. Then the most amazing thing happened. As the demonstrators ran, the cops broke their ranks and became dispersed. Somewhere, out of the fire and smoke and screaming and sirens, a chant began: "Don't run, don't run. Turn around, turn around. Slow down, turn around, fight back . . ." It rang louder and louder and faster and faster until thousands were shouting, "Fight back, fight back! . . ."

And this chant communicated itself throughout the crowd and people did indeed begin to slow down and turn around and fight back. They threw themselves on the police. The cops were armored in protective gear and had nightsticks, but they weren't prepared for guerrilla warfare. I saw skinny little gay boys wearing nothing but T-shirts and jeans hurl themselves at the gladiators, jumping on their backs and trying to tear the clubs away. Everywhere I looked people were wounded, either bleeding or holding broken arms, or on the asphalt writhing in pain. And this continued for what seemed hours, with the cops advancing, then falling back and then advancing again, until the streets around city hall were secured, a wasteland of burned cars and shards of glass.

I was with Bill Kraus, who was an aide to state assemblyman Phil Burton at the time, when we eventually fled Civic Center to stand a few blocks away at the corner of Van Ness and Market Street in front of the Bank of America. Knots of rioters were racing all around us, kicking over trash cans and smashing windows. I asked Bill if he'd ever broken a window. He had not, and neither had I. Tonight, I said, I want to break a window. Bill grabbed a chunk of stone and threw it against the Bank of America window—and it bounced off, not even leaving a scratch. I cracked up and said, Bill you're such a sissy, you can't even break a window. So I picked up a rock and threw it hard as I could. Nothing. Bill started laughing. Then up walked a big butch woman and hoisted a garbage can over her shoulders and smashed it through. And then she walked off, not saying a word, just raising her fist as she headed, incredibly, back to city hall.

The police came around the corner soon after, so we ran and I somehow was separated from Bill. There were bands of motorcycle cops chasing protesters through the Tenderloin, and residents six stories up throwing bottles and garbage down at the police. All the shops and restaurants had closed their windows, locked their doors. The city was under siege, and we ran like rats in a maze. I ended up at Union Square, and a spike-haired punk who looked like Debbie Harry roared up on her motorcycle and said, "You better get on, girl, the pigs are coming!" And we tore up Market Street, all the way from Powell to Castro, maneuvering around cops and barricades and dodging burning piles of debris, broken glass, and clusters of gays wandering around and chanting.

The Castro was remarkably calm. A lot of people wanted to avoid the riot and had collected in the bars. I stopped by my house for maybe fifteen minutes; when I came back out there were cops everywhere. A pack of them came down Castro Street—sirens blaring, lights flashing—and formed a cordon around the Elephant Walk, trapping everyone inside. All of them had flipped their badges backward. They charged in, beating everyone there to the ground. The cops wanted revenge. They'd gotten their asses whipped at Civic Center and so had invaded the Castro, aiming their retribution at the largest bar in the neighborhood. From the outside I saw the shadows of people being knocked down and punched and kicked. It was a horror film framed by the windows of Harvey's favorite bar.

Up Nineteenth Street, another line of cops began forming and then swept up the street in a flying wedge, laying about with their clubs under a rain of abuse and debris from apartments above. I looked up and saw people with guns on the rooftops. I didn't know if they were police or mad queers, but the sight of men with rifles pointing down onto the street was terrifying. I ran back to my apartment, and Eric and I crouched behind the front door, an old Victorian door with frosted glass, through which we could see silhouettes of police with their clubs. When the coast seemed clear, we'd sneak out and grab the wounded and drag them up to our apartment. It was a battle-zone infirmary. Bodies on the couch and beds, lined up on the floor moaning. There was blood everywhere, in handprints on the door and in smudged red footprints on the floor.

By this time the chief of police, Charley Gain, had arrived and was negotiating with poor Harry Britt, now supervisor. Neither made much progress. Gain wasn't trusted by the police; Harry wasn't trusted by the gay community. In fact, as Harry stood there trying to save our necks, he was being jeered and mocked by the crowd. Thank God for cameras and Super 8 movies; they seemed the only thing that slowed the onslaught. Once the police realized they were being photographed, they began to pull back. They had, after all, made their point.

CHAPTER SEVEN

GRAND JURY
AND THE
AFTERMATH

THE DAY AFTER the riot, I was called into Mayor Feinstein's office for an 8 o'clock meeting. All the gay and lesbian city commissioners were there, along with several heads of gay political organizations. The purpose of the meeting was to inform us that the National Guard was being called in. None of us wanted a second riot, but we were unsure of Feinstein and extremely wary of the Guard. There was little response, particularly when she asked us for permission to say her actions had our approval. I was sitting in the back, listening. Finally Jim Foster, a city commissioner and former president of the Toklas Club, said, "We can't help you. You're going to have to talk to Cleve. He's the one with the permit to close Castro today." Strangely enough, this was true. We had planned a big birthday party for Harvey, booked acts, and, unlike the old days, made everything kosher with city hall by taking out a permit. It was a strange situation. Feinstein had changed. No longer the nervous local politician, she was now a leader of substance and power and was clearly comfortable with that power.

"I just can't allow that party to go on," Feinstein declared. "It would be irresponsible after last night to encourage people to congregate." I paused, stood up, and said, "You can't stop them. No amount of barricades will stop people from coming. They're conditioned to come to the Castro whenever there's trouble, whether it's Anita Bryant or John Briggs or berserk cops or killers going free."

And then I told her a bald-faced lie. "I have four hundred trained peacekeepers to take care of things. All I want from you is a promise that there will be no visible police presence on Castro Street."

"You really have four hundred monitors?"

"Absolutely."

And . . . she agreed. "I won't call in the National Guard today. We'll give it twenty-four hours. You can give the party for Harvey Milk but there will be police, though they'll be out of sight."

I left quickly, feeling weighted with a responsibility whose implications I hadn't really considered. The first thing I had to do was come up with four hundred peacekeepers. I had an old-fashioned telephone tree where you call ten people and tell them what's happening and then they call ten people and so on. And the word went out. Late that afternoon we had five hundred volunteers gathered at Douglas School. I explained that they were not ad hoc cops, that their job was to protect people's ability to exercise constitutional rights. We would carry no weapons, nor would we use any force. We were going to preserve the peace, not promote violence.

Despite our efforts and the mayor's promise, we were convinced the police would attack. Feinstein may have been sincere, but Charley Gain had proved himself to be a weak commander and worse, an indulgent one. There were reports that he'd intentionally slowed his approach to the Castro last evening to let his boys "blow off steam." I believed them. Our only choice was to prepare for a battle. Hidden infirmaries were set up, complete with doctors, nurses, cots, and supplies, in nearby apartments and shops and in the parking lot behind the Castro Theatre. We asked for and received legal observers from the ACLU and the American Bar Association; they were designated with green armbands. Also, in order to document any infractions by the police, we positioned photographers on roofs and in apartments along Castro Street. If a fight did come, we'd be ready, not just for that evening, but for later in the courts.

As the late afternoon came on, the team leaders for the monitors, medics, and photographers sat down in my apartment to go over plans. There were quite a few people there that I'd never seen before, and I suspected some might be undercover cops. The one thing we feared most during a riot was to be corralled, blocked off on one of the Castro's narrow streets with nowhere to run. We had plans to deal with such a charge that included escaping through buildings on Castro Street, if necessary. And these plans would be useless if they'd been exposed.

I called a neighbor, and a few of us slipped out of my apartment and went over to his. My suspicions were immediately confirmed. No sooner had we begun talking than there was a knock at the door. It was Captain Jeffries and the head of police intelligence. Were they tapping my phone line? Bluntly, they asked what our intentions were. We told them: a peaceful memorial party for Harvey Milk and George Moscone. They probed for more information and we outlined our preparations. As I left, Captain Jeffries gave me a police-band radio. I looked at it doubtfully and asked, "You're giving me a police radio?" "Yeah, we'll be in touch," said Jeffries.

Just after sunset, I climbed onstage and picked up the microphone. The juice came on, my taps on the mike echoed over the crowd, and everyone looked up, waiting. So many faces, so much in the balance. There was a cop at the door of my apartment, a cluster of them at a command post above Cliff's Hardware in the middle of Castro Street, and thousands more out of sight, all of them on alert and ready to pour into the streets at the least sign of trouble. The crowd for the most part was rather calm, groups arm in arm, candles flickering. But of the forty thousand who'd come, one in ten were rigged out for a fight, wearing hard hats, masks over their faces, and carrying baseball bats or crowbars. What the fuck could I say? I'd had no time to prepare anything, and I doubt that I could have focused enough in the previous twenty-four hours to write anything sensible. Here I was in front of tens of thousands, at a crucial time in our history, and I had to deliver. I had to say things that would heal and help turn the previous night's disaster into a unifying event, without glorifying or reigniting the violence. Somehow I had to reach them all, bridge the divisions, and if not salve the grief and the rage, give our still raw emotions direction and purpose. I wish I could convey the sense of certainty that came over me and replaced the panic. I thought of Harvey and began:

"Thank you for being here. Last night the lesbians and gay men of San Francisco showed the rest of the city and the rest of the world that we are angry and on the move. And tonight we are here to show the world what we are creating out of that anger and that movement. A strong community of women and men working together to change our world.

"It seems highly appropriate to celebrate Harvey's birthday in this manner, a party on the street he loved. Castro Street was Harvey's home. Where he lived , worked, and organized.

"How many of you have moved here to this new home from somewhere else?

"How many of you are not native San Franciscans?

"We have come here from all the old hometowns of America to reclaim our past and secure our future and replace lives of loneliness and despair with a place of joy and dignity and love."

After my speech I introduced the singer Sylvester, who got everyone dancing to his latest hits. We smoked our pot and drank our beer and celebrated a community that could riot one night and disco the next. We were dancing right in the cops' faces, all forty thousand of us. And there was no trouble.

As the party wound down, a group of us got onstage and began singing: "Happy Birthday to you . . ." Thousands of voices in the night singing, "Happy birthday, dear Harvey, happy birthday to you."

WITHIN TEN DAYS of White Night, as the riots came to be known, a grand jury was convened to investigate and bring the culprits to justice. You could almost hear sighs of relief from city hall, the courts, and the police department, none of which wanted to have the responsibility of deciding who was wrong or right. It seemed a tidy way of satisfying public opinion, which, though divided on the verdict, was overwhelmingly disapproving of the demonstration and the resulting destruction.

The curtain went up on the grand jury melodrama in a scene worthy of French farce. It was morning, about 8 A.M., and I was shaving. My one suit was laid out on the bed, my shoes had a nice shine—all in order to clean up "radical homosexual activist Cleve Edward Jones," as that morning's *Chronicle* had dubbed me. The doorbell rang and I answered with my face lathered in shaving cream. "Cleve Edward Jones?" "Yes." "I hearby serve you with a subpoena to appear before the grand jury. Sign here." I signed. He left, and in a couple of hours I took the bus to city hall—not to answer the subpoena, but to be appointed to the City of San Francisco's Committee on Juvenile Delinquency.

I was not the only one called to appear, of course. Every gay activist within miles of the riots was on the hangman's list. Reporters were also subpoenaed and ordered to produce their notes. News organizations were told to hand over all pertinent pictures and footage. Noncompliance would mean a search-and-seizure order along with a contempt citation. This obviously brought up all sorts of First Amendment issues, but grand juries exist in a kind of netherworld, with tremendous overriding powers. Witnesses are not even allowed to bring an attorney, and all the proceedings are secret and sealed.

All of us were thus placed in a double bind. Refusing to testify guaranteed jail, and testifying would give the appearance of ratting on friends. We were scared and more than a little paranoid. The first option came with the penalty of lost wages, lost jobs, and wrecked careers. The alternative was betraying the community, which is how we all expected to be judged, whether or not we'd implicated our comrades. Not a nice spot to be in.

Some people felt the demonstration to have been nothing more than childish, mindless violence. I was criticized as having tried to lead a mob, then failing to control it. There were a lot of us caught in the middle. Most of the activists were glad the violence had occurred, but that was not a responsible thing to convey. Some conservatives gays wanted to apologize and raise money to do things like repair the ornamental grill-work on city hall, buy the police more squad cars. But the "no apology" response was consensus. We would not try to justify our actions, but neither would we condemn them. Harry Britt articulated that.

My head spinning, I went to Matt Coles, a tough and clever lawyer who's now with the ACLU's gay rights division. He loves complicated cases, and this one had enough twists and turns to get his engine going. After a few days he came up with a bold but simple strategy. I would answer any and all questions from the grand jury to the best of my ability—but at the end of each day's testimony I would release exact transcripts of the questions I had been asked and the answers I had given.

This elegant solution had one more wrinkle, and it too rested on a strict interpretation of the laws governing grand jury proceedings. Though witnesses were not allowed to appear with counsel, they did have the right to leave the hearing room to speak outside the chamber with a legal representative whenever they needed guidance. There was no limit to the number of times a witness could seek his attorney's aid. That was the key.

Here's what happened: I'm seated in the witness box facing jurors with little mountains of evidence laid neatly in front of them—stacks of photographs, notes and affidavits from my old friends at the SFPD. Grand juries tend to be conservative, and this one fit the mold. The men were all in suits, the women in dresses. As I studied their all too serious faces I saw only three jurors of color, two African Americans and a Hispanic woman, and not a single likely gay. The room was still and quiet when the foreman boomed out, "Will you please state your name." I took out a pen and pad of legal paper, and asked him to repeat the question. He repeated it and I wrote it down. Then I said, "I respectfully request permission to consult with my counsel before responding." I stood up and walked out. The jurors just sat there, mouths agape. I went out, lit a cigarette, finished the cigarette, trembling, and returned to the witness box to give them my answer: "Cleve Edward Jones."

The thing dragged on and on, with me invoking the excusal clause after each question, no matter how banal. By the time they got through determining my address ("593a Castro Street") and my whereabouts on May 21, 1978 ("San Francisco"), the afternoon was shot. It was a standoff. I was exhausted, and most of the jury was obviously bored with this stillborn drama.

Exasperated, the red-faced foreman threatened to indict me with contempt of court. "Will you cooperate?" I left the room and came back, after a few nervous minutes, with a statement: "It is my intent to answer completely and honestly all questions posed to me by the grand jury. It is also my intent to publish all questions asked and answers given." Lots of furrowed brows on the jury. The foreman did his job and I was reminded, again, that my behavior would not be tolerated and asked to "consider the consequences, young man!" And then the grilling began: "We want you to describe in detail the manner in which you proceeded from Castro to city hall." Once again I left the room, talked with Matt, returned to my seat, leaned into the microphone, and gave my answer: "On foot."

Lots of shuffling of papers, raised eyebrows, and the sole Hispanic woman in the jury hid a smile behind her hand. "Are you or are you not willing to answer our questions, Mr. Jones?" I did my routine, Matt gave me a thumbs-up, and I went back in. "Yes," I replied.

The sham ended as ridiculously as it began. At the end of the day I was dismissed. The grand jury never did call me again. Editorials called for an accounting and kept pointing the finger at me, saying it was Cleve Jones who'd led the crowd to city hall, but Mayor Feinstein restricted herself to arm's-length involvement and the inquiry fizzled out.

The aftermath of White Night—the ensuing political machinations at city hall, the scapegoating grand jury, and the controversy surrounding it all—was absurd and missed the importance of that night by sidestepping the whole tinderbox of emotions behind the murders, the trial, and the verdict. To consider the idea that the riot could have been a spontaneous uprising against a flagrant miscarriage of justice would have acknowledged that there had been real issues. It was much easier to single out a few targets, blame them, lock them up, and shelve the mess in a tight legal box. Luckily, we found that the box was easily escaped. None of us had to implicate friends or in any way compromise our beliefs. Afterward, Gwenn Craig, an articulate black lesbian activist, spoke for us all in a dramatic speech to the Harvey Milk Gay Democratic Club when she said, "We were pushed to the wall—no apologies."

DURING THE GRAND jury I was getting an extraheavy dose of death threats—nothing out of the ordinary, just the usual letters saying that I was a faggot and should be killed for being a pervert. Harvey had gotten hundreds of similar notes and we'd pinned them to his office's "wall of shame" as badges of honor, proving that you can't change the world without upsetting a few crazies. I wasn't too concerned, but many of my friends were, especially since my phone number and address were known to so many people. I was more frightened of the police, who I knew would love to get me, especially since I'd slipped through the grand jury's net.

Our paranoia came to a head on a Sunday in June 1979, coincidentally just two days after I'd been dismissed by the grand jury. Two hundred fifty thousand people were expected to attend the gay pride celebration in San Francisco, and I'd be marching with the Harvey Milk Gay Democratic Club for six miles along crowded city streets. If anyone wanted to hurt me, they'd have an easy target. The assailant could easily disappear into the crowd.

Had the atmosphere of that winter and spring not been so fogged with conspiracy and violence, such thoughts would never have occurred to any of us. But they did occur, and so as we marched along, several people walked close beside me. About halfway through we relaxed and were getting into the mood of all the festivities when all of a sudden a man rushed out of the crowd, grinning, but wearing a drab gray business suit. I was scared stiff, and the famous photograph of Jack Ruby shooting Lee Harvey Oswald flashed through my mind. My protectors gathered around me, worried, defensive; we had no idea what to do. And then this scarily ordinary man planted himself right in front of me and pointed his finger in my face, yelling at the top of his lungs, "You're Cleve Jones! You're Cleve Jones!" And then he waved his arms above his head and burst out, "I was on the grand jury! You were *fab-u-lous!*"

I was so relieved that I hugged him. Then that frozen moment out of time dissolved and I began to hear the marching bands and feel the excitement of the day, and as my unknown fan melted into the cheering crowds, the parade moved on.

CHAPTER EIGHT

SACRAMENTO
AND
JANE FONDA

T HROUGHOUT THE LATE '70s it became more and more obvious that gays and lesbians around the country were asserting themselves and claiming rights and freedoms long denied. Some of us had feared that the backlash begun in Dade County and filtered out to so many other states would slow the progress and expected also that Harvey's assassination would cripple our own courage. But the opposite took place. The attacks only woke people up to the reality of homophobia. It truly surprised some of my friends to discover that they were hated. What seemed so obvious to activists like me was a revelation to many who'd never questioned society's assumptions. But once out, very few were willing to return to the closet, and most were discovering the simple notion that maybe they weren't so bad after all and that our rights were just as sacrosanct as the straight world's. Our homes and bars shouldn't be raided, our jobs should be secure, and our voices should be heard, not only in the urban centers but everywhere.

In the summer of '79 I began traveling a lot, and saw the change with my own eyes. My calendars for this period read like a campaign schedule, with speaking dates all over the country. For gay pride events alone that year, I was in Sacramento, Miami, San Jose, Houston, New York, and Seattle. I had a series of expendable jobs, and when life in the city seemed too crowded, I'd resign and hop a Greyhound, leave town for a few weeks, and give a speech or visit friends in New York or Boston. Overnight the gay world in cities along my cross-country routes seemed to come alive, even in Middle American towns like Kansas City and St. Louis. The large cities on the coasts began hosting enormous pride parades, film festivals, newspapers, literary journals, religious groups, gay Republican clubs, gay Democratic clubs, gay Libertarian clubs, gay Marxist clubs, gay professional associations for gay doctors, gay lawyers, gay sporting groups . . . It was just this phenomenon mushrooming all over the country in just a few years.

Here in San Francisco, we not only survived Harvey's death, we thrived. Mayor Feinstein replaced Chief Gain with Cornelius Murphy. A reliably loyal captain from the ranks, Murphy assuaged gay fears and by 1980 was recruiting gay and lesbian officers as a matter of course. Of personal importance to me was Harry Britt's conduct as supervisor. He'd surprised us all with his grit and refusal to knuckle under and downplay the gay rights agenda. I'd been impressed, particularly with his "no apology" stance on the White Night riots, when he'd told reporters that "society is going to have to deal with us not as nice little fairies who have hairdressing salons, but as people capable of violence. We're not going to put up with Dan Whites anymore."

My own star was also rising at the time, thanks to a big-hearted politician named Art Agnos. By the cutthroat rules of politics, Art Agnos should not have become my friend, let alone my mentor. Philosophically, he was much more centrist. He was part of the liberal northern California Democratic machine that believed in business as usual and viewed "radicals" like Harvey and me as dangerous and disruptive upstarts. We were the lunatic fringe. In response, the democratic political machine had consistently backed Harvey's gay opponents in his first two runs for supervisor, in '72 and '74. And in 1976, when Harvey ran for assemblyman, Agnos himself ran against him. The Assembly race was very contentious, particularly bitter in the final weeks as the polls tightened and the Committee to Elect Art Agnos hit us with the not-so-subtly homophobic ads that eventually won Art his seat. The next year, 1977, when Harvey ran for supervisor the third time, Art was again on the offensive, backing Rick Stokes, a "toilet trained" gay candidate, for the supervisor seat that Harvey eventually won. Agnos and I had history between us, across a rather wide divide, none of it amicable. But with Harvey's win, he'd gained credibility in Agnos's eyes and so had I.

I was at loose ends those months after Harvey's death, and my office comrades had gone their own ways. Anne Kronenberg had left town to start a new life "anywhere but San Francisco." Dick Pabich was doing fine with his new partnership in Rivaldo-Pabich, but had no time for me. I'd gotten a clerking job in a bookstore, Noe Valley Books and News, making just enough to pay rent and buy a few drinks at the bars. On the whole, I'd had come through it all relatively intact. The recurring nightmares of running desperately through city hall, chased by Dan White, seemed to be subsiding. My parents, with whom I'd reestablished relations, offered to help pay for tuition at SFSU so that I could finish up my undergraduate degree, but after life in the real world, sitting in a classroom and knocking out term papers seemed pretty pale. I didn't really know what to do.

Still, I stayed politically involved. I was appointed to the Mission Mental Health Advisory Board and won election to the San Francisco Democratic County Central Committee. I also signed on as a Britt supporter in his bid for reelection and worked on the campaign. One of the statewide organizations that came on board Britt's campaign was the CED, the Campaign for Economic Democracy. The CED was Tom Hayden's vehicle, a coalition of left-wing groups cobbled together from socialist, antiwar, and environmental organizations, and they offered to help us get Harry Britt reelected as supervisor by lending us financial support, along with a little movie-land pizzazz—Hayden's wife, Jane Fonda.

Nowadays every minority group has celebrity backers, but back then it was something new, giving reporters yet another angle to cover in stories with headlines like "Gay Hollywood Connections" and "Hanoi Jane Comes to the Castro." And we were grateful. It's only now, when stars acquire activism like a new mink coat, that cynicism has set in. At the time we accepted the support at face value and thought Fonda brave. I still do. Whatever her motivation, Fonda's aura lent us credibility and some welcome glamour. She spoke at various fund-raisers about brotherhood and loving your neighbor and the world as one big family, and everybody just loved her. She was the perfect one to get the bar queens out and into the voting booths, and I took her on a tour of several saloons. We went to the Midnight Sun, to Oil Can Harry's. Britt, a tad deficient in the charisma department, was happy to give her the stage. The star turns culminated in a very dramatic procession down Castro Street—Jane and Harry leading arm in arm, followed by an entourage of CEDers lapping up the spillover adoration.

After the election, which we won, I had no illusions of being offered a job in the city's current administration. Though Britt and Feinstein respected my speaking ability and regarded my capacity to bring out a crowd with a certain fearful admiration, I wasn't quite their cup of tea. Too outspoken, too "combustible," as a friend once chided, and no jobs were offered. I'm not sure I was ready to return to city hall so soon anyway.

Naturally, I was not the sort of person Assemblyman Agnos chummed around with, and I didn't have any sort of contact with him until an evening in December 1979 when I went to a meeting called by the Alice B. Toklas Memorial Democratic Club (which, along with the Harvey Milk Gay Democratic Club, was one of the most powerful gay organizations in the city, started by an old friend of mine from early days,

Jim Foster). The city was reeling from a huge influx of crack cocaine at the time, and my friend Felix Munoz and I were there to lobby against budget cuts that would stall funding of drug-prevention programs and a mental health treatment center in San Francisco's Mission District, a heavily Latino and gay area.

Art was the good Democratic soldier defending the system. I was pissed off that once again minorities were being cut out, and I really went after him: "Do you know what's going to happen if they shut down that program? Have you ever been on Sixteenth Street, Mr. Agnos? It's in your district. . . ." Art, who's a master at handling crowds and deflecting bullshit, was extremely smooth in answering my questions.

Afterward he came over and patted me on the shoulder, saying, "You're really obnoxious. Maybe you should get a real job in politics." "Oh that would be great," I said. "Why don't you find me a cool job in Sacramento?" I was just being a smart-ass, and we laughed about it. Some two weeks later, Art telephoned me at the bookstore: "Hey, smart-ass, I got you that high-powered job in Sacramento if you want it." So in the first week of January 1980 I moved to Sacramento. I was the first openly gay person hired to work in the capital—an olive branch to the Milk faction—and, as I would find out, a relatively naive newcomer to the sometimes clandestine ways of state politics.

It was, as Art had so trenchantly put it, my first "real job," complete with a reliable check every two weeks (twenty-three thousand dollars a year, not bad for a twenty-six-year-old), health insurance, and even a pension plan. I got my first-ever driver's license! My parents were happy, Art was happy, and I was willing to give the traditional side of politics a shot.

Agnos had introduced A.B. 1, which would have outlawed discrimination based on sexual orientation, as soon as he took office. Throughout my four years in Sacramento, pushing that bill was a spring ritual. Though Governor Jerry Brown had indicated he would sign the legislation, in those days we often did not even have the votes to get A.B. 1 out of the Labor Committee and you could count our supporters in the Assembly on two hands. Even so, Art insisted every year in launching a full-fledged campaign. Art recognized that gay rights legislation would never pass until a solid majority of legislators understood that they too had gay and lesbian constituents; the difficulty was in finding them outside the urban centers. So every year he'd hit the road, traveling throughout rural California to debate the right-wingers and fundamentalists, just as he'd done during the Briggs Initiative battle. I traveled with him on many of those trips. At every stop, Art would passionately articulate our community's hope for equality under the law and an end to violence and injustice. Usually there were more opponents than supporters, but he countered all the old myths with statistics that proved their fallacy.

I was assigned to the office of Majority Consultants, a semiprivate consulting outfit under the control of then–Assembly Speaker Leo McCarthy, head honcho of the California Democratic Party. During the legislative session, I worked on health issues, which meant I was the liaison between McCarthy and the Health Committee, reporting to the Speaker and then back to Agnos and the other Democratic members of the committee on the Speaker's position. I liked the work and quickly found it so absorbing that I spent a lot of nights poring over issues ranging from asbestosis to Alzheimer's to laetrile.

It was fascinating to see close-up the inner workings of a big party machine that ran a state whose economy rivaled that of most nations. Millions of dollars were spent on this, on that, depending on what, I wondered—the party platform, campaign promises, the Speaker's whim, the state's needs, or a blend of it all? I expected a larger version of the bargaining I'd known well among San Francisco supervisors; that wasn't the problem.

Majority Consultants was a pool of political advisers who during the legislative session worked for the state on legislative issues. As the campaign season began, they went off the state payroll and onto the Democratic Party payroll as shock troops deployed by Speaker McCarthy to support his candidates in the primaries and in the general elections. When does the payroll switch occur? As late as possible, of course. It's a fundamentally exploitive system that diverts taxpayers' money for purely partisan political efforts that inevitably strengthen the incumbent party leadership, but it continues to this day.

Majority Consultants was run by a man named Paul Kinney, who still does political legwork. One day, Kinney asked me, the only gay guy, and Tyrone Netters, the only black guy, to stay late. He had something for us, the only two minority staffers, to do. He led us up on the roof and, what do you know? There were trucks on the roof, empty, with their doors open. Kinney handed us rolls of tape and told us to go back down to the office and cover up all the tags marking the furniture as property of the state of California. We were to then load all the desks and credenzas and chairs, typing tables and bookcases, into the trucks and drive the booty over to campaign headquarters. Hmmm. It was nighttime; we were a couple of blocks from the capitol. Just over the skyline we could see the lights of the city, and beyond them, I knew, was Folsom Penitentiary. All we needed were a few trench coats to make the scene properly sleazy. With his tasseled loafers, pleated pants, and news-anchor coif, Kinney had his role down pat.

This was the smarmy side of machine politics. Going to jail just to save a few bucks wasn't what I'd bargained for. I called Agnos and said that I really appreciated his getting me work, but if petty theft was part of the job description, I wasn't interested. He was furious. "Just you go home," he said. "I'll stop that." And he did. Kinney wasn't so friendly after that little dust-up.

THOUGH DEMOCRATS HAD done well in San Francisco and in California generally, Ronald Reagan's landslide in 1980 and a surprising number of Republican victories in the House and Senate had the pundits predicting a new conservative trend in American politics and tolling a death knell for the far left democratic groups like the CED. Certainly Hayden's candidates had been steamrolled, and after a few months of soul-searching and sifting polling data, the CED began a series of conferences to map out a comeback strategy. Despite the climate and faltering membership rolls, it was flush with money thanks to Jane's wildly popular exercise videos. And with money came ambition. Hayden was writing a philosophical book on his vision for the country and devoting a lot of energy to expanding the CED into what he envisioned would become a force not only in the state of California but on the national political landscape.

I was considered a rising star in some circles, and found myself invited to spend the weekend at Tom and Jane's ranch in the Santa Barbara mountains for one of the CED comeback conferences. It was to be a select gathering of activists from around the state to analyze the results of the election and talk privately among ourselves about the future and how we'd get there.

I drove down with Gwenn Craig, who was a great barhopping friend of mine. We made jokes along the way (I was to stay in the "Cesar Chavez" room) and pretended not to be impressed that we were spending the weekend with Barbarella and one of the Chicago 8.

We spent a good portion of our time in the main room of the lodge. There was a circle of chairs and worktables, and we'd watch and dissect and discuss hour upon hour of political commercials from around the country, both Democratic and Republican. But mostly we were lounging and playing around in a fabulously located compound with panoramic views of the Santa Barbara mountains. It was very exciting to lie by the pool with Jane Fonda and make small talk. She was gracious and easy to get along with. I went jogging on the mountain trails with her and she showed me caves whose walls were inscribed with old Indian paintings. Ronald Reagan's ranch was on the other side of the mountain, I learned. During all this time the only really serious faux pas I made was a crack about the extreme right and extreme left hiding guns in the same hills. No one laughed except Gwenn.

The last day, we were told in hushed tones that Tom Hayden would be giving a speech. The solemnity of the messenger made it quite clear we should be grateful that we had been chosen to hear this oration. Some of us had wondered where he'd been.

At the appointed time, we filed into the main room. But instead of our familiar "nonhierarchical circle," the chairs had been arranged in neat rows in front of a lectern next to which was a single straight-back chair. We waited in reverent silence. Tom walked in and began a turgid analysis of where the liberals had gone wrong and what they'd have to do to recapture power.

The chair beside him remained empty until, right on cue, a side door opened and Jane demurely glided in and took the acolyte's position in the ostentatiously plain wood chair, her hair pulled back in a ponytail, wearing a down vest and no makeup. Staring earnestly up at Tom at the lectern, she looked like a lovesick Ivory girl or a more youthful version of Nancy peering earnestly up at Ronnie. Very touching.

Tom Hayden droned on and on, and then just as we were about to nod off he caught fire and began bellowing faster and louder: "I know many of you are disappointed now, and tired. But I want you to remember the soldiers of Valley Forge. Though their feet were cold and cracked and bloody, they marched on. We will march on in the factories, in the fields, in the ghettos of America. . . ."

The entire tableau was hysterically theatrical, and Gwenn and I were clutching each other's arms in a desperate attempt to keep from laughing. When Hayden's chin started crinkling up, I leaned over to Gwenn and gasped, "If he cries, if he cries. . . ." And she whispered, "I'll leave, I'll leave!" Then we look over and there's Jane sitting there with her hands on her knees, tears pouring down her face. And Tom builds and builds to the climax: ". . . and we shall be like those soldiers in Valley Forge and we shall prevail!" Then he slammed his fist down on the lectern and they both stood up and, in a final bit of over-the-top chore-ography, embraced and then walked out the door to deafening ap-plause. Gwenn and I fell on the floor in convulsions and hightailed it out of there.

After the Hayden fiasco I returned to Sacramento and found things at a similarly unsatisfactory pass. With the Democratic majority split al-most exactly between McCarthy and Berman loyalists, Willie Brown stunned the entire state by persuading the Republicans to support him for Speakership. In the first of his signature presto-chango leaps, Brown was elected Speaker by the Republicans, plus one Democratic vote—his own. As the McCarthy troops were replaced by Brown loyalists, I went to work each day expecting a pink slip. I was spared the guillotine, thanks to Art's intervention, but it was clear that my climb up the political ladder was now on hold. Willie Brown, as everyone knew even then, has the memory of an elephant and wasn't about to promote a former McCarthy man. Still, I was a good soldier, taking Agnos at his word that he'd allied himself with Brown and I had nothing to worry about. As it turned out, thoughts of career were about to become much less important.

CHAPTER NINE

AIDS

W E FORGET TODAY how long we had to operate without any real information on AIDS. The first time I heard of it was in 1981 in a few lines of a UPI press clipping that I pinned to the wall of my office. Within months it became probable that this little-noticed disease would engulf a generation in a mass wave of death. I, along with almost everyone I knew, was already carrying it within my body like a ticking bomb. It was the dawn of the plague years. Back then we didn't even have a name for this silent killer.

As the Speaker's legislative aide on health concerns, it was my job to read all the governmental reports of disease in the Eighth District, the eastern end of San Francisco, including the Castro. Foremost among the reports was the Centers for Disease Control's *MMWR,* the *Mortality and Morbidity Weekly Report,* which chronicles the occurrence of every deadly disease. Cancer is there in a bewildering number of mutations, and sometimes a virus of little-known origin will crop up. In a port city like San Francisco, with ships docking from every other continent in the world, strange diseases are not abnormal. But among the entries there was something new coming on: *Pneumocystis carinii* pneumonia, or PCP, a rare pneumonia, often appearing with an equally rare cancer,

Kaposi's sarcoma—or KS, as it quickly became known. There seemed to be a connection, but the only hard fact we could discover was that all the patients were homosexuals.

I'd get calls in my office all day from people finding purple spots on their calves and feet. Some were panicked, barely able to tell me their symptoms. Many were so numbed and frightened that I had to lean forward in my chair to hear their whispers. It was heartbreaking. I couldn't do much except listen and take down their names and refer them to a doctor who knew nothing about their disease but would at least treat them with respect and not be afraid to touch them—a rarity in those days.

In April 1981, I got a call from Dr. Marcus Conant. As the only openly gay person on the Speaker's staff, I took hundreds of calls a week, but Marcus's call stood out, largely because of his voice. He speaks softly, with a slight southern accent, and there was something compelling about his tone. He was very concerned about the appearance of a usually rare cancer called Kaposi's sarcoma and thought the state government needed to be involved. He made dinner reservations at the Zuni Café, where he told me what he knew about the outbreaks, describing in his gentle drawl the heinous symptoms, how the telltale purple lesions signaled a complete collapse of the immune system. And then he made a wild leap and said emphatically that he was sure it was a new virus and that it would turn out to be fatal. He explained that it seemed to be transmitted sexually and that there would of course be a pyramiding effect if the virus had a long incubation period. A slow onset of symptoms would hide the disease, and carriers would inadvertently spread it, perhaps for years. My mind refused to add up the numbers of people one man could infect. And I remember leaving there thinking, *If he's right, we're all going to die.*

Shortly afterward, on a beautifully clear day, Marcus took me up to UCSF Hospital to a balcony that overlooks San Francisco Bay. I distinctly remember the long soft fingers of fog just beginning to push through the Golden Gate Bridge. He introduced me to a wonderful nurse named Angie Lewis, a very brave and no-nonsense woman who took us in to meet Simon Guzman. Simon was the first person I saw at the end of his struggle with AIDS. I should have been hardened by all the people who'd come through the office, but this was different. Perhaps it was being in a hospital, or maybe it was Simon's birdlike fragility. Though his eyes were bright, he couldn't speak; there were hollows at his temples; and when he coughed, those dry hacks racked his chest so violently I was sure each one would be his last.

He had photographs on the table showing what he'd looked like before the virus, posing poolside in a swimsuit, obviously proud of his sculptured body, big flashing white teeth, and beautiful eyes. A handsome Hispanic man with a knockout, mile-wide smile, he was just my type. But this person on the bed had orange-sized tumors and his skin was covered in huge KS lesions. He'd lost so much weight that the sheet rose off the bed in points at his hips, knees, and feet. After I'd seen Simon, all the studying and theorizing seemed pretty empty.

While we knew that most of the affected were gay men, quantifiable information was so scarce and contradictory that we could only track its effects. Dr. Selma Dritz, at the San Francisco Department of Health, had blackboards mapping the disease's progression, which seemed to concentrate in the large coastal cities. The first identifiable diagnoses came in groups—or *clusters,* as they were known. All these were connected with chalk lines forming a sort of spiderweb or some weird cell structure. We knew there was a house in the Castro on Eighteenth Street where successive tenants had come down with KS. There were two households in Los Angeles and three in New York City. Though it was as yet unproven, sexual transmission seemed to be the link. We knew that our work was potentially explosive and so coded names as X_0, X_1, and onward. One of those individuals, the only common link, was Gaeton Dugas, the now infamous Patient Zero.

The day I walked into Selma's office and learned that Paul Popham's house at Fire Island was on the map, it was all I could do to stay cool. My friend Marvin had spent time there, and I'd heard of it before only as a wonderful beach house in one of the legendary gay resorts. What could I say to Marvin that wouldn't sound like killjoy paranoia? I called him anyway, with a warning that came years too late. That was very strange, to be tracking this mystery killer, and all of the sudden to see a friend of mine listed as X14.

WE HAD SO little support back then. The newspapers, if in fact they knew of it, gave it little or no coverage. The gay papers, sensitive to what seemed a sardonically homophobic disease, were both skeptical of this "fluke" and fearful of hurting their advertising base. And there was a great deal of reluctance on the part of government officials. I remember asking Pat Norman, the director of the Office of Lesbian and Gay Health in the San Francisco Health Department, for a list of doctors I could refer people to. The idea of a list made her nervous. "We don't want to panic the public," she warned, and then reminded me of the implications of panic in the gay community as well as the potential to ignite an antigay backlash. We needed to be careful, she said.

It was an incredibly frustrating time. I knew we were doing good and necessary work and that people like Selma Dritz and her colleagues supplied the essential groundwork for gearing up the complex machine that would hopefully eventually bear down and crush the disease. But I also knew that I wasn't cut out for desk work. Even if I'd had the training to read lab results, I couldn't make the abstract jump required of a good researcher to translate statistics and from them build the sort of arguments to help win the long bureaucratic battle. But on the front lines I felt alive, worthwhile. I needed to be with people, as much to help them as to be helped.

One day I called Marcus and told him how I felt. I couldn't be anywhere else but in the streets. Did he understand? After a pause, he said, "I may have something for you." And then he went on to outline a plan for the Kaposi's Sarcoma Education and Research Foundation, which later became the San Francisco AIDS Foundation. He was working on putting together a board of directors; did I have any suggestions? Could I get Agnos to give me time off to work on that? I told him I was sure Agnos would support the project and that I was more than ready.

The original board consisted of one of Marcus's friends, a lawyer named Frank Jacobsen, as well as Bob Ross, publisher of the gay weekly *Bay Area Reporter* and Dr. Paul Volberding, a doctor who, like Marcus, was treating the first cases of AIDS. They were to supply the legal, media, and medical expertise. I was operations director in charge of setting up the office, distributing literature, and making presentations.

All the organizing was important, but my first responsibility, and the one I was most qualified for, was enlisting volunteers. For the first few months my "office" was at the crossroads of the gay world, Castro and Eighteenth. I jokingly anointed it Hibernia Beach, after the Hibernia Bank whose sidewalk has historically hosted activists pressing a cause and sun worshipers getting tanned. After work downtown, I'd sprint up to the Castro just in time to catch the rush-hour crowd and set up a folding table piled with fliers and leaflets. When somebody went by that I knew (or wanted to know), I'd grab him by the shoulder and say, How would you like to come with me and serve your people? It was a hell of a pickup line.

Though most of my recruits would have preferred to cruise the happy-hour crowd at any of the scores of teeming Castro bars, enough agreed to work that within days we had a staff and a complement of volunteers were fanning out into the neighborhoods, spreading the news and information about the disease and signing up people for exams. One of the guys I grabbed was Chuck Frutchey, who stayed with the organization for many years. He and I had a friendly competition, not only over who could sign up the most people, but over whose recruits were the cutest.

After a few months, I became alarmed by our lack of progress and wanted to do more. I went to Art and told him that I didn't want to work in the office any longer, asking for permission to work full-time on Castro Street with the foundation. He wasn't surprised at all. Actually, I think he expected something of the sort. But beneath his nodding encouragement I felt a degree of disappointment. There is something in all politicians—a little boy playing king of the mountain, perhaps—that craves a follower, a believer, someone to back him up and take his lead. Art is tall, dark-eyed, and charismatic, seductive, like all successful politicians. I wanted to please him; he'd been a mentor to me, after all. But one of our ongoing arguments was about his vision of my future. "Don't you understand, Cleve? You're my Jackie Robinson! Look farther than the Castro! With all your talents, you could do so much more. . . ." Supervisor Jones, Congressman Jones. He'd let the potentials dangle. And I would waver. The only problem was I didn't want to leave Castro Street. Castro was my home, its natives my people. And now there was something wrong. We didn't know exactly what it was, when we could stop it, or even how we'd survive. But I had no other choice, I told him, even if it came down to quitting my job.

Fortunately, since the foundation had no money for salaries, Art not only agreed to my request but also suggested we write a funding proposal. Ed Power, an early foundation volunteer, and I went into Art's office late one night and drafted a funding proposal to be spent on new diseases: ten thousand dollars for the city. The day we opened the office, we had a line of people going down the staircase into the streets. Our phone, which we'd not yet listed, began ringing off the hook within an hour. In September 1982 we organized a community forum on AIDS, held at Everett Middle School. It was the first public event to discuss the epidemic. Attendance was high, and the local papers all covered it. We made the front pages, finally.

We had many comrades in the effort to raise the alarm, and the fight, as we saw it, wasn't only about AIDS. It was about being honest concerning this new disease, and part of that honesty was coming out. One of the early gay activists was my friend Hank Wilson, a handsome public-school teacher. One of the pioneers of our movement, he is still alive, working today on youth awareness programs. I'd met him in the late '70s, when he was part of a gay teachers' group; I also knew him through BAGL. Of all the activists he was the most likable because he was least concerned with ideology. He was purely focused on encouraging gay people to come out of the closet and be strong and clear about who they were.

In the '70s, Hank, Randy Alfred, and I, together with several others, had started the Butterfly Brigade, which distributed whistles to gays and lesbians all over the city. Yes, it was funny name, but the idea was to turn the perception of gays as weak fairies on its ear. There was a constant threat of bashers in those days, so we told everyone, "If you hear a whistle, blow your own and come running and beat the shit out of whoever's causing trouble." Instead of just taking a beating quietly, we had to change. "Fight back! You don't have to take it anymore, and you don't have to do it alone. Just whistle."

One Friday night I was on Castro Street when a carload of punks pulled up looking for a fight. We started blowing our whistles and confronting them one-on-one, two-on-one, and very quickly there must have been fifty of us to their four. There was a lot of shoving and yelling, but I don't remember anyone throwing punches. Then, like in an old war movie, the cavalry came to the rescue. One of the stores across the street, Cliff's Variety, was undergoing renovation, and there was a Dumpster on the street. A bunch of us climbed in and started hurling plasterboard at the bashers. They ran to their car and tried to get away but it stalled, and chunks of garbage rained down, smart bombs aimed at the getaway car. By then it was a rout and our anger had changed to triumph. When that once shiny sedan finally limped away down Castro, we'd completely trashed it. I'll never forget one guy's face, cowering behind a cracked rear window. Score one for the good guys.

Another friend, met through Hank, was Bobbi Campbell. Bobbi was the first person with AIDS to go public. He wrote a column for the *Sentinel* (one of San Francisco's weekly gay newspapers) titled "The

Gay Cancer Journal." I'd read his first two installments, and when Hank introduced us, I told him I was grateful for his decision to brave the publicity and write the column. He had a sleepy kind of smile and a softness that belied his tenacity. He said he'd do anything to stir things up: "I want to live, anything for that."

Then he took off his shoes and showed me the KS lesions on his feet. He was very articulate, with a quiet intensity—qualities that seared audiences when he spoke for funding measures or in community awareness meetings. Later, he and his lover would appear on the cover of *Newsweek* magazine in one of the earliest attempts to "put a face on AIDS." The article didn't mention that he was one of the first members of that new holy order, the Sisters of Perpetual Indulgence, an activist organization of men dressed as nuns that to this day has raised hundreds of thousands of dollars to fight AIDS. His drag name, since he was also a nurse, was Sister Florence Nightmare, R.N.

I remember once talking to Hank and Bobbi at the Twin Peaks. Perched at the top of Castro and Market, Twin Peaks is famous for being the first gay bar to conduct business openly behind clear windows rather than behind the usual cavelike walls of most other homosexual saloons. I was in a low mood that evening. Here we are, I said, in the middle of the capital of the gay world, spoiling the party by shouting that something is rotten. Bobbi would have none of that: we couldn't keep quiet, no matter how unwelcome our message. We got very drunk that night.

I've always liked parties, especially giving them, and on New Year's Eve—I guess it would be the beginning of 1983—my roommate Donald Currie and I gave one a hell of a celebration. There were motorcycles and cars clogging the streets. And jammed inside our two-bedroom Victorian flat were all these Democratic Party hacks mingling with buffed-out tank-top boys, cops and bikers and punks and bull dykes and a few sweater fairies. There was a judge dancing with a hustler to the beat of Sylvester's "Dance, Disco Heat." There was lots of laughter. We were all high, not only on whatever we were drinking or smoking or cadging in quick trips to the bathroom, but on San Francisco and its magic, incomparable mix of people.

As if to put a higher peak on an already glorious night, in came Bobbi, who'd been so sick so many times, like a street fighter diva in this incredible silver sequined floor-length dress and towering mile-high hair. And pinned to his huge bust ("My balcony, darling. Like it?") was a plate-sized button emblazoned with "I Will Survive." The perfect top note of glitter and grit.

It was just a party, like so many others, but it has stuck in my mind because Bobbi's entrance was in such contrast to the next time we met. Not long after New Year's, I got a call, then another, and then a third—each from someone who'd seen Bobbi at the baths. Although none of them had seen him having sex, they were disgusted that he would show himself in such a place, sores and all, as if he still belonged to the world of carefree pleasure. It made them angry and frightened that he was "flaunting it," as one of the callers said. "Why can't he just stay home!" This was really the first time I'd had to face something that grew quite common—anti-HIV prejudice within the community. Now, of course, we know that AIDS is transmitted through blood and semen (neither of which Bobbi was passing on), but hysteria was rampant and even a sick person's handshake was suspect.

For whatever reason, I was enlisted to talk with Bobbi, and I did, reluctantly, relay the message. He was enraged. "Who are these chicken-shits?" he demanded. "Why don't they talk to me face-to-face?" I just managed to say that fear distorts everything, that it's part of the price of going public in a column on AIDS: "You're a target now. . . ." What did Bobbi say? What could he say? He was being told the boat was full, that he was no longer a member of the club. Life, as he knew it, was over. And I was delivering the news. I remember tears in his eyes, but beyond that, memory is blurry. I see only his face, white with shock and betrayal. . . ."I'm not doing anything unsafe," he whispered. "I know you're not, Bobbi."

The people who were frightened of Bobbi Campbell, surely one of the gentlest people God ever created, were heartless and wrong, but we were all scared shitless. And whether we were projecting our fears cruelly onto others or just kidding ourselves into believing it couldn't happen to us, we just didn't want to believe that our dreamworld was part nightmare.

When I attended the first National Lesbian and Gay Health Conference in Dallas in August 1982, AIDS was still a small part of the agenda and only fifty of us showed up for the AIDS forum. The caliber of participants, though, was heartening. I was especially impressed with Paul Popham and Larry Kramer, founders of GMHC (Gay Men's Health Crisis). Unlike in San Francisco, where we had a few strong supporters in city and state government, these men had little or no government backing. In spite of this, they'd developed a support network of over three hundred volunteers to feed, house, and inform New York's burgeoning AIDS population. GMHC, like the KS Foundation, was establishing the outlines for AIDS treatment and care that would soon be the world model.

Still, despite all the activity, the forewarning from Marcus Conant, from the people who'd come through my office, from Bobbi's example, even I myself did not understand the full implications of the signs of the approaching epidemic. I remember one evening visiting my boyfriend at the time, Felix Velarde-Munoz, a handsome young lawyer. We had met one glorious afternoon in 1980 at a tea dance at the I-Beam. He was extraordinarily handsome, but it was his clompy way of dancing that charmed me, the way he threw his body about to the music with such abandon. Later that afternoon, we exchanged numbers and parted. As he walked up Haight Street, I turned for one last glimpse and saw him jump up and kick his heels. We had a wonderful, lighthearted affair, and he was always full of explosive energy. But that evening in '82, as I excitedly told him of my day's frustrations with complacent politicians, he was unusually unresponsive. Wrapped up in my monologue, I barely noticed his lack of interest. And then he suddenly leapt up from the table and ran outside to vomit. I dismissed it as a passing flu. A year later Felix was in the hospital with PCP. He'd never told me he was ill with AIDS, never told anyone.

Another man I was seeing when I'd first met Felix—Frank, from Long Beach, with whom I worked on Agnos's gay rights bill—mysteriously began breaking dates after what seemed like a promising first few months. I assumed his ardor had cooled. Then, in 1982, I heard Frank's name being read on the Assembly floor in Sacramento in memory of his recent death. Looking back, we all held tight to a sense of normalcy, even as reality broke inevitably through.

Strangely enough, even with the dreadful undertow of sickness, the early '80s were a golden time. There was so much excitement in those days. Most of us had cut ourselves off from our hometowns and families and launched ourselves into an unknown territory. We knew we were participating in some kind of birth and self-consciously carving out own rituals and insider codes, creating, however crudely, a culture. There were sweater queens and clones and biker dykes and lipstick lesbians—niches for everyone in the emerging gay culture. And every week held a first: the first gay pride parade, the first gay and lesbian film festival, the first gay and lesbian church service, the first Sunday afternoon tea dance, where T-shirts doubled as swirling banners. I remember Jon Sims pulling me into Orphan Andy's for a coffee and excitedly telling me he was going to start a gay marching band "with a brass section and woodwinds and majorettes and *faaaaaaaabulous* uniforms!" Everything was fabulous, wonderful. I remember a breathless Dr. Tom Waddell telling me of his idea to start a gay Olympics: "Think of the potential!"

During that brief period between White Night and the plague we all felt that something big was happening in San Francisco. It seemed like every other week a new celebrity would drop in for a fund-raiser of one sort or another. I remember being very excited about a party Matt Coles and Don Knutson threw for the novelist Christopher Isherwood. He'd long been an idol of mine and when I was in Europe I'd traced the routes he'd described in his *Berlin Stories*. The reception was actually a stuffy affair with mostly academics and lawyers and very well off society swells gathered to raise money for Matt's group, Gay Rights Advocates. I got there a little late and, along with my friends, was about thirty years younger than most of the other guests, who were clearly boring Isherwood to death. After catching him smiling in our direction, I shouldered my skinny little self through the surrounding gentlemen and said, "Mr. Isherwood, would you like to come in the living room and talk to a few young people?" With a twinkle in his eye, he said, "I suppose I must." He told us wonderful stories of returning to Berlin after the war and finding his old haunts in the bombed-out streets.

Gore Vidal came to San Francisco back then. I met him on a fundraising trip for his New York Senate campaign during a very formal luncheon at the Belli mansion. Vidal's main topic was puzzlement. He couldn't understand why his campaign seemed unable to gain traction even among San Francisco's supportive population. Finally, responding to crashing sounds from the kitchen, Lia Belli, our hostess—the trophy wife of Melvin Belli, the famous "King of Torts"—stormed from the table to scream at the servants. I turned to Vidal and said, "I'll tell you what's wrong with your campaign. It's your hostess." Without blinking, he whispered back conspiratorially, "Yes, she's deeply stupid."

B UT THERE WAS a terrible stalker shadowing this gaudy, never-ending party. By 1984, San Francisco had become "Ground Zero of the Plague" as *Time* magazine famously called it. People died fast then. One day you would see someone who looked fine. A month later he looked bad. Two weeks later you'd see his name in the obituaries. The pace became so rapid and the numbers so overwhelming that the gay papers had to work out a formula to handle the flood of notices: one picture, preferably a head shot, and two paragraphs, two hundred words to sum up a life. Sometimes there was no obit, just a tape recording saying the line had been disconnected or a returned envelope stamped "Deceased."

I blunted the feeling of rage or powerlessness (it changed daily) by living in a frenetic, very '80s style. My routine was to get up in the morning, drink coffee, shower, examine every inch of my body for lesions, shave, get into a suit, do a line of coke, and grab the subway. Once in the office I'd decipher the CDC reports and cross-check them with our ever more crowded blackboards. Then I would leave the office and go straight to Castro Street, to the Midnight Sun, and drink until the bar closed. Two A.M. found me stumbling down Eighteenth to my apartment. If I was extremely lucky, those nightmares of running without being able to move would hold off so I could have a few hours' rest. Next morning, I would get up, do a line of coke, shower . . . And this went on and on.

In other campaigns, there was always an underlying excitement about what lay ahead, either freedom from repression when we fought Anita Bryant or a victory at the polls when Harvey was running for office. We had an enemy with a face. This fight against AIDS was different. There was the disease itself as well as layer upon layer of ignorance and fear. Our goal was to wake people up to the reality of its existence and gather information. Without a concrete objective, something more substantial, it was frustrating—especially so when all our warnings were so vague. The virus hadn't even been "isolated," as the medical community was quick to point out.

The first clear-cut evidence that I was HIV-positive came in a nasty bout with herpes. Herpes zoster, or shingles, lives in the nerve endings of anyone who's had chicken pox. It's one of those things a healthy body deals with invisibly and capably. But when the immune system is weakened, it escapes like an evil genie and literally burns a path along the nerve endings it's been locked inside. Sometimes the sizzled nerves erupt through the skin, leaving pits and scars. Today there are pills to stop its fiery march, but back then you just waited it out and dulled the pain with whatever you could find. In my case it was scotch.

I couldn't go outside. Most of the lesions were covered by my hair, but enough were visible to pique my vanity. If I wore a hat, the pressure was unbearable. If I didn't wear a hat, the slightest breeze would ruffle my hair and send waves of electric needles jabbing painfully into my skull. Instead of going to Marcus, I went to my HMO, Kaiser, which I could afford to pay. That was a mistake. The doctor I saw was rather typical of those days. After inspecting my sores, she stepped back and pulled off the rubber gloves, finger by finger. "Mr. Jones," she said, "you have shingles." She was cold and matter-of-fact. "Are you gay?" "Yes." She nodded with what I took to be smug satisfaction and began writing a prescription—for Tylenol 3. About as effective as stopping an iceberg, which she was, with an ice pick. As she handed me the scrip she said, "I'm sure it's AIDS." She gave me a blank look, and left.

It was inconceivable that I would be spared. I had watched boy-friends and lovers get sick and die. The KS Foundation, through which I had known hundreds of the earliest victims, was now well established and changing its name to the San Francisco AIDS Foundation. I had the signs, too, in swollen lymph nodes and night sweats. Along with most, I'd long since stopped going to the baths. But still, I just wasn't ready to hear the final word that I was positive. What was the logic of knowing? We had the antibody test and AZT coming on, but very little reason to get confirmation. If you believed that it was transmitted sexually, you just learned to make do with the new rules of safe sex. Whether you had five hundred T-cells or fifty, doctors, cruelly or not, routinely suggested that their patients get their affairs in order: "Is there anything you've always wanted to do?" The disease, or GRID, as it was called then—Gay Related Immune Deficiency—was unstoppable. Bobbi died. Enrique committed suicide. Everyone's address books were a mass of scratch-outs.

My out was a one-way ticket to Hawaii. I did, of course, flop around in the waves, and there were a few adventures, but for the most part it was not a carefree tourist time for me. I was becoming increasingly depressed. I remember once sitting alone in my apartment on Maui and blowing my whistle. No one came to the rescue.

T HAT SUMMER IN Hawaii was when Rock Hudson was failing. He'd been in Paris doing the same experimental treatment that Bill Kraus was exploring. I was sitting in the apartment watching the evening news when they showed Hudson being flown back from Paris. All the networks had rented helicopters to get that famous aerial shot of him being transported by ambulance from the airport to the hospital. And it really enraged me. The media were paying attention only because someone famous was dying and the story had the underlying titillation of homosexuality. Here was this sex symbol to millions of American women, the embodiment of broad-shouldered manhood, star of *Giant* and beloved hero of *MacMillan and Wife,* and now, after all these years, he had AIDS? Only fags got AIDS. What a delicious, sickening betrayal. The only glimmer of light in that horrible episode was Elizabeth Taylor. She supported Hudson and refused to back away from her friend. Her grief came across as genuine, and there was no question of blame or judgment; he was simply her friend, and now he was sick. It was extremely brave of her to speak up while the rest of Hollywood kept silent. She was the very first celebrity to publicly embrace a person with AIDS.

We all knew Rock Hudson was gay. Friends like Armistead Maupin and Ken Maley had attended parties and met his boyfriends. There had been speculation for a few years that he was sick because of his sudden thinness, grayness. Now he was being served up to the public as a warning, another Hollywood comeuppance tale by the nightly news. The whole thing was pathetic, vulturelike, maddening. Unfair to Rock Hudson, and to us all.

CHAPTER TEN

A VISION
OF THE
QUILT

AFTER EIGHT MONTHS on Maui I was back in the Castro. I had no job, no money, and was sleeping on a friend's couch (Jim Foster had taken me in). But I had a plan. I'd written a speech that I hoped would reignite the will to fight. I would give my speech at the candlelight march commemorating the day Harvey Milk and George Moscone had been shot. After that, who knows? I never really worried about career and fortune in those days. I was surviving, and that seemed quite a lot.

It's hard to communicate how awful it was in the fall of 1985. I'd left town out of my own fear and frustration. And somehow that sabbatical had been recuperative. Physically I felt fine. The shingles had left with only lingering tingles. And I'd gotten myself out of the coke and drinking routine thanks in part to Randy Shilts, an old friend from the Haight-Ashbury days. He, alone among my friends, had encouraged me to go to an AA meeting. It was hard as hell to attend those first meetings. Then, slowly, I broke the pattern and eventually learned to sleep without numbing myself with drink.

But there was something different in the San Francisco I returned to. Everyone seemed exhausted, almost fatalistic about AIDS. I understood that, certainly; but I also detected signs of hope within the despair. For one, the media had caught on to what was happening. Randy, who'd been a staff writer for the *Advocate,* was hired full-time by the *Chronicle* to write weekly AIDS columns, and he was extremely dogged in his attempts to puncture all the myths. There was a piece on the fallacy of AIDS being transmitted by mosquito bites, by tainted water, by waiters handling dinner plates. He went into AIDS wards and interviewed the nursing staff and doctors, and the truth was coming out.

Other newspapers followed his lead, and the public began to learn, if not always to accept, that this disease was not divine retribution. And other "points of light" flared up. Bobbi Campbell and his lover sat smiling on the cover of *Newsweek* in an article on the new disease—appearing shockingly alive and productive. There were respected physicians speaking out and against the panic. These were all important achievements, but still it was just so much whistling in the dark. We desperately needed an immediate fix, and it wasn't even on the horizon.

Seven years before, on the night of Harvey Milk's murder, I swore to myself that he would not be forgotten and began organizing a candlelight march to mark the day of his and Mayor Moscone's deaths. It had become a ritual, with thousands attending every year. A few days prior to the 1985 march, my friend Joseph Durant and I were walking the Castro handing out leaflets reminding people of the candlelight memorial. We stopped to get a slice at Marcello's Pizza and I picked up a *Chronicle.* The front-page headline was chilling: "1,000 San Franciscans Dead of AIDS." I'd known most of them from my work with the KS Foundation. Virtually every single one of them had lived within a ten-block radius of where we were standing at Castro and Market. When I walked up Eighteenth Street from Church to Eureka, I knew the ugly stories behind so many windows. Gregory died behind those blue curtains. Jimmy was diagnosed up that staircase in that office behind the venetian blinds. There was the house Alex got kicked out of when the landlord found an empty bottle of AZT in his trash can: "I'm sorry, we just can't take any chances." I wasn't losing just friends, but also all the familiar faces of the neighborhood—the bus drivers, clerks and mailmen, all the people we know in casual yet familiar ways. The entire Castro was populated by ghosts.

And yet, as I looked around the Castro with its charming hodgepodge of candy-colored Victorians, there were guys walking hand in hand, girls kissing each other hello, being successfully, freely, openly who they were. So much had been accomplished since the closeted days when the community met furtively in a back-alley culture. The Castro was a city within the city, an oasis and harbor for thousands who lived there and millions of gay men and lesbian women around the world for whom it symbolized freedom. And now, in what should have been its prime, it was withering.

Angrily, I turned to Joseph: "I wish we had a bulldozer, and if we could just level these buildings, raze Castro . . . If this was just a graveyard with a thousand corpses lying in the sun, then people would look at it and they would understand and if they were human beings they'd have to respond." And Joseph, always the acid realist, told me I was the last optimist left standing: "Nobody cares, Cleve. This thing doesn't touch them at all."

November 27, 1985, the night of the memorial march, was cold and gray. As we waited for people to gather, Joseph and I handed out stacks of poster board and Magic Markers, and through the bullhorn I asked everyone to write down the name of a friend who'd been killed by AIDS. People were a little reluctant at first, but by the time the march began we had a few hundred placards. Most of the marchers just wrote first names, Tom or Bill or George; some of the signs said "My brother" or "My lover," and a few had the complete name—first, middle, and last—in bold block letters.

That Thanksgiving night we marched as we had for six years down Market Street to city hall, a sea of candles lighting up the night. One of the marchers asked me who else would be speaking this year and I said, "No one else. Just me. People are tired of long programs anyway." I was an angry, arrogant son of a bitch. The candles we'd been carrying were stumps by the time we'd gathered at Harvey Milk Memorial Plaza at city hall.

". . . We are here tonight to commemorate the deaths of Supervisor Harvey Milk and Mayor George Moscone, victims of an assassin's bullets seven years ago this very day . . ." I talked of Harvey and how even back then he was not really our first martyr, that we'd lost many people to murder and suicide and alcohol and AIDS. "Yes, Harvey was our first collective martyr, but now we have many more martyrs and now our numbers are diminished and many of us have been condemned to an early and painful death. But we are the lesbian women and gay men of San Francisco, and although we are again surrounded by uncertainty and despair, we are survivors and we shall survive again and the dream that was shared by Harvey Milk and George Moscone will go forward. . . ."

Then we moved down Market to the old federal building. At that time it housed the offices of Health and Human Services—not such an effective rallying point as city hall, but perfect for our next demonstration, one that turned out to have more impact than I ever imagined. Earlier in the day, Bill Paul, a professor at San Francisco State University, and I had hidden extension ladders and rolls of tape in the shrubbery around the building's base. As the federal building came into view, I ended the chanting ("Stop AIDS now! Stop AIDS now!") and explained through the bullhorn that we were going to plaster the facade with the posters inscribed with our dead. And that's what happened. The crowd surged forward, the ladders were set in place, and we crawled up three stories, covering the entire wall with a poster-board memorial.

It was a strange image. Just this uneven patchwork of white squares, each with handwritten names, some in script and some in block letters, all individual. We stared and read the names, recognizing too many. Staring upward, people remarked: "I went to school with him"... "I didn't know he was dead"... "I used to dance with him every Sunday at the I-Beam"... "We're from the same hometown".... "Is that our Bob?"

There was a deep yearning not only to find a way to grieve individually and together but also to find a voice that could be heard beyond our community, beyond our town. Standing in the drizzle, watching as the posters absorbed the rain and fluttered down to the pavement, I said to myself, *It looks like a quilt.* As I said the word *quilt,* I was flooded with memories of home and family and the warmth of a quilt when it was cold on a winter night.

And as I scanned the patchwork, I saw it—as if a Technicolor slide had fallen into place. Where before there had been a flaking gray wall, now there was a vivid picture and I could see quite clearly the National Mall, and the dome of Congress and a quilt spread out before it—a vision of incredible clarity.

I was gripped by the same terror and excitement that I'd felt standing before other large works commemorating other large issues. Not long ago I'd seen Christo's running fence in Sonoma County. It was a beautiful and moving sight, and I was struck by the grandeur of those vast expanses of shimmering opalescent fabric zigzagging up and down the golden hills. How it billowed in the breeze with the light playing off it, like a string of azure tall ships sailing on a golden sea. And there was the memory of Judy Chicago's *The Dinner Party.* This was a long table, maybe one hundred feet in length, with each place setting designed by a different artist. Both Christo and Judy Chicago had taken a commonplace items, sheets drying on a line in his case, plates and utensils in hers, and by enlarging them had made the homely a dramatic, powerfully moving statement. It seemed an apt synthesis: individual quilts, collected together, could have the same immense impact.

When I told my friends what I'd seen, they were silent at first, and as I tried to explain it, they were dubious: "Cleve, don't you realize the logistics of doing something like that? Think of the difficulty of organizing thousands of queers!" But I knew there were plenty of angry queens with sewing machines. I wouldn't be working alone, I told my friends. Everyone understands the idea of a quilt. "But it's gruesome," they said.

That stopped me. Was a memorial morbid? Perhaps it was. And yet there is also a healing element to memorials. I thought of the Vietnam Veterans Memorial wall. I did not expect to be moved by it. I was influenced by the Quakers, who are suspicious of war memorials, which they believe tend to glorify war rather than speak to the horror of it. But I was overwhelmed by the simplicity of it, of that black mirrorlike wall and the power it had to draw people from all across America to find a beloved's name and touch it and see their face reflected in the polished marble and leave mementos.

So I thought about all these things and also about how quilting is viewed as a particularly American folk art. There was the quilting bee with its picture of generations working together, and the idea that quilts recapture history in bits of worn clothing, curtains, jackets—protective cloth. That it was women who did the sewing was an important element. At the time, HIV was seen as the product of aggressive gay male sexuality, and it seemed that the homey image and familial associations of a warm quilt would counter that.

The idea made so much sense on so many different levels. It was clear to me that the only way we could beat this was by acting together as a nation. Though gays and lesbians were winning political recognition in urban centers, without legitimate ties to the larger culture we'd always be marginalized. If we could somehow bridge that gap of age-old prejudice, there was hope that we could beat the disease by using a quilt as a symbol of solidarity, of family and community; there was hope that we could make a movement that would welcome people—men and women, gay or straight, of every age, race, faith, and background.

To this day, critics ignore one of the most powerful aspects of the Quilt. Any Quilt display, no matter how small or large, is filled with evidence of love—the love between gay men and the love we share with our lesbian sisters as well as love of family, father for son, mother for son, among siblings. Alongside this love, the individual quilts are filled with stories of homophobia and how we have triumphed over it. There's deep and abiding pain in letters attached to the quilts from parents bemoaning the fact that they didn't accept their dead son. And there's implacable anger in the blood-splashed quilts blaming President Reagan for ignoring the killing plague. All these messages are part of a memorial that knows no boundaries. We go to elementary schools, high schools, the Bible Belt of the Deep South, rural America, Catholic churches, synagogues, and wherever we unfold this fabric we tell the story of people who've died of AIDS.

That night, standing with those few men and women in the damp and dark, I saw a way out for all of us, a method of surmounting our fears and coming together in a collective memorial of our experience: all the sadness, rage, and anger; all the hope, all the dreams, the ambitions, the tragedy.

Eleven years later, this picture in my mind's eye became reality. But that night in November 1985 it was just an idea, and on the 8 Market bus up to the Castro, my friends Joseph Durant and Gilbert Baker and Joseph Canalli were unimpressed. Reagan will never let you do it, they said. Straight families won't join any cause with a bunch of San Francisco queers. It was late, they were tired. An AIDS quilt was a sweet idea, but it was morbid, corny, impossibly complicated. Give it up. But I was on fire with the vision. The idea made so much sense, in so many ways—the irony and truth of it. I couldn't get it out of my head.

CHAPTER ELEVEN

DIAGNOSIS POSITIVE

T HAT NIGHT GAVE me the push I needed to take the antibody test. It had been around for perhaps half a year, and I'd put it off. But now I didn't have quite the terror of dying. I had a purpose and wanted to know how much time I had left to see my quilt happen.

Since I'd been part of a hepatitis study, I was spared the usual two-week wait from blood draw to sentencing. All I had to do was pick up the phone and call the lab, which I finally did one day, and this very polite woman said, "Sorry, Mr. Jones, we don't give out that information on the telephone." I'm afraid my response was pretty rude: "Yes, I know. I made those rules!"

When she came back on the line she said that Bob Stempel would take me out to lunch the next day. The name alone gave me a warning chill. I had nothing against Bob; quite the contrary, I thought only fondly of him. He was one of those people who dropped into my life in the early '70s when I was on the street; he had given me a place to stay and, a few weeks later, money to buy my first Thanksgiving dinner away from home. We had remained friends, nodding on the street and talking over coffee or in the bars. Now he was head of the study.

Well, I figured right then you don't get a free lunch with the program director unless it's terminal. We met at the Village Deli café. Gentle as always, he bought me a turkey sandwich "for old times' sake"; then we sat down and he asked me what I thought. What I thought? How could I make sense of a death sentence? I told him I thought I was infected, and he told me I was right.

I don't think anyone who faces an HIV-positive diagnosis is ever prepared for it, even if you've told yourself over and over that you know what the answer is going to be. You're always surprised at the amount of hope you've harbored away there deep inside. Despite all my resolve and telling myself I just needed a few years to complete my plan for the Quilt, the news hit with the same deep blank despair I'd felt when I heard that friends had died. It seemed that my life was over and that everything I loved most had been taken from me. I felt . . . nothing—terrifying, absolute nothingness.

We didn't know about the incubation period back then. It just seemed people tested positive and then got sick and died. And you want so much to try to live normally, but normal life for most people is based on the assumption of endless time. I kept hearing that phrase: "Sorry, Mr. Jones."

My friends and I dealt with the knowledge of being HIV-positive in different ways. Hank redoubled his activism and began investigating the link between poppers and KS. Gerry Parker, a big bear of a man, became the scourge of every political gathering. Whether a public hearing was gathered to discuss rent control or bus service, he was there to refocus the topic on AIDS. I used to sit and wait for Gerry to explode. The barest hint of hesitation on the part of a speaker would give him an opening and set him off. Eyes glittering, spit dripping from his beard, he'd erupt from his seat and begin shouting, "When are you going to do something about AIDS, goddamn it!"

These people had the energy to fight. Others didn't. Some of my friends dealt with being positive by saying they'd commit suicide when the symptoms became undeniable. Others tried, often unsuccessfully, to go back to their families. I couldn't go home: to die in Phoenix would be redundant. Neither could I commit suicide. It just never seemed an option, and had I ever entertained such a notion, I doubt I'd have had the guts to pull it off.

Basically I just floated aimlessly through a few odd jobs. Though I did think about the Quilt, I lacked the will to work on that or much of anything else.

A FEW MONTHS LATER I got a call from Mike Wallace of CBS. He'd seen a videotape of the speech I'd given on the steps of city hall on November 27, 1985, the same night we'd put the name signs up on the old federal building. He thought it was a compelling speech and suggested he come out and interview me for a *60 Minutes* segment. I didn't know quite how to react.

Six years before, in 1979, CBS had done a special called *Gay Power, Gay Politics,* an incredibly biased prime-time hour of antigay propaganda. In the serious, somber tones of a documentary, it depicted gay men as wild dogs in heat and I was named as one of the top dogs. It opens up with Harry Reasoner admitting he is puzzled about the whole idea of "political power for homosexuals." "Like every other new minority group," Reasoner intones, "gays are pushing their own special interest" and raising troubling questions for society as a whole. The "troubling" aspect was sex. George Crile, the reporter, cites statistics saying that "the average gay man has had sexual encounters with at least five hundred different men, and as many as a fourth of the population has been with more than a thousand." All this is confirmed in interviews with "typical" gay men. To underscore the fact that all gay men are sexual predators, Crile visits an S&M shop. As the camera pans past harnesses, whips, and masks, Crile asks, "Who buys this stuff?" The shop owners says, "Everybody does." What viewers didn't see was the shop owner clarifying his response, saying that 90 percent of his customers were heterosexuals. That ended up on the cutting-room floor, leading everyone to understand that gays were not only sodomites but aficionados of pain and torture. The "high" point of the piece was a visit to Buena Vista Park. The film goes murky and dark and shows shadowy figures walking the paths and meeting—for more sex. The implication was obvious. Be wary, America, gays are taking over your parks. The same leafy nooks where your children play are scenes of bestial orgies after dark.

I was given star billing both throughout the documentary and in the promotional clip. Just before Reasoner's introduction, Crile asks me, "So what's the message today?" "Look out, here we come!" I say. My enthusiasm confirmed the paranoia: gays are on the march, assaulting the cities and suburbs in a tidal wave of evil.

Even now I cringe at the episode. We were so naive. Crile and his partner, Grace Diekhaus, had wined and dined us all, encouraging us to confide in them as old friends. It was all a set-up. Later, CBS grudgingly admitted that the show was warped. But that really didn't matter once the piece had aired. I was ashamed, and shamed, to have been so foolishly trusting. People would come up to me on the street and in the bars, asking me what I was thinking: "How could you let yourself be a part of that lynching, Cleve?"

Later, in a rebuttal on PBS, I was sputtering mad and made a total fool of myself. More effectively, Randy Alfred nailed CBS before the National News Council and orchestrated their censure. George Crile was also the one who was sued by General Westmoreland and lost. (I sent the general a note saying I sympathized, but he never responded.)

Still, all this had been six years before. The idea that millions of *60 Minutes* viewers could witness what AIDS had done to San Francisco and how we were coping with it seemed worth the risk. It turned out fine. They did an excellent piece on how ordinary citizens were stepping forward into an absolute vacuum and without federal assistance, dealing with the epidemic and caring for sick people and trying to educate the public with the Buddy Programs, and with speakers' bureaus that featured doctors who told the truth about transmission. Wallace proved not be to be the right-wing jerk I'd imagined, and it was amazingly satisfying to walk around the Castro with a parade of cameramen and introduce Wallace to people with AIDS and others who were fighting it. I felt like a local official welcoming an ambassador from another, much larger country. Wallace himself seemed awed at being confronted with the enormity of it all, of the wasting and sickness that made men half his age look like his grandfather. It was as if Wallace were heterosexual America, and that as he came face-to-face with his own ignorance of AIDS he mirrored the country's ignorance and was now experiencing for the first time and in a personal way the intense suffering and needless cruelty. All the stereotypes, all the fictions that had built up around gays males—that we are rich, pleasure-mad creatures, a somehow dangerous foreign breed—melted away. We were the sons and uncles, the fathers even, of regular, run-of-the-mill citizens.

WHEN THE SHOW aired, I'd moved to Sacramento to work for the Friends Committee on Legislation, a Quaker undertaking, primarily as a watchdog over the prison construction program of George Deukmejian, then governor of California. Aside from my grandmother's rather humorous take on my good looks, the only immediate personal impact of the *60 Minutes* episode was slight. I got a few calls from friends, and the *Sacramento Bee* wrote a couple of paragraphs on the piece and made a few remarks about local efforts in the battle with AIDS. That, I thought, was that. But two days after the newspaper write-up, the death threats began. Every morning at six o'clock, the phone would ring and this kid would come on and tell me he was going to kill me: "You fucking queer, we're going to kill you." I've had many death threats in my life, and I've never gotten used to them. But what I really object to is when they come early in the morning. It's kind of a drag to begin the day with a murder threat. I'm not a morning person.

Still, I wasn't very rattled, because the guy sounded so young. Calls like that are just part of the territory, I told myself. I remember discussing it with my friends, and we agreed that this kid was just confused and that in a couple of years we'd see him down at the bar. I thought about calling the phone company and having my number unlisted but never got around to it.

There wasn't much time to worry about it anyway. My job for the Quakers was to monitor the prison program and find out how deeply it would cut into social programs. I was in way over my head and working late trying to understand all the ramifications for the budget. My view was that the whole prison expansion idea was insane, that we had more people behind bars in California than most countries do, and that now, instead of spending money on prevention, we were about to build yet more prisons. To fend off critics, the governor was proposing to many of the penal system's current administrators that it be privatized, thus further entrenching an already bloated and corrupt organization. Great, so now we make money off incarceration?

One night I left the capital building at about ten o'clock. It was hot and humid, and by the time I got to my apartment all I wanted to do was change my suit for a T-shirt and go down to the corner store for ice cream while the air-conditioning cooled the apartment. As I left the complex, I noticed two young guys glaring at me as I walked by. I didn't hear anyone following me, and so I was surprised to see them blocking the sidewalk just around the corner.

You always wonder how you will react when confronted with violence on the streets. I did everything correctly—no eye contact, I just kept walking. But as we passed each other, one of them said, "Too many goddamn queers in Sacramento." That struck me oddly, because I'd been looking everywhere and I felt there were far too few queers in Sacramento. I said nothing, of course. Then I heard a sound and turned, and one of them was right there with his fist up in the air and brought it down with such force that I fell to the ground. They began kicking me and screaming over and over, in high, shrill voices, "Faggot, faggot, faggot." I was lying on my back when the one who'd hit me first came at me with a knife. It bounced off my chin and onto the pavement, and they ran off laughing and shouting.

When I tried to stand up I realized that the first blow must have been a knife, not a fist. There was blood spurting out of a hole above my shoulder blade. I lay there taking deep breaths, listening to my breathing and thinking quite dispassionately, *Well, it didn't get your lung.*

I managed to stay conscious and stumble back to the apartment, where I blacked out by the mailboxes in a pool of light. Fortunately, one of my neighbors had forgotten to pick up his mail and came out to get it soon after. He found me in a lake of blood and called the police. When I came to in the ambulance, bouncing along, hearing the sirens, I must have been delusional. I opened my eyes and saw an angel hovering over me, a beautiful man with full lips and giant liquid brown eyes and the smoothest skin in a white gown with a badge. He gazed into my eyes and I could feel his hands on my chest. He was putting sensors on, but I felt as if I were being caressed. As I was looking up into his face I saw that blood, my blood, had splashed all over him. And I felt this horrible wave of panic and I said, "I have AIDS, I'm HIV-positive." And he took my hands and leaned closer and said, "I'm sure we've all been exposed by now; just relax and let me take care of you."

At the hospital they discovered I'd been stuck with a seven-inch dagger under the right shoulder blade, severing the flesh so close to the carotid artery that they suspected internal hemorrhaging. I had an angiogram, an incredibly painful procedure in which they open an artery in your groin and insert a catheter; dye is then injected to follow the course of the veins. If my carotid had been cut, they'd see it on the X rays. This may hurt a little, I was told. It hurt like hell; the dye felt like boiling water.

When it was over, they sewed me up and said there was nothing serious about my wound. I don't remember feeling much relief, just a dull hunger for sleep. But as the gurney took me to the ICU, I heard excited voices at the other end of the hall. They were saying my name, and I realized it was my friends come to see me. "Oh my God, it's Cleve." "Is he going to be OK?" As they wheeled me down the corridor, I watched the light fixtures go by on the ceiling. I thought, *If I'm going to risk death, I should at least get some ink out of it.*

And the voices got louder. I closed my eyes and waited until I knew everybody was all around me. Since the doctor had been in such a rush to check my artery, they hadn't cleaned me up and I looked a wreck. Not only did I have an IV and bandages; my chest was covered in blood, mud, and bits of dried leaves I'd collected while crawling to the apartment. With the stage set and the audience ready, I opened my eyes and yelled out, "Don't just stand there, call the *Chronicle*!" I gave them Randy Shilts's home phone number and passed out. Sure enough, it was the front-page headline the next day.

Anyone who's been through trauma has a reaction to it. Certainly I had nightmares about getting stabbed, and those kids' screams of "Faggot" echoed in my head long afterward. And it made me angrier than I think I'd ever been. I had been a part of the gay liberation movement since I was seventeen years old. I believed I was a fully realized person, free of the scar tissue of heterophobia. But in the months following the attack I was consumed with hatred and fear of heterosexuals. Particularly of straight men for their violent response to anything they thought was threatening their turf. How do you fight some sort of genetic weirdness going back to the days of cavemen? Evil was not an abstract thing; it was two guys in leather jackets. When the cops told me that the two guys were neo-Nazi skinheads, it got worse. Later the police got an anonymous letter saying the next time the attackers would be sure they finished the job. It was a nightmare. Another one.

WHILE I WAS recovering, my best friend, Marvin, was dying in his parents' house in Rhode Island. I'd first met Marvin in 1975 during the Haight-Ashbury period, when we were two broke kids making the rent by selling Time-Life books over the telephone. That was the most godawful boring job I ever had in my life, cold-calling strangers over four-hour shifts and making my pitch at machine-gun speed: "Hi good to hear your voice I'm calling about one of the books in our Wilderness Library it's a really great book called *High Sierra* and what I'd like to do Mrs. Smith is send you a copy show it to the kids and if you like it and I know you will I'm sure you'll like the other books in the series. OK?"

To enliven the routine, I would come up with different *noms de phone*. "Hello, Mrs. Smith, this is Willy Loman calling from Time-Life Books . . ." And no one ever got it. One day in the middle of my spiel, I heard laughter from two desks behind me. I turned and there was one of the most beautiful boys I'd ever seen in my life. He was short, with longish curly brown hair, big gray-blue eyes, cheekbones for days, a great dancer's body, a dancer's neck. I was smitten. Not only had he gotten the Loman reference, he was howling about it.

We had our first date that night at the Stud, one of my favorite '70s haunts, and made out by the cigarette machine between songs. He walked me home and I asked if he would come in with me. "Cleve," he said, "I think we're going to be sisters." And then, in a gesture I was to come to know very well, he tilted his head to the side and smiled impishly: "Don't you just hate it when that happens!"

Instead of lovers, we became best friends. Marvin was very involved with theater, both acting and, at that time, directing. I didn't know

Samuel Beckett from Jerry Herman, but whenever Marvin was onstage I was in the audience. He had very little interest in politics, but when I was on the podium he was in the audience. We lived together in San Francisco and I stayed with him in New York and we traveled all over Europe and the Middle East. We had a wonderful circle of friends. He introduced me to Erica Van Horn, an artist, and I introduced him to my friend Scott Rempel, and our group grew to include Danny Rounds and Dennis Oglesby. We were all very close, constantly on the phone or at the bars, swapping stories and urging each other on in whatever we were doing.

Although his mother had called me to let me know he was sick, I wasn't sure how Marvin's gay friends would be received. I'd met the Feldmans only briefly, but I knew they were religious and that a rabbi would be there. More deeply, I was frightened about what Marvin would look like. I'd watched so many friends die and knew all too well what the last days of AIDS could be like. The thought of looking into Marvin's eyes and not finding him there was unbearable. All during the plane ride and until the moment I walked up the house steps I really felt that all I had to take to him was my own fear of death.

When I stepped into Esther Feldman's kitchen, that fear evaporated. The whole clan was there, jolly and welcoming, though their eyes were dark and troubled. Everyone kept pushing food on me, and when I finally made it through to Marvin's room, there was one of those awkward emotional scenes. I started to hug him and juggle the plate of food at the same time. And then we laughed. Marvin's eyes had been spared, but his body was so ravaged he was barely able to pull himself up onto the pillows. I climbed into his bed and held him in my arms. His eyes were clear and bright, the same wry humor, the same loving nature—he was all there.

Esther and Sid made a bed for me in their reading room, next to Marvin's bedroom. At night I could hear Marvin's labored breathing on one side and Sid and Esther weeping on the other. And we waited.

The second day, he got out of bed and sat at the dining room table pretending to eat lunch. That afternoon he and I went through his correspondence and decided where his belongings were to go. The next day he went into a coma.

We all have to make these journeys. Sometimes it's only a crosstown taxi ride, sometimes it's longer. In my case it was a five-hour Pan Am flight to Rhode Island. Either way it's a hard journey to say good-bye to someone you love, knowing you'll never see them again. But it's worse when you leave. Sid drove me to the airport, never once mentioning Marvin. Instead, he told me about liberating the death camp at Ohrdruf during World War II, and about prisoners so weak and thin that it hurt them to be moved even onto a stretcher, so frail that they would choke on a spoonful of soup. There was so little Sid could do to ease the pain for those men, or for his son.

I'm not a very spiritual person, but I do believe in holding people and memories in your heart, and always trying to keep them in your mind. I had started the habit of putting up photographs of my friends in a hallway in my apartment. Nothing so grand as a shrine, but seeing all my friends made me feel connected somehow and less lonely and morose over the fact that so many were sick or dead. But now I couldn't face the reminder of so much loss. When I got back from the Feldmans', I stripped the walls bare. I really felt I had to find a way to bury the memories along with the people. The day Marvin's mother told me he was dead, it all came crashing down. I felt like a rat in a cage with all the gates closing and no means of release. First I'd been diagnosed positive, then the stabbing, and now I'd lost my best friend. I walked around in a state of shock.

Sometime later that fall, I got an invitation to appear on *Oprah*. She was doing a show on gay bashings. Though I was reluctant, it seemed that any sort of publicity for this always ignored problem would be worthwhile. I knew we were in for it when we were shown to the green room, where we were expected to hang out before the show with self-avowed bashers: us on one side, skinheads on the other. A very tense stand-off. Oprah was just coming on then, and although she steered the conversation as best she could, it was a tough situation. As a young woman from Indiana told of being gang-raped and pistol-whipped, the audience applauded. During the station break a nut stormed the stage with a Bible raised up at us like a sword, yelling out that we deserved to die. When it was over, we all felt like specimens in an experiment gone wrong.

That winter on the street one day, I saw Joseph Durant, with whom the year before I'd marched in the candlelight march and put up the posters. He didn't look good. He was very skinny and his face was gray. I said, with a warmth I didn't feel, "Joseph, what's up?" He said, "I don't want to talk about me. It's time you started the Quilt."

He was right, of course. I couldn't let anger and despair poison my life. None of my friends would have wanted that. It helped no one to continue down that road and become, as I'd seen others become, a tightly wound ball of hurt and anger and fear.

- -

CHAPTER TWELVE

THE FIRST
DISPLAYS

D.C. AND S.F.,
1987

WHEN PEOPLE ASK me today when I knew the
Quilt would catch on, I say always. From that first
night at the federal building I just knew it would work—that people
would be touched and respond. But for all my sureness, it was maddening trying to explain the idea, because I didn't have anything to show.
When I told friends I wanted to take ten thousand quilts and lay them
out on the Mall in Washington, D.C., on October 11 for the National
March for Lesbian and Gay Rights, they really thought I'd lost it.

Finally, after a year and a half of thinking and scribbling on napkins, Joseph Durant and I sat down and made a list of forty men we felt
we knew well enough to make quilts for and in February began crank-
ing them out, each of them three feet by six feet. The panels were that
size because of the vision of bulldozing the Castro and leaving only

corpses lying in the sun. I wanted to show the space that would be taken up by each of those bodies, about the dimensions of a grave. I told Joseph that we'd sew them into twelve-by-twelve-foot squares, large enough to be efficient and small enough that people could reach out and touch the fabric as they walked around them. Joining them together that way also allowed flexibility so that some of the panels could be made horizontally and some vertically, like the parquet pattern on the floor of my grandfather's house.

All this was fine with Joseph until he started talking about how we were going to have to build scaffolding to hold it up. I said no, the power of it comes from laying it flat on the ground. Joseph was adamant that it should be up in the air like a flag, but I knew that that would totally alter the experience. We use both methods of display today, and you can see the difference. If you view the Quilt hanging upright, you have a very different experience from what you have when it's flat on the ground. You're much less conscious of your surroundings when you're looking down and more likely to pause and perhaps kneel and touch it. The argument spiraled out of control, and unfortunately, Joseph decided he couldn't work with me any longer.

I knew then, as I've always known, that I couldn't do it alone, and I asked Gilbert Baker, who I knew was a good seamstress, to become technical director. But Gilbert, who'd created the rainbow flag, wanted to be called artistic director. And then Ron Cordova came on board also demanding that title. I told them both that there was to be no artistic director. The only artistic director would be the people who made these things. All we do is gather them, uncensored, unedited, and sew them together. Our only job is to display them. Fortunately, Ron decided to put up with me in the end, agreeing to become technical director, and he worked like a dog getting things ready for October.

With the Quilt itself begun, we needed someone with management experience, able to oversee the resources and the money I expected to start coming in. I was living at the time with Atticus Tysen, a sweet young man I'd met at Quaker meeting. He told me about Michael Smith, a fellow Stanford M.B.A., who was looking for work. I couldn't offer a salary, but I had something better, a cause. Mike was the first person I convinced to give me his life. We were a terrible mismatch, and for three years we treated each other with incredible cruelty. But we worked together starting up the Quilt, and it wouldn't have happened without him.

The key to getting any idea off the ground is reaching people, letting them know and see what it is you're pushing, and so sometime in May we called a public meeting. We plastered the Castro with flyers and rented the Women's Building for a couple of hours for our meeting, but as the time drew near I was stricken with anxiety and became convinced that no one would show up. I was wrong. Two people came: Cindi "Gert" McMullin and Jack Caster. They'd both made quilts, much more sophisticated than Joseph's and mine. Gert's was for AIDS activist Roger Lyon, an intricate design containing eighteen notes written to Roger from a class of fifth-graders he'd spoken to. The notes were really wonderful, and captured the fierce loyalty and love these kids felt for Roger. They said such wonderfully innocent things, like "I hope you get out of this tuff spot" and "If you don't get well you owe me 5 dollars." She'd eventually make two more for him.

The quilt Jack made for his lovers Wade and Joe has always been one of my favorites. It's a double panel connected across the top with a ribbon spelling out a line of mystic gibberish. Just before he died, deep in dementia, Wade lifted his head off the pillow and with this joyful look said, "I've got it, the median above to be three!" Jack had no idea what this message meant, but I think it reflected the confusion we all faced—nothing made sense. I love quilts inscribed with something nonsensical, code words and pet names or an evocative sentence like *Remember that night in August* . . . You're allowed a glimpse of the intimate communication that existed between these people. That's what matters most about the Quilt, that it allows us to lose our cynicism in connection with someone we love and to make private declarations public.

Although Gert and Jack were treasures and quickly became an integral part of our team, the meeting could be looked on only as a failure. The idea was catching on too slowly; we'd never get to D.C. if the Quilt remained an underground effort largely confined to the gay community in San Francisco. In spite of our fears, not one of us gave in to hopelessness. We all had so much riding on it, and so all of us—Gert, Jack, and Mike, the nucleus of the early days—tried to analyze exactly what would make it work. The one thing we'd always had trouble with was explaining the idea in conversation. People needed a visual representation to grasp the idea, something they could see and touch.

Getting the Quilt out there, in front of as many people as possible, became our goal that late spring of 1987. We expected to get a good deal of publicity at the upcoming gay and lesbian pride festival. There'd be upward of 250,000 people attending the event, and we would be able to talk with hundreds of them as they stopped by our booth. Also, I'd been invited to speak at the opening ceremonies and would talk about the Quilt and invite all 250,000 to join us, both in making a quilt and in making the presentation in D.C.

Jack came up with a great idea. I remember him saying, "Cleve, you know Mayor Feinstein. Why don't you get her to hang the Quilt in front of city hall during the week of gay pride?" We were all immediately excited. City hall sits on one of the busiest streets in the city, so no one could miss seeing those panels hanging on the ornate neoclassical facade. It would be a coup. I'd known Mayor Feinstein casually when I worked for Harvey while he was a supervisor, but our relationship had been a little cool since White Night and I wasn't sure how she'd react. But as always in those early days, we had to make the effort. Also, as Jack quite rightly pointed out, with elections coming up, Dianne's support might help her chances of retaining the mayoralty in ways a refusal would not. "It would be good for her," said Jack. It made sense, so I dredged up the only decent shirt in my closet and went down to make my pitch. It was easy. I remember the mayor twiddling with that ever-present red silk bow at her neck and saying, "I think it would be wonderful." She's got a firm handshake.

Soon after, Warren Caton sent us the stunningly beautiful panels he'd made for Liberace and Rock Hudson. Exquisitely embroidered and dazzling when the light sparkled on the sequins and glitter, these two were like the first in a series of good-luck charms to come. The next break we got came thanks to Scott Lago, who also joined our team. Lloyd Phelps, a co-worker of his at Neiman Marcus, had died, and Scott suggested that a quilt would be a wonderful memorial. The company loved the idea, and the entire staff of the visual-display department created a quilt for Lloyd. It was beautiful, a block of golden beige with two kittens on the left side playing with a strand of yarn that curled from their paws into Lloyd's name and then rolled into a ball on the right. Accompanying the quilt was a dedicatory note: "Lloyd Phelps—an Illinois farm boy with a talent for producing the most elegant and sophisticated table settings. He loved his cats and working on his Victorian flat. He was the gentlest of men, with an improbably deep voice. He was kind, giving, and talented, and all of us who worked with him miss him very much."

His panel, along with forty others, was featured in the forty-foot-high front window of the San Francisco Neiman Marcus store in August 1987. The NM display facing Union Square, San Francisco's choicest shopping area, really helped us break through the perception that the Quilt was for and about activist Castro clones. We now had chic! And our new legitimacy translated into a big jump in volunteers, donations, and quilt makers.

Things were really breaking our way in those early months. But as our profile grew, so did the flak. The Quilt was fast becoming "our thing," meaning the property of those who'd lost and continued to lose their gay friends. Feeling ownership of something so explosively emotional was only natural and has propelled the Quilt to its current stature. But in some cases, that proprietary interest fought against the Quilt's overarching goal, which was to connect all people, regardless of age, race, and sexual orientation, in the fight against AIDS.

All this came to a head over the pope's visit to San Francisco in June. He was coming to Mission Dolores, which is right in the middle of the gay and Hispanic neighborhoods. When the pope visits a church, the local congregation decides how to welcome him, and the people at Mission Dolores had asked us to bring some sections of the Quilt to the ceremony.

That set off an uproar. While I saw the pope's acknowledgment as a useful breakthrough, others were outraged. They said the Quilt was made for gays by gays and it was sacrilege to present it to a homophobe, the man who represents the Catholic patriarchy, two thousand years of oppression. The loudest naysayers were the ACT-UP people, a new generation of gay activists for whose identity AIDS was an explosive part. It's not enough to make a quilt, they sneered; the Quilt is a passive thing. The pope's blessing, they felt, would be a mockery of everything they had fought for. I took a few deep breaths and told them then, as I tell them now, that we never said the Quilt is enough. It's one response among thousands, not the final answer. Their faces would harden and I'd repeat that we would never restrict participation, that we weren't going to exclude anybody. It was no use. I was an Uncle Tom, a sellout, afraid of my own sexuality . . . and on and on. I didn't know it then, but Mission Dolores marked the beginning of a long argument with a small minority of people who hate the Quilt. There's nothing to be done about turning them around.

By mid-July, we had about one hundred panels, all of them stored on Mike Smith's back porch, and we began to look for a workshop to display and assemble them. Though we had absolutely no money, we leased an empty storefront on Market Street, just by its intersection with Castro. This was a huge move for us. Having a space really made us feel as if it were all going to happen. It seemed cavernous—especially when we set up our single sewing machine, a brave little Singer, on a rickety table. We had nothing else back then—no chairs, no tables, nothing but an incredible amount of light fixtures: the previous tenant had been a furniture store, and the ceiling was a maze of track lighting.

I still marvel at our optimism. I just taped a sheet of butcher paper on the front door with the announcement "This is the new home of the

NAMES Project and here is our wish list..." We needed everything from sequins, beads, fabric, and glue to extension cords, computers, telephones, lights, and furniture. At the end of the list I added, "back rubs, hugs, and money."

The response was incredible. Within two weeks we were given ten sewing machines (three industrial models!), and volunteers started streaming in. Mike always says it couldn't have happened anywhere else in the country, and he's right. Local merchants paid the first month's rent. Someone left an anonymous gift of five hundred dollars in the donation box, and a hunky chiropractor regularly gave free massages to volunteers who sewed evenings until midnight. Very soon our shelves were overflowing with needles, bobbins, thread, and fabric.

The workshop was magical and at the same time devastating. Every day someone would walk in and recognize a name on the panel, learning for the first time that a friend had died. Guys with AIDS would come in to make their own quilt, then stop coming as they became too sick to work. Sometimes a friend or family member would come by and take the panel to the sick man's house or hospital bed so he could work on it. More often, we just went ahead and finished it for him. There wasn't a day that I didn't cry, but the miracle of it was that over the sound of the sewing machines you'd hear laughter, and it got to be a tradition to sing a rendition of "There's No Business Like Sew Business." Everyone was finally able to train their emotions and energies on something concrete.

Though the majority of volunteers were gay men, there were also lots of straight people coming through our doors to donate time and money: children walked in with their fathers; mothers came by with a quilt they'd made for their husband or son. After a few weeks we realized that the epidemic reached far beyond our little world. And that the Quilt meant something outside the Castro.

In midsummer the *New Yorker* ran an article and then *People* magazine did a story, as well as the *Dallas Morning News*. After each burst of publicity, we'd get more quilts, including some from people who'd never known the person they were memorializing. When *Newsweek* published a series of photographs profiling 302 people who had died of AIDS, panels began arriving from people who'd been moved by that piece. There was one we received from a man named Michael Lueders to honor Curt Norrup. Curt had broken up with his lover and attempted suicide. The hospital would not release him until he found a place to stay. Michael, who'd never met Curt except though the article and who had no experience with AIDS, took him into his home and nursed him through the last months, quickly learning how to handle the mundane chores of caring for a bedridden patient as well as the more difficult tasks, like handling Curt during his seizures.

The quilt he made for Curt is simple: black cloth letters sewn into gray fabric with pink elephants. Attached was a note: "I spent 14 hours sewing with a lot of love and needle pricks but it was well worth it. I knew nothing of his life when I took him in and because of that we became good friends. I pray that our short time together provided him some laughter and hopefully some joy."

DURING THAT FIRST summer it felt very much like we were launching a small business on a shoestring budget. Nothing was easy, and most of the day-to-day strains fell on Mike Smith. He was part sergeant, part nanny, dealing with everything from overdue bills to staffing problems. While Mike was putting out fires, I was on the road trying to raise our national profile. Begging plane tickets from rich friends and flight attendants, I'd go to cities around the country, hit every gay bar, and convince the manager to let me into the DJ booth and make an announcement about the Quilt presentation at the National March for Lesbian and Gay Rights in Washington. I learned to keep my speech short or suffer the taunts of queens impatient for a disco fix. But for every jerk there were ten or twenty men and women who listened and promised to come.

Every morning I was at home, I'd go to the post office on Eighteenth Street to see if there were any packages. It was a great day if there was one. Usually there weren't any, and as we went into summer things looked bleak. By mid-July we had less than a hundred quilts, and those were overwhelmingly from the Castro. We'd set the deadline for August 1, just a few weeks away.

One day in late July, having returned from a weeklong swing through Texas, I was standing in line at the post office when one of the clerks looked at me and said, "Oh, it's Mr. Jones!" And his pal raised an eyebrow and chirped, "Does Mr. Jones want his mail?" I was used to a certain amount of ribbing. I knew I'd been a pest and that the Castro post office had a high camp quotient, but I was really puzzled when they opened the door to the back room and asked, "Did you bring a truck?" I went through and saw bins, big canvas postal bins, filled with paper packages, hundreds of them.

I called over to the workshop told them to bring whatever cars were available and park them on Eighteenth and Collingwood. We set up a relay line, picking bundles up out of the bins and passing them through the post office lobby and over the sidewalk into the cars. As we did this I read out the postmarks and everybody cheered. Two more from Texas! *Yeah, Texas.* Here's some from New York City! *Yeah, New York City.* Here's one from Delaware. *Yeah, Delaware!* Here's one from Virginia! Montana! . . . *Montana?*

After several minutes, it got very quiet. I think all of us, without saying anything, realized how weird this was, that all across the country people were taking the names of their dead loved ones and pouring all their anger and pain and grief and love into creating works of art and then sending them to a group of strangers at a post office box.

Seeing these panels piled up in the workshop got me thinking about how we'd display them. We all agreed it was very important for people to be able to get close enough to touch the quilts they'd made. We expected they would want to leave mementos like flowers or notes. So we decided to take four of the twelve-foot squares and link them together with grommets and cable ties to form a larger square that was twenty-four feet by twenty-four feet. Canvas walkways would separate each square, so everyone would be able to get within twelve feet of a panel.

The next question was, How do we present it? How do we unfold it? Is there a ceremony, a ritual? Many ideas were advanced, but with all my Quaker mistrust of rituals I did not want anything fancy or portentous, no music or fanfare or sermons. What we needed was a very simple, dignified, powerful way of revealing the Quilt. Nothing seemed quite right. One morning Jack Caster stumbled in with a terrible hangover and pockets full of wadded-up cocktail napkins, which he excitedly unfolded on my desk. "I've figured it out," he announced. With a rather grand flourish he said, "I call it the lotus fold!" He showed me sketches of a twelve-by-twelve section with eight panels, then began folding them in, corners to the center, corners to the center, until it was a neat bundle. The idea was to position one bundle in the center of each twelve-by-twelve square of the grid. "When it comes time, we'll have a team of eight people do the unfolding. The first four will reach in and pull out the first four corners, the second four will do likewise, and so on until it's flat. Then we'll just pull it out and it will fit into the grid." Sheer genius.

We all agreed it was a simple and elegant solution. But what would the unfolders wear? Should they be dressed alike? If they wore street clothes, wouldn't the colors clash with the Quilt? Black seemed too dark and Druidic; maybe something neutral would work best. White was suggested, then shot down as too nurselike. I thought of the all nurses I'd met in the last few years in AIDS wards across the country and how much love and support they had given. Maybe that wasn't such a bad idea. They were heroes. Many were lesbians who had volunteered to care for the AIDS patients others feared to touch. So we decided that the unfolding ceremony would consist of teams dressed in white, unfolding the lotus-folded panel squares while the names were being read. We went to practice at the Stanford University football field and got it all down.

That final week before the display was exhausting and inspiring. Everything was coming down now to hours and minutes. Though we'd moved the deadline to September 15 and had by then received 720 panels, another 1,200 had just arrived. Each one had to be hemmed to exactly three feet by six feet, then sewn into a twelve-by-twelve square, and then the entire piece again edged in canvas. Grommets were sewn on to hold the fabric in place within the grid of intersecting walkways. The walkways were made of nine-foot-wide white fabric, which in turn had to be measured and cut to the exact size that Ron Cordova, the technical director, had worked out over so many nights pacing up the street from our warehouse to the Café Flore, precisely the right distance.

We had so much help from so many people. Jeff Kuball, an attendant for the air-freight company Flying Tigers, not only had organized a quilt to be made in honor of three co-workers, but had persuaded seventy Tigers employees to donate time and money so that we could fly the Quilt to D.C. and back. It weighed just under seven thousand pounds. Thousands of yards of fabric, thousands of metal grommets, 1,920 names, so much love and loss.

When we got to D.C. for the display, Michael Bento snuck us into some empty dorms at Georgetown University (which had just voted to ban gay and lesbian organizations). We used their computers and phone lines to prepare for our invasion of the District of Columbia.

At about one in the morning on October 11, 1987, ten years after Harvey Milk first called for the National March for Lesbian and Gay Rights, we formed a caravan and made our way through Georgetown up Pennsylvania Avenue to the Mall: the trucks with the Quilt, a thirty-three-foot Winnebago, and a pickup truck with a four-ton scissor lift. It was eerily quiet, and so dark that we used flashlights to lay out the walkways and set up the tables and microphone. Plastic sheeting was set down to protect the cloth panels from the damp grass. At 5 A.M. we were only halfway through laying out the grid, but at dawn we were ready, bundles in position. At 7 A.M. the set-up team held hands in a circle. We'd done it! Ron Cordova's calculations had worked out, Steve Abbeyta's grommets held the panels in place—my vision had come true.

And then things went wrong. At the precise moment we began the unfolding, a panicked voice hissed urgently on my earphone, "We fucked up, it doesn't fit." Somehow, we'd set the bundles at wrong angles and when the Quilt was laid out it extended over the walkways. Thank God for Gert. Very calmly and without the least hesitation, she got on the radio and told the unfolders to lift the Quilt in unison, move it a quarter turn to the left, then set it down. They performed faultlessly. The fabric billowed skyward, catching the first rays of sunlight on the sequins and rhinestones, and then settled gently, perfectly, into place—now a permanent part of every display procedure.

As dawn became day, thousands of people lined the perimeter and I stepped slowly to the podium in the shadow of the Jefferson Memorial. I have almost no memory of walking to the podium, no words to describe the emotion flooding my heart as I read those twenty-four names, each so precious and containing in a few syllables entire lives. I began with Marvin Feldman. It was extremely difficult to speak slowly and deliberately, pausing between each name, and my voice began breaking down at the end of the list. Other readers were Art Agnos, Whoopi Goldberg, Robert Blake, Lily Tomlin, Harvey Fierstein, and Congresswoman Nancy Pelosi. Joseph Papp, producer of the New York Shakespeare Festival, ended his list of names with a tribute to "my dear friend and colleague Michael Bennett." Then, in front of photographers, with his wife, Gail, at his side, Papp untied the ribbons around the red fabric roll under his arm and flourished a shimmering panel emblazoned with Michael Bennett's name and a metallic sunburst, the design from Bennett's most famous Broadway production, *A Chorus Line*. He then walked over to the check-in area and turned it in with the other panels that continued to arrive through the day.

And so, a year and a day after Marvin's death, on October 11, 1987, we unfolded nearly two thousand quilts on the National Mall. It looked incredible. Nothing prepared me for its beauty. There were plain panels of stark white with black lettering, and extravagant ones with gold lamé encrusted with rhinestones and silver braid. There was every material from tweed to leather to silk, and of course ribbons and beads and glitter galore. And everything you could imagine was sewn onto the fabric: locks of hair, record albums, souvenir postcards, a Barbie doll, whistles, crystals, a motorcycle jacket, a tuxedo, a shard of glass, foam-rubber french fries, toy cars, a thimble, a cowboy hat, teddy bears, a pink Lacoste shirt, a Buddhist's saffron robe, and even a padded jock-strap. Notes were scribbled in corners; others were sewn in. Some panels held the ashes of the people they memorialized.

And then there were the letters, hundreds of them, that people had sent along with the panels they'd made. On the back of one of those, decorated with a drawing of twelve candles, three lighted and nine extinguished, Lance Hecox wrote, "To 12 men I expected to grow old with. Nine who have passed on and three who will join them soon."

My friend Gert McMullin wrote of her own grief in one of the most touching letters of them all:

> *Roger, The day I met you, my best friend of ten years told me he had fallen madly in love with you and that you would be living together. Oh yes, and that you had AIDS. Oh Roger—please forgive me for the ten minutes that it took me to stop hating you. I didn't know you and all I could feel was anger and then panic that David might become ill. And I had loved him for so long and I didn't know you at all!*
>
> *Memories of you are not ones most people share. Wheelchairs, hospital waiting rooms, watching you fall, trying to help you up*

without you being mad that someone had to help you, watching
you sleep, and (the most fun!) talking about all of David's faults
and nasty habits while lying in bed.

Few memories, true . . . but what I have is all stored very ten-
derly in my heart.

Roger, I have learned one thing in my life. Don't get to know
someone and become friends after they died. I never got the chance
to run and play with you or to watch you have the time to be happy.

You have given me one thing—a determination to be the kind
of person you would admire. One who touches, wants to be
touched and cares. Your respect is my ultimate goal.

Love you so, Gert

Most of the letters came from men mourning their dead lovers. This
one, from Paul Hill, talked of the secrecy that was necessary even after
his friend's death:

Out of all those people who loved Ric and attended his funeral,
only a handful knew that he died of AIDS. Being gay and having
lived a lie, it was no problem lying about death as well. My lover
who died of pneumocystis quickly became a roommate who died of
viral pneumonia. This sham angers me now, but during that period
of vulnerability which occurs immediately after a great loss, one
can be talked into just about anything. This scenario repeats itself
many times a day all over the United States. There are just too
many people who don't realize that this awful disease has already
touched their lives.

Art Peterson from Atlanta made a quilt for his lover Reggie
Hightower and enclosed this note:

Ours was a unique relationship. We had lots of obstacles which
we overcame to make our relationship grow: He was deaf, I was

hearing; he was black, I was white; we were both gay and proud.
We agreed that these were the happiest times of our lives. We lived
and shared a totally "married" life.

I don't have many ideas on how he should be memorialized—
perhaps a carving on the side of Stone Mountain here in Georgia. I
feel it's a shame that I can't convey to others how great a life he
lived—for he left no mark to be forever immortalized except deep
within those people he loved and those who loved him. How do I
fully express his life to those who never met him? The memories are
so wonderful and yet they cause so much pain.

His panel is composed of shirts that he wore—some his, some
mine. They were hand-sewn (by me) with double thread and
double sewn in places for strength and durability. Please display
it prominently.

The handsign in the middle is sign language for "I Love You."

Sincerely, Art

There are so many stories from that first display. Years before, Hank Wilson had introduced me to Donald Montwell and Jim Maness. They had organized the protest when Dan White was released from jail and fifty thousand people shut down San Francisco. By 1987, Jim was very ill. At the behest of Donald, who'd managed the Valencia Rose cabaret, where Whoopi Goldberg got her start, Whoopi agreed to come to the first display. On Saturday, before we opened the Quilt to the public, Whoopi and Donald and I took Jim out in his wheelchair for a private viewing. As it was quite chilly, Jim borrowed Whoopi's jacket, a shiny silk road crew jacket emblazoned with "Whoopi." He never gave it back and was buried in it not long after returning to San Francisco. I think he was holding on just to be at the display. It meant so much to so many people.

The response to that first display was overwhelming, something I had not imagined or planned for. I'm convinced that every single person who saw the Quilt with their own eyes became an evangelist, telling a few friends who told others, really turning the tide of grassroots support. And certainly the newspaper coverage spread the word. We were on the front page of newspapers around the world, even as far away as New Delhi.

But the thing that put us front and center in millions of Americans' minds was the night I was profiled on television by Peter Jennings as a "Person of the Week" on the *ABC Evening News*. I first heard about it just two hours before airtime in a phone call from ABC. I thanked the man and hung up, not really believing it. A few friends came over and we sat around the TV. Nobody bothered to set up a VCR. Jennings started out by saying, "This week the plight of a little girl who fell down a hole has drawn us together . . ." and I thought, *OK, I've been bumped by little Jessica McClure.* And then he went on, "But tonight we're honoring another person who's brought us together in a different way . . ." And there I was, big as life, walking around the Quilt on television in living rooms all across America. If we thought press coverage had been good, it soon became great. The impact of the Quilt beamed to millions of homes, with mourners walking among two football fields of panels, packed an incredible emotional wallop. It seemed like the whole country was watching television that night, and the calls and letters just poured into the workshop.

When we got home to San Francisco, the mailbox was overflowing. People all over America had been inspired by the panels and had sent us poems and photographs, paintings, screenplays, and play scripts. There were designs for posters, for T-shirts and caps. And every day brought letters from all over the country and around the world, many accompanied by quilts. I remember one letter from a mother whose two sons had died. She opened by saying she hoped it was acceptable that she had put their names together on a single panel. They were very close friends, she explained, and then she asked to pray for all of us: "I have two more gay sons. I live in fear." Another woman wrote of her ignorance and shame, telling of a time when a dying friend who'd been deserted by his lover and family had reached out for a hug and she'd hesitated, afraid of being infected. She hoped he would forgive her.

Some of the letters came from people who'd made quilts for a person they'd never known. "I'm just a housewife," wrote a woman from Nebraska. "I thought there would be no recognition from his family. I felt bad about that. I feel bad about all the people who die of AIDS that nobody knows."

Every letter was different, but they all said that same thing: please bring us the Quilt, let us remember our dead. And that's when I knew that we couldn't close up shop. We had to go on the road and bring the Quilt to everyone, in whatever town they lived, large or small. The letters and the quilts have never stopped coming.

We had no idea the Quilt would last beyond that day. I was looking for a symbol to focus the nation on the epidemic at a time when many of us had lost hope. I hoped it could be a tool for healing families divided by homophobia and believed it might unite the nation against the plague. But I saw it mainly as evidence, as mediagenic proof of the enormity of the crisis killing thousands. For all the beauty and tenderness of each panel, the hard fact was that someone of value had died to make it happen. The Quilt was and is an activist symbol—comforting, yes, but mortally troubling. If it raised a single question, it was, What are we going to do about it? That was the challenge we laid at the national doorstep.

ON DECEMBER 17, 1987, we displayed the Quilt in San Francisco. I'd like to say we had a sense of returning victorious to our hometown and that, back with so many familiar faces, we had a feeling of accomplishment, but for me it was a bittersweet time. Even the fact that the display was held at the newly built Moscone

Center, named for Mayor George Moscone, contained an element of ambiguity. And I couldn't help wondering, as I walked among the panels, which of my friends would soon have their names stitched with so many others.

I don't mean to suggest that any of my reflections betrayed doubt of our mission. Of that I was rock certain. Neither then nor in the intervening years, over innumerable interviews with reporters and journalists, did I ever flag in telling the story of the Quilt and what we stood for and what we were trying to do. My date book for that month is filled with appointments with ABC, CBS, the *Chronicle,* the *Examiner,* and many smaller local papers. Telling one person who would tell hundreds or thousands of people what we're about has always given me a sense of fulfillment, and in that sense the Moscone display was wonderful.

Certainly, the red-carpet embrace from our fellow San Franciscans was encouraging. All the politicians were there for the opening ceremonies, including Art Agnos, then the newly elected mayor, along with Congresswoman Nancy Pelosi, who'd been one of our earliest supporters and has continued to steer us around bureaucratic tar pits to this day. It was through her good offices that we'd secured space on the Mall in D.C. just weeks before, and later, in February 1989, she nominated the Quilt for a Nobel Prize. I remember one conversation with her at the San Francisco display when I'd thanked her for the fund-raisers she'd hosted early that summer. She smiled and said with a combination of relief and amazement that she and other politicians had helped raise money out of loyalty to me, admitting that for all her enthusiasm she'd never imagined that the Quilt would catch on as it had. In this and so many other instances it was wonderful to be able to return in faith to the people—especially the volunteers and donors—who'd placed their trust in us.

For all the good strokes and sheer relief of being home, I had a sense that we had just begun, that we must hurry. Being HIV-positive may have played a part in my wanting to rush on. I was symptom free, but many others were not. Though we had elevated AIDS to a new level of aware-ness, mobilized hundreds of thousands of people in the fight against the disease, there had been no accompanying breakthrough in medicine. The fear that dogged my trail that fall was a very simple question: Had our work come in time to make a difference?

One evening after the closing ceremonies I returned to the work-shop, exhausted both physically and emotionally, and sat down alone in that quiet, cavernous room, sorting through the stacks of mail at a small table in the back. After a while, I got the feeling I was being watched. We never did lock the doors in those days, never saw the need. I turned and saw an old black woman staring through the front win-dow. She had on a blue dress and matching hat and had a deeply lined, dark face. I went out and said, "We're open, if you want to come in." She just crossed her arms and looked down, wouldn't make eye contact, and came in sideways through the door without saying anything. I went back to my desk and she walked around. I saw her touch one of the quilts. She picked up a brochure and left without saying a word.

A few days passed. I was again at the workshop. The radio was blaring, the sewing machines were going, there was a couple crying in one corner, there was a group laughing in another corner—just this general chaos and hubbub. And in the middle of this confusion I again got this back-of-the-neck sensation that I was being watched. I turned and it was the same woman, standing on the sidewalk, scowling through the door, her arms across her chest, wearing the same blue dress.

As she came in the door, I noticed a bundle of fabric in her arms. She walked straight over to me and began her story. She'd come on a Greyhound bus from a small town in Kentucky. A year and a half ear-lier, her oldest son had returned from Los Angeles, where he'd settled after being discharged from the army. He'd come home to die. Though she was the choir director at her church and had a large, close family, she cared for her son for a year without ever revealing the nature of his disease to anyone.

When it was time for her son to die, she took him to the county hospital. After two days he died. She walked back home and, opening the front door, looked across the living room to her son's bedroom; and through the doorway she could see the hospital bed, the stack of towels, the IV rack, the bedpan. She closed door to his room and locked it shut.

Several months passed and she grieved alone, never uttering a word of the truth, never opening the door to her son's room. One day, while she was waiting at the dentist's office, she happened to read a story about the Quilt in a back issue of *People* magazine, went home, and packed a bag. For four days she'd ridden the bus from Kentucky to San Francisco, and now, she said, "I'm at the end." The whole time she'd talked she had been standing ramrod straight. Now she handed me the bundled quilt in her arms and said, "This is my son. I'm going to go home now and clean out his room."

There was nothing to say to this woman that she didn't already know. I stood still and she made her quiet way out the door, pausing only once to give a quick wave—not to me in particular, but to all of us and the quilts and what it all meant. And I felt so proud at that moment, that we in San Francisco, who were mainly young and white and gay, had created a symbol that had traveled across America to this old black woman alone with her grief in the hills of Appalachia and connected her and her son and their struggle with all of us.

I never doubted the Quilt or my place within its mission, but whatever lingering fears I had at the end of that first year about whether I would be up to the task of shepherding a national, even international project simply vanished after my encounter with that old black woman. Her fortitude gave me the strength and confidence to carry on and brought me to a final acceptance of something I'd struggled with for a long time—my place as a gay man in the world.

The Quilt required me to change. Whether it is the pope or the woman from Kentucky, the Quilt touches something intensely private and personal in everyone who sees it. I had to learn to listen to those feelings, those fears and hopes—not just of my sorrowing brothers, but of everyone who even for a moment had opened up and recognized a common humanity, a link between all of us. For ten years I'd lived in the gay ghetto, shouted through the bullhorn, marched and been arrested and jailed. My friends were gay, the music I listened to was gay oriented, the movies I saw had something to do with being gay, and except for a few family holidays it was a closed world. But now our goals demanded a different attitude, a wider reference. Certainly I wanted to startle Middle America and shake them up, but shocking people, hollering, "Look out, America, we're coming!" just didn't work. Times had changed, and the Quilt was part of the way we would survive and possibly prevail.

M Y GRAND-
mothers,
Helen Rupert Jones
and Vera Davy Kirk.
Grandma Jones's
mother, Irene, sewed
a quilt for me with
tigers, dragons, and
dolphins on it, made
out of my great-
grandfather's old
pajamas.

A S A YOUNG
woman, my
mother studied under
the legendary dance
choreographer
Martha Graham.

M E AT AGE six with "Papa,"
my paternal grandfather,
Blythe Randolph Jones.

M Y CAREFREE days kicking around Europe. This is me in Amsterdam in 1975. I'm on my way to Munich, home base for further travels, including a trip to Barcelona where I witnessed the first Gay Pride March after Generalissimo Franco's fall.

W ITH HARVEY Milk at a march in San Francisco against the vote in Wichita, Kansas, one of the many copycat measures that came up after Anita Bryant's "Save Our Children" crusade.

T HE NIGHT after the public television debate with John Briggs, we all went to the Elephant Walk, Harvey's favorite bar. Harvey surprised me by remembering that it was my twenty-fourth birthday. Note the donut with a candle on it. Doug Perry is on the left, and gay historian Eric Garber is on Harvey's lap.

I WAS SERVED THIS subpoena to appear before the Grand Jury investigating the White Night riots on the same day I was to be sworn in as a commissioner of the city's juvenile delinquency panel.

A VERY YOUNG me graced the cover of *Christopher Street*, an early national gay magazine.

ON NOVEMBER 27, 1985, after the candlelight march for Harvey Milk and George Moscone, we wrote the names of friends who had died of AIDS and attached them to the front of the old Federal Building in San Francisco's United Nation's Plaza. It was that night that my idea for the Quilt was born.

F OR GAY PRIDE IN 1987, Mayor Dianne Feinstein allowed us to hang our first quilts from San Francisco City Hall. It was one of our first major publicity breakthroughs.

H ERE'S THE ORIGINAL Quilt crew sitting on the back of Stella, the truck that carried us from Los Angeles to Boston and back to San Francisco on that first national tour in 1988. From left to right, back row: Jack Caster, Joey Van-Es, me, Gert McMullin, Evelyn Martinez, Michael Smith, Debra Resnick. Front row: Scott Lago, Sandy O'Rourke.

T HE WORKSHOP WAS an amazing place, full of incredibly dedicated people working, crying, and laughing as we tried to recapture our friends' lives in cloth. Here are Joseph Durant (above) sewing and Jack Caster (right) being particular about where to attach a belt to a panel, 1987.

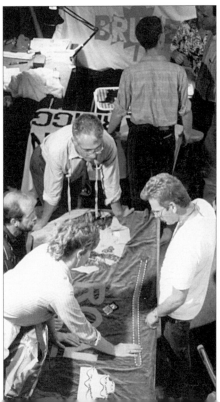

Here i am with the friends of Zoel St. Sauver at his panel, 1988. For many of us, AIDS was our World War II, our Vietnam. This photograph reminds me of the classic memorial to Iwo Jima. All of us in the picture were HIV positive, caught in a nightmare that seemed unending.

Rosa parks, icon of the Civil Rights movement, is a wonderful inspiration to me. Her steadfastness, courage, and nobility set an extraordinary example. Here she is at work on a panel in the Detroit Chapter of the NAMES Project, 1989.

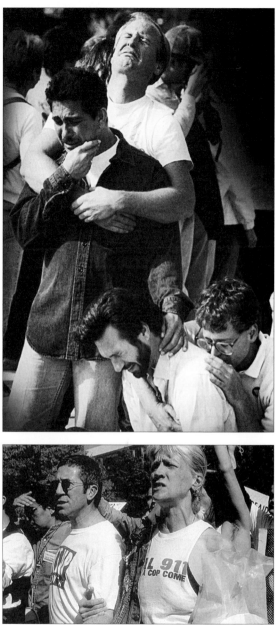

This is Rick Solomon and Gert McMullin at the protest at the White House gates. The plastic bag in Gert's hand held the ashes of our dear friend Joey Van-Es, which Gert emptied onto the White House lawn.

A CIRCLE OF volunteers preparing to unfold a 12 x 12.

REVEREND JESSE JACKSON, San Francisco Mayor Art Agnos, and me in 1991 at a rally against measure K, an attempt to repeal an early version of the domestic partners law for San Francisco. We won!

LILY TOMLIN has been with us from the beginning, appearing at countless AIDS benefits and Quilt displays around the country.

Here I am at the '96 display with my parents, my sister Elizabeth, and her husband John. We're all together, still happy, and still alive. Dad had beaten prostate cancer, I had triple-digit T-cells again, and for the first time in years there was reason for hope. We were very proud and grateful that day.

Elizabeth Taylor at the '96 display, inspiring us all with her elegance and her beautiful speech: "The Quilt shows us that although we are all different, we are all the same." The reading of names continued throughout the day with Maya Angelou, Mikhail Barishnikov, Judith Light, and many others.

For the first time a President of the United States visits the AIDS Memorial Quilt. The Clintons were moved and both found panels for friends they had known.

THE QUILT DISPLAYED in full on the Washington Mall, on October 11, 1996. It was my 42nd birthday. Over 12,000 volunteers had worked together to unload and lay out 43 tons of fabric, the size of 24 football fields. They also had to handle 21 miles of walkway fabric, 36,000 tent pegs, and 20,000 boxes of Kleenex. There were 1.2 million people in attendance at that display.

line between the Capitol dome and the Washington Monument, the Quilt had meandered—a little to the left, a little to the right. With our typical acid humor, we dubbed it "the Cordova Curve."

Far from a gilded band of acolytes whose halos shone with goodness, we were each of us irreverent, sarcastic, hard-assed, and hard-drinking (or recently recovered from hard drinking). There was nothing remotely angelic about us; we were just a collection of sharp-tongued, driven people who dropped everything—quit jobs, left relationships—and devoted ourselves to the Quilt. Our edginess brought us problems, but also an incredibly focused energy.

Mike, the Stanford M.B.A., had a by-the-numbers attitude that was summed up in the Brooks Brothers shirts he wore like armor. Gert's previous job had been at the cosmetics counter at Macy's, where she'd coo to customers all day and agitate for the union at night. Sweet Evelyn was a straight Mexican-American woman who carried the shadow of the loss of her husband even at her most lighthearted moments. Jack was a gentle, funny, and dirty-minded man who'd sold his successful antique business after his partners and roommates of twenty years had died. There was also Debra, who never liked me. She was a lesbian separatist with arms like a lumberjack's. She arrived during our the first week in the workshop; she came in, sat down, and didn't get up from the sewing machine for six months. One day I thanked her, and she flexed her arms and narrowed her eyes and said, "I'm not a fan of yours."

Though superficially very different from each other in most respects, we had two things in common: the soul-deep wound this disease had inflicted, and a passion to use the Quilt toward its healing. To this day, there's really no one else I know who has the experience of the epidemic that Gert and I share, having lived in the Castro for twenty-five years and watched so many people die and yet survived ourselves. After the first showing in D.C. in October 1987, we had some money from selling T-shirts and buttons, so we began paying out small salaries—fifty dollars a week, I think it was. One day at the workshop, the phone rang on

Lance's desk; he was the office administrator. He was out, so I picked it up and began rummaging through his desk for a pen. And I found a stack of all his paychecks. He had never cashed any of them. Jack Caster paid us a thousand dollars a month for the privilege of being a volunteer. When he died, he left us his life insurance, which was our first major donation.

I loved them all. And it was wonderful to have friends again—people who I knew would, were we allowed to live, share the intimacy that comes from long-term friendships, something I thought I'd lost forever.

THOUGH THE QUILT seems a fixture in American life today, we thought of the 1987 D.C. display as a one-time event. Once the nation had seen the Quilt laid out on the Mall, read the names, and felt the love in these profoundly American panels, we idealistically thought, the entire country would be mobilized, the government would fund research, families would unite, and our job would be done. After that? I hadn't guessed where our individual lives would go. And yet every day we went through stacks of letters containing hundreds of testimonials asking us to continue.

Once, during this time, I went across the bridge to Oakland and met with a group of ninety mostly African-American women who had banded together as a group. As we went around the circle, I asked each to state her name and why they had organized to fight AIDS. As they stood up and said their piece, I got goose bumps. Each spoke of seeing the Quilt, of how personal the panels were, and said that now they understood our struggle and saw that it was theirs, too. It was wonderful. We'd made an impact, just a few miles across the bay from San Francisco, but across a wide chasm of cultural differences.

We had indeed unleashed an untapped reservoir of emotion in the heart of the nation. All the personal appeals amounted to a popular edict: bring the Quilt to us, to our hometowns, large and small. We need to see it, to be part of it.

The idea of a national tour was daunting, to say the least, especially after the marathon of starting the Quilt, getting it to D.C., and then transporting it back home to San Francisco. We needed a break to think things through, so I took us up to the Russian River—a beautiful out-of-time pocket of ancient redwoods set by a lazy river. The largest of the towns is Guerneville, with a population of twelve hundred, ten times the size of what is now my own hamlet down the road, Villa Grande. Though the "River," as we call it, had once been a popular summer re-sort for San Franciscans (Tommy Dorsey played there in the '30s and '40s), it had fallen on hard times and was a sort of forgotten treasure. The little ramshackle cabins with hand-painted signs over their doors like "River Nest" and "Doc's Reward" and "The Carter Family Camp" were being abandoned by the later generations, and many had been sold off as the economy and younger generation moved elsewhere. Just two hours from San Francisco, relatively isolated by redwood-covered hills on one side and the Pacific on the other, the area had been discov-ered in the '70s as a cheap, safe place for gays to gather. Although there was an eruption of homophobia every so often, most of the locals were glad to see their villages repopulated. A few resorts turned gay or gay friendly and fueled the emigration. One of these, a series of cabins spread out along winding woodland paths, was called the Woods. It was there, under the redwoods, that we developed the outlines of the organization you see today.

Though I'd helped found the San Francisco AIDS Foundation, our decision to start a nonprofit was based on very thin experience. Mike and I tried various names, like the National AIDS Memorial Education and Support, but finally settled on just the NAMES Project. It was simple, and people understood what it was about.

None of us had any idea that from the national tour we were plan-ning would come the structure of the world's largest community arts project, but that's what happened. We began by mapping out the route. It wasn't too difficult to estimate the costs for gasoline, for lodging, for mundane things like thread and batting. Mike and Ron took care of that. And Debra had found an old but very large truck to carry everything, a thirty-foot bobtail Ford. I was dubious that the old rust bucket could make even two blocks, but she gave me one of her "Don't cross me" looks and mumbled, "I've already named her Stella." "Lovely name," I said and quickly agreed. Mike was never comfortable with naming the truck, especially when he discovered that along with the name came two chrome busty ladies facing each other on the mud flaps. But even he was no match for Debra.

We then developed a list of contacts in various cities we'd visit on the tour. Most came from AIDS service organizations across the nation, members of which we'd met at the first display and the March on Washington. Our approach was simple: find us a display site, then help feed us, house us, and set things up. None of the organizations had much money, and so we offered the Quilt as the centerpiece for a fund-raiser. In order to finesse the inevitable jockeying between groups, we asked that the host committees be made up of a representative from each local organization. As it turned out, those committees were the embryos of what has become the backbone of the organization: the Quilt chapters in fifty cities all across America, from Los Angeles to Topeka to Boston.

Along with the tour, there were other things to consider. We'd been approached by HBO about a movie on the Quilt, to be directed by Rob Epstein. I'd met Rob in the early '80s, when he directed a movie called *The Times of Harvey Milk*. It was a wonderful, groundbreaking documentary, narrated by Dustin Hoffman, that featured many friends of mine, including Sally Gearhart. My good friend Bill Kraus, with whom I had a long history, was also in the movie. He'd been one of the prime gay activists and worked for Phil Burton (who engineered Moscone's winning coalition); on the night of the murders, he and David Weissman and I ended up in my apartment, talking and drinking, trying to imagine what the future would hold. He'd also helped steer Harry Britt through those tumultuous first years. The night *The Times of Harvey Milk* premiered at the Castro Theatre marked the beginning of what would become a proud history of debuts of gay films at the Castro. Bill died not long after, but it is wonderful to have him recorded on film.

I knew that Rob was warm and bright, but I was hesitant: he'd spent a lot of time filming interviews of me for *The Times of Harvey Milk*, which won an Academy Award; but when the film was released, I discovered that none of the footage of me had been included. Still, the new project was obviously worthwhile, and we agreed to let Rob and his crew come in and start shooting in late December.

The resulting film, *Common Threads,* turned out to be a beautiful essay, not so much about the Quilt itself—there is only a brief view of the workshop where it began—but about five people struggling with AIDS at a time when hope for survival was nonexistent. I think the filmmakers selected them very well. One of them was Vito Russo (the author of *The Celluloid Closet*), whom I loved dearly. In March 1990, *Common Threads* won the Oscar for Best Documentary.

I should not have been surprised that the Quilt would, like any other work of art, be interpreted and reinterpreted in many ways. Indeed, that is one of its strengths—that it can be so much to so many different people. But what we learned the hard way was that to preserve its richness we'd have to defend the simplicity of the Quilt itself. Just laying out the quilts, letting people see the panels, that spare presentation, allows everyone open access, unencumbered by embellishment from one group or another. Whites, blacks, poor, rich, straight or gay— no one is excluded by signs or symbols from joining our effort to put a face on statistics. To maintain this defensive, even conservative stance was a constant struggle those first years as we learned over and over that we must protect the central message and keep it clean.

In what would turn out to be one of the most spectacular tests of our resolve to be inclusive, the first showing of the tour took place in Los Angeles. We "went Hollywood," as they say. It was a disaster.

We were excited, our L.A. friends were up for it, and we all thought a spring debut display in Hollywood would make for one heck of a kickoff. I must admit to having some of the northern Californians' distrust of Los Angelenos. They were in my mind a polo shirt and khaki crowd, whereas we were jeans and flannel. But much of my attitude had changed a few years earlier after I'd come down to speak at a memorial for Harvey and George. It was late at night, and thousands of us had marched in the traditional sea of candles and gathered in a parking lot. I mounted the podium and began telling stories, and then I noticed something that surprised and moved me. Nowadays, it sometimes seems I don't even have to say a word; I just get up there onstage and the weeping starts. But back then, as I looked out at the front rows, it was unnerving to see people holding each other, trembling and crying. It shook me up, and I decided that I'd underestimated my Angeleno friends.

Because of his background, Mike Smith, our managing director, was the designated negotiator with all the tour-city host committees. For Los Angeles this was not an easy job since it, like the other large cities in the late 1980s, had hundreds of AIDS groups, each composed of strong-minded and opinionated people on a mission as heartfelt as ours. I was on the road constantly during this time, doing interviews, and I left negotiations in Mike's hands. Although the L.A. committees had come up with many creative ideas, we were all unified—or so I thought—on the importance of enforcing our views on how the Quilt should be presented, and I relied on Mike to take care of that. At first things seemed a little overproduced, but not too much so—just a mention of a light show and the possibility of a few celebrities. A dash of stardust seemed natural. But as the date drew nearer, things got out of hand. The event became longer and more elaborate. There was to be a light show and celebrities, as well as an orchestra, and the local TV stations were sending cameramen, reporters. There were even complicated plans for valet parking! Just weeks before the display, the L.A. host committee sent us a script that began with the following: "Darkness. A single light comes from the heavens. A note, sad. It is Rachel crying in the wilderness . . ."

Exasperated, I asked Mike somewhat sarcastically if Bob Mackie, of Cher fashion fame, would be designing the car attendants' outfits. He didn't laugh, but just went on saying that some big people were going to be part of the presentation. Whoopi Goldberg was to be involved, as well as TV vamp Morgan Fairchild and her then boyfriend, Alan Cranston, the cadaverous senior California senator. I had horrible visions of the Quilt trotted out as a glitzy movie-land backdrop, lit by tiki torches and carried by Lycra-clad rollerbladers. Had Mike set up a review in *Variety*, maybe seeded a headline like "Boffo Quilt Bash"? Mike and I had a huge fight, probably the most serious of all our fights. Partly because of our own increasingly tense relations and partly out of deference to the very classy L.A. crowd and the work they'd already done, Mike capitulated to everything. I was furious.

Apparently, the spirit of the Quilt agreed with me. At precisely 8 P.M., as the spectacle was about to begin, the power went out at UCLA's Pauley Pavilion. The entire arena, filled to the rafters with thousands of people, was plunged into absolute darkness. People screamed and hooted, creating a carnival atmosphere. A moment later the orange emergency lights came on under the seats. There was no power, but somehow Whoopi was given a bullhorn and went down onto the center of the floor to calm things down. Though it was a noble effort, it caused mayhem. As she stepped out among the Quilt panels, so did the camera crews. As Whoopi began telling jokes, the cameramen chased her around the floor, and as they pivoted to get the best angles, the quilts became tangled in cables and churned up under wheels.

Backstage I was seething at the circus of it all, but had no idea what to do. The stage manager came up and told me that the emergency power would last only twenty minutes and that we needed to get everyone out while there was still light. I looked over, and there was Whoopi holding forth to a barrage of flashing cameras and the TV crews were swiveling their minicams and wheeling dollies, knocking a bundle of panels aside. I walked out onstage and took the bullhorn from Whoopi and said to her, "Thank you, Whoopi." I turned to the crowd, my voice trembling, and said, "There is only fifteen minutes of emergency power left, and you must all leave the building now, every one of you."

And they booed.

It was humiliating. I felt I'd betrayed every person on every panel and also those people who'd made them. Marvin, Ed—their memorials had been trashed, and I was to blame for not protecting them. Those boos rang in my ears. Shaking with fury, I told Mike and everyone near me, "That's it. Tomorrow's display is off. We'll learn from our mistakes and we'll go on."

And then I was given another lesson. Instead of being allowed to help gather the quilts and repack them, I was told by my friends to go home. I was stunned. But they stood together. Danny Sauro, Ron Gray, Sandy O'Rourke, and Scott Lago took me aside and said, "Cleve, you need to go to the airport and get on a plane and go home. It's out of your hands. There are hundreds of people down here to make this happen. And they've been working and we've been working and you no longer have the right to just say this is being shut down." And I looked at them, numbed and totally disarmed. The last of the crowd was filing out the doors, the staff was quietly folding the quilts and setting them aside—all of it bathed in the strange orange glow of the emergency lights. No one was speaking. "You're right. I'm out of here," I said, and left.

The most lacerating aspect of the confrontation was not the overwhelming shame and anger I felt, but a strange sense of loss. Somehow my dream, my child, was no longer mine. It was everyone's. Here were my friends, people I trusted, looking beyond me toward a larger goal, and my own obsession suddenly seemed small. Everyone takes an inordinate amount of ownership in their own creation. True, Mike had fucked up, but I'd let my obsession obscure the reason we were there. I couldn't deny the Quilt to all Los Angeles. I would eventually find a place between ownership and independence, but it would take many years.

Just after the Los Angeles debacle, we came across another example of overweening possession. About midway to Phoenix, just before we were to cross from California into Arizona, Stella was pulled off the road by a large group of motorcyclists: women, radical lesbians, in leather jackets and chaps, roared up beside the truck and herded us off the side of the road like a lost calf. With military precision, they boxed us in, front and back. Nobody knew what to expect. They sat there in formation, revving their engines, not taking their helmets off. It was intimidating. Then one woman swung off her bike and strode up to the truck: "No straight hands must touch the Quilt," she announced.

Evelyn and Debra get a lot of credit here. Very quietly and diplomatically, they informed these women that the hands of heterosexuals had been touching the Quilt from the beginning; indeed, they'd sewn it together. This very severe, black-leather-clad woman asked, "Are you straight?" I don't know what the hell that had to do with anything, but for this woman it was vital. Without flinching, Evelyn said, "Yes." Debra said, "I'm a dyke. So, what?" This was puzzling to the radical lesbian, and she marched off. Seated in the old rusted cab out in the middle of the desert, Evelyn and Debra waited. Eventually, the spokesperson strode back up to the cab and said, "We'll take you in." She stuck out her hand to Evelyn, shook it, looked at Debra, and walked back to her bike. With its motorcade escort, Stella made a rather grand entrance into conservative Phoenix. With that sad twinkle in her eye, Evelyn said she felt safer than she had in years.

Whether the attacks have come from the far right or the far left, the attempts to subvert the Quilt's message have always just dissolved. In thirteen years the only people who've taken potshots at it have been extremists; everybody else seems to understand it and be inspired. What we've found is that the best way is to simply lay the Quilt out and let people read the names. Don't have preachers, don't have politicians; just let people walk through the Quilt and feel its power.

HAT FIRST TOUR started in early spring and continued through the summer. Two of the seven-member
crew would ride in Stella and the other five would be in an RV that
Mike had got us for a song. After L.A., we were always concerned
about the Quilt's fragility—roof leaks if the display was to be inside,
and rain if it was to be outside. And there was a lot of worry about
leaving the Quilt out in parking lots, especially when we stayed in cheap
hotels in rather dicey areas. None of our fears about attacks from right-
wing nuts came true, and Stella was surprisingly reliable. We took a lot
of hits, including a fire scare in Illinois, but we got pretty good at pre-
cautions and miraculously kept on. Aside from two fender benders, the
only problems we encountered were at the weigh stations. After we'd
picked up so many quilts, Stella began to wobble at high speeds, making
it obvious we had exceeded our load limit. Even this was got around. If
it was a man in charge, Debra would have Gert change into tight pants
and a sexy top. "Smile now, chippie. Flirt with him!" she'd say, "and get
us through here." And they always let Stella pass, wagging those tacky
mud flaps.

I was spared the driving routine to concentrate on the overall publicity. Typically, I'd fly in a day or two before the road crew arrived,
meet the committees, and do interviews with the local papers and television news. I'd stay for the opening ceremony and then head off for the
next town.

Once at our destinations, we were totally dependent on the community. Our hotel budget was always low, so housing was often donated by
local supporters, who were wonderfully generous with very much appreciated home-cooked meals. It was great matching faces to the voices
we'd talked to on the phone as we'd tried to rent a stadium or arrange
for shipments of quilts. Everywhere we found what seemed like old
friends as we met the people who had created the panels we admired and
had written the letters that had so deeply moved us back in the workshop. It strengthened our bonds and made the hardships worthwhile.

Most of the volunteers were gay men or lesbians, all of whom felt a great deal of pride in the Quilt because it had debuted at the March on Washington and also because it had carried on as a visible sign of hope in a time when the public perception of AIDS remained mired in fear and prejudice. The new treatment with AZT offered a glimmer of hope in battling the disease, and ACT-UP's famous battle cry, "Silence = Death," gave us all a certain sustaining courage. But there were scant symbols for the AIDS community to gather around in a country where the death toll was reported at 27,900 and when HIV-positive children like Ryan White were shunned by their neighborhood elementary schools. A recent study had found that 14 percent of those who tested positive contemplated suicide. I knew it was even worse.

Our tour began soon after the release of Surgeon General C. Everett Koop's report on AIDS. The report had a huge impact, not so much on the already well-educated gay community, but on straight Americans, who were just beginning to feel the effects of the epidemic. Here was the revered and respected Dr. Koop speaking out about AIDS as a disease like any other communicable disease. He talked of the prevention and treatment of AIDS as a public health problem, arguing against the homophobic bias that had so wrongly colored the debate on what to do. Among the falsehoods he batted down were the wild-eyed speculations about infection from drinking fountains and from going to the dentist. Part of the solution he outlined involved education and condoms. The sad state of government leadership was succinctly described when the Institute of Medicine of the National Academy of Sciences described the Reagan administration's response to the epidemic as "woefully inadequate." If Dr. Koop, with his stolid, grandfatherly style, could stand up and tell the truth, so could many of the families whose sons were sick and dying. As the tour went on, we saw an increasing number of straight attendees. This was most moving when a gay family had made a quilt and a biological family had made a quilt and they'd both show up for a display looking for their quilt and meet each other for the first time. Even in this bleak atmosphere, we had proof the Quilt was doing its job.

Some of the displays drew hundreds of people, some only a few. No matter the crowd size, we kept to the full Quilt presentation ritual. The volunteers would roll out the canvas grid, then put in place the panel bundles, then unfold the bundles. With a volunteer at each corner point, the quilts would be lifted up, catch the air, and turn to settle gently in the square. After the display the quilts would be refolded, and once they'd been returned to the truck we'd begin checking in new panels—a task considered among Quilt people to be the most difficult. People would line up to present the new panels on the far side of an empty grid. If I wasn't there, someone else was, but it was always a single person who stood and received the new quilts. One by one the panel makers would walk alone across the empty grid carrying the cloth memorial of their lover or brother or sister or child.

When the displays were not well attended, there was a special poignancy to the new-panel check-in. However isolated or friendless their lives, in that moment of handing over a loved one's panel to be joined with the Quilt, they are with people who understand their pain. To this day, especially among those intimidated or overwhelmed by crowds, there are many who believe that the Quilt is most powerful when viewed in single and solitary moments.

If on some days we gathered only a few quilts, others brought us hundreds, and they added up quickly. City by city, the Quilt was growing visibly. Every time it was unfolded it was bigger, and each display increased our awareness of its power, at times leaving us almost giddy. You could see people grow as they walked around it and see the depth of emotion in their faces; you could see what they were experiencing and feel it. The messages in the quilts were so simple and yet so eloquent. Jim Brumbauh's panel superimposes his name and dates over a Halley's comet sparkling across the sky, signifying his sense of awe. Duane Kearns Puryears's message was starkly affecting: "I was born on

December 4, 1964. I was diagnosed with AIDS on September 7, 1987, at 4:45. I was 22 years old. Sometimes, it makes me sad. I made this panel for myself. If you are reading it, I am dead."

About midway through the tour, the mythic qualities of the Quilt began to reveal themselves in mysterious, portentous moments that point to something more than coincidence. Over the years we've had hundreds of these incidences. Once a reporter came late to a display just as we were packing up at the end of the day. She was upset that she'd lose her story and distraught that she'd let down her friend. As she began helping us reload the quilts, she stumbled backward and a bundle tumbled down. There on the ground was the one panel out of hundreds that she wanted to see, the one for her roommate.

Volunteers can be extremely nervous about loading and unloading the panels. They're juggling emotions and yet trying to be skillful and tender. Many times in my experience people have reached up to carry off a bundle and the bundles have fallen open on the ground—revealing the name of the volunteer's lover, or a brother or a son.

These kinds of magical coincidences kept happening over and over. We'd see a volunteer shudder or gasp as she was unfolding a panel and then learn that, contrary to what chance would dictate, the panel they were holding was the one they'd made. Another time we discovered that two lovers, separated for years in different parts of the country, had been reunited in the Quilt, their panels stitched side to side.

I was never prepared for the spiritual power and the artistic beauty of the Quilt. People say the world is becoming more secular and cynical. What I saw then, and what I see so often today, is a great empathy as well as phenomenal connections—which, though they may come outside the dogma of religious structure, affirm something quite wondrous. If you talk to any of the Quilt dinosaurs, as we old-timers call ourselves, you'll discover that Quilt magic is something everyone remembers.

I loved those moments and did think of them as affirmation of our work, but I was also concerned that they could be distorted into something beyond their individual meaning. I can't remember if it was in Boston or New York or Chicago, but as the tour went along we became uncomfortably aware that the Quilt had developed a strange following of fanatics. At successive stops I'd see a face I'd seen before, then a few from Atlanta and Houston were now in St. Louis and a guy in a red jacket kept reappearing like déjà vu.

The devotion the Quilt engendered was amazing to me and a little scary, especially when we'd drive to a site and out of the shadows would walk the same people, who would literally throw themselves on us. They were harmless, I suppose, but it was kind of creepy to be hugged and cried over by people who seemed to think we were something we were not. We called those people—the camp followers—"Threadheads," like the devotees of the Grateful Dead.

One time, as we were working an assembly line to pack quilts before sending them off to a display, I was smoothing a panel and felt a hidden pocket. Something was concealed there, and I couldn't figure out what it was. Chances were that it was innocuous, something personal, but I couldn't in good conscience send the panel up in a plane full of people without first investigating. Gert thought it might be drugs. When we opened it up we found ashes. Someone, somewhere in the Midwest, had sewn his lover's ashes into a panel and sent it across the country to people he'd never met. I was stunned by the incredible faith evidenced by this and so many other gestures.

We tried not to react too strongly, as we did understand how they felt. We were all desperate for a cure, and willing to sacrifice anything for a chance to beat the odds. Many of my friends pinned their lives on the slimmest chance offered by the newest exotic herb or promising concoction against the virus, none of which ever worked.

And we ourselves were very vulnerable. Back then you would call home after a couple of weeks of travel only to find that friends and volunteers were gone. We knew that almost all of the guys involved with the Quilt were infected. So the fear was constant. When we lost one of our own, everyone just shut down, sometimes for weeks.

On those rare occasions when all the staff were together, I cautioned people about using certain words and phrases with religious connotations or the New Age vocabulary. One day in Chicago I began to get particularly uncomfortable as Scott Lago led volunteers through the unfolding procedure. He'd come from Atlanta, Georgia, but had rapidly mastered the phraseology of the human potential movement. He talked of the "spiritual essence" of what we were doing, of "trusting the flow of feeling," and wrapped our simple, stripped-down ceremony in all sorts of gauzy euphemisms. I pulled him aside and told him he was scaring me, that we weren't trying to build a cult, that we were not a church. He was offended, but soon after, I made a list of banned words, like *empower,* and phrases, like *share the enshrinement.*

I deeply distrust these West Coast words, and the constant use of indirect phrasing. Don't say, "I have issues around survival"; say, "The issue in my life is survival." Choose words carefully, words that are evocative, that will perhaps punch little buttons in people's subconscious. It's become a joke among old-timers, but I would doggedly admonish everyone not to gab away about the "solidarity" of people of different classes; instead, talk of Conestoga wagons, talk about your grandmother. When you are talking to an American audience, there are all sorts of things you can speak of that make connections. When I talk of my grandmother making quilts, I can see the people nodding their heads with like memories. I told the crew to listen what people are saying. At one display I heard a woman tell her friend, "When Mark got sick I felt like our family had been canceled—like we were a TV show and the remote had clicked and now we were in some awful episode of *General Hospital.*" This is how real people talk about real lives, and the Quilt, among all things, must reflect that.

THOUGH I DID often feel I was in the center of a storm, most of the winds were blowing our way. In January 1988 the NAMES Project received nonprofit status from the Internal Revenue Service. Simon and Schuster was about to publish *The Quilt: Stories from the NAMES Project,* a beautiful photo book concentrating on the previous year's D.C. display, written by Cindy Ruskin, a young South African woman.

And the tour had been successful. After four months we had raised five hundred thousand dollars for hundreds of local AIDS service organizations in Los Angeles, Phoenix, San Diego, New York, Houston, Dallas, Baltimore, Chicago, Cleveland, Detroit, Kansas City, Minneapolis, New Orleans, and Providence, Rhode Island. More than nine thousand volunteers across the country helped the seven-person traveling crew move and display the Quilt. Local panels were added in each city, tripling the Quilt's size to more than six thousand panels by the end of the tour. In May we inaugurated our first Quilt chapter in Atlanta, setting up the form soon to be followed in Boston, St. Louis, New York, Atlanta, Houston, and Dallas.

Just after the tour, I placed a call to Dr. Jonathan Mann. I'd heard of his work with AIDS in Africa and that he was one of the strongest voices arguing that AIDS was a worldwide problem. With his recent appointment as founding director of the World Health Organization's Global Program on AIDS, I thought we could work together extending the Quilt's reach beyond the United States and around the world. Actually, he'd had the same idea. Surprisingly, he had already envisioned the Quilt as an integral part of his idea for World AIDS Day. And he wanted it soon—that summer, actually. "We've got a lot of work to do," he said. "We're going to make the world understand that AIDS is not an American disease, not a gay disease, but a world epidemic that is incidentally going to kill half the homosexuals in America."

If I'd known his entire staff consisted at that time of just him and his secretary I'm sure I would still have been as enthusiastic. He was charming, persuasive, and best of all, he spoke not in bureaucratese but in real terms about what was happening, about the cost of homophobia in the affluent West, and the sheer ignorance of the coming storm among the impoverished Third World peoples. He was not a chalk-board theorist; he was a doctor trying to save live patients, and he saw the Quilt as an important part of his global efforts. Even then he had no patience for the party line among most governments, which counseled us all to proceed with caution. Instead, he was pushing for immediate implementation of research and prevention programs that on average were mired in a seven-year process.

Mann never thought small. The first effort he envisioned was a European tour modeled on our recent tour of the United States. He believed the Quilt carried a message that would cross cultural and language barriers and saw it as the foundation for establishing a world-wide ritual to be called World AIDS Day. It was a huge undertaking, but nothing seemed to faze him. Language barriers disappeared with access to his multilingual staff, and logistics would be handled through the United Nations, the WHO's parent organization. I was hesitant to bring up our costs and worried that our meager resources could not finance such a tour. Not to worry, he said; just give me a general budget and I'll fix everything.

At the World AIDS Conference in Stockholm, Sweden, held that summer, Jeannette Kojain (who was so important to establishng our international chapters), Mann, and I met to go over the details. Located close to the Arctic circle, Stockholm is an enchanting yet sometimes unnerving city. In summer, daylight lasts through the night, so that even after midnight there's a eerie glow as you walk down the streets.

Among the people Jonathan introduced me to, all of whom seemed to be fluent in English, as opposed to my embarrassingly hobbled "menu" French, was Viola Mukassa, a wonderfully warm Ugandan woman who worked with the AIDS service organization of her country. She was as disoriented as I by the constant twilight, and we became friends over "breakfast coffees" at all hours of our disjointed days. She loved the Quilt, and I thrilled to listen to her beautifully accented English. She spoke at the candlelight march in Washington during the display that October. Once again, Dr. Mann's generosity came through, not only for Viola but for a number of other women from Third World countries who bore witness to the epidemic and memorialized kindred lives. Later that year, after she returned home, she and other people from TASO, the Ugandan AIDS service organization, sent us the first African quilts. They were made of strands of tree-bark fiber.

By summer Gert, Jack, Scott, Lance, and I were scattered throughout Europe helping guide the various displays. With the Quilt's reputation and the imprimatur of the United Nations, it all went rather smoothly. We were waved through customs in Paris, Stockholm, and Berlin, and though Jack was increasingly weak and fatigued, he seemed to be having no serious problems in London.

Gert and Lance went to Geneva, Switzerland, for the World AIDS Conference. Lance had previously been a vice president at Dean Witter stockbrokers, so I figured he had the polish to deal with all the bigwigs they'd meet. They both reveled at being seated in the grand, forty-foot-high-ceilinged Geneva conference rooms, wearing those translators in their ears like any of the other cabinets ministers and heads of state. Gert and Dr. Mann quickly became buddies over a mutual love of sweets, and they'd sneak chocolate doughnuts to each other while the dignified droning went on; she quickly became a favorite of his.

In addition to the formal presentations in the big conference hall, Dr. Mann scheduled personalized introductions to the Quilt for each of heads of state. And that is where we almost lost it, in a NAMES Project version of the Cuban missile crisis.

The thunderclouds began to gather when word came down that the papal delegation was coming to see the Quilt. Gert had misgivings, strong ones, about any sort of papal blessing. In spite of Lance's reassurance that it was only a ceremony, she was adamant: "He'll bless these panels," she said, "over my dead body."

Luckily for my blood pressure, I was spared the minute-by-minute countdown. But here's how the legend goes:

Flanked by his uniformed entourage, the Vatican's representative made his call resplendently attired in brocaded robes and headpiece, about as royal as they come. As head of our delegation, Gert stood protectively before a folded bundle of panels, facing his Eminence's approach. All this was fine, except she may as well have been invisible. The cardinal began speaking not to the woman he was facing, but crosswise to Lance, standing to her side. *"Buon giorno ..."* "Good afternoon ..." "Welcome ..." All the pleasantries ricocheted about like an absurd Marx Brothers routine—an amusing (at least at this remove) bit of sexism. Gert waited equably through it all until, finally, Lance said, with some exasperation, "I don't know what you're doing. You're looking at me, and she's the one you have to talk to."

Then Gert came right out with it: "Are you here to bless the Quilt?" *"Sì,"* said the cardinal and clasped his hands. "No," said Gert, "we can't allow that." And in a very even voice, Gert let him have it: "As you know, the Catholic Church has not been sympathetic to homosexuals or very compassionate toward gay men with AIDS. If you'd like to see the Quilt, we'd be very happy to have you view it, but you can't do any kind of ceremony."

To everyone's relief, the cardinal made a slight bow and smiled. *"Bene,"* he murmured, and the tension broke. And then Gert knelt down and began unfolding the bundle, corner by corner, and then the cardinal too swept his skirts aside and carefully joined in until at last it was laid flat. "Much love," said the cardinal, in English, as he ran his fingers along the stitching. As he was about to leave, Gert handed him one of our souvenir buttons and said, "I'll give you a button ... but you can afford to buy one of the books." *"Bene, grazie . . ."* A flick of his ring-laden hand and the Vatican made its contribution.

Good old Gert. When Mike got all over her about respect and how important it was to treat everyone diplomatically, especially the "vice-pope," she retorted, "Oh, come on, cardinal what's-his-name is just another man in a skirt!"

I later found out that Gert's mother had been one of the last Americans excommunicated from the Catholic Church because of divorce. She died very young, and shortly afterward, as little Gert was lighting a candle at the altar, she contributed a nickel instead of the quarter that was the cost for the large eternal flame. A nun came up and blew out the candle, sending Gert into a horrific state, sure her mother's spirit had been evaporated once and for all. Gert is a deep one; she'd kept it to herself.

The European displays were a huge success, raising over five hundred thousand dollars and making great strides in waking the world up to the fact that AIDS was not, as common wisdom held, an "American disease." Everyone was further united in plans for World AIDS Day that December 1, with displays and candlelight marches all over Europe. It was during this time of the tour and coordinating World AIDS Day that many of the international chapters were established. Today there's a Brazilian quilt, an Israeli quilt, a New Zealand quilt, a Thai quilt, a huge Canadian quilt. All in all, there are thirty-eight independent Quilt organizations throughout the world. Hardly a week goes by that we don't get a photo of an international display; one came in from Taipei just last week.

T HE MORNING OF our second D.C. display, October 11, 1988, came on cold and damp. The Washington Monument was shrouded in fog; the Capitol dome sat proud and unreflective under gray skies. Between the two, the Ellipse, our display field, stretched out in five sections. At a distance I could see the small figure of Mike Smith bent over his viewfinder, peering into the scope, waving his arms to the left, to the right, determined to make sure the Quilt laid out straight this year. Crews of volunteers clustered at the midpoints of each segment. One group was being led through the unfolding by Scott Lago: "Raise the Quilt up to your chin, turn clockwise, and make a square within a square—higher! That's not your chin! . . ." Another group was listening to Sally, from Boston, as she explained that the orange caps she and her friend wore marked them as crisis counselors: "If someone breaks down, just wave us over and we'll deal with it." As the rolls of canvas were unfurled to form the grid, a camera crew interviewed a panel maker from Boston: "We couldn't afford a workshop, so we used my apartment, all thirty of us. It will be a mess when I get back, but a beautiful mess."

Just down the way there was a man dressed in the white of the un-folders, carrying a clipboard, methodically recruiting among the sparse early-morning visitors for volunteers to sign up as monitors. We had one hundred, and needed one hundred more. A man in a green sweater turned away weeping: "I can't do this, I just can't." Over in the RV, Gert and Evelyn were frantically sewing "just a few more panels." Very often we receive unfinished panels in bits and pieces—fragments of a favorite shirt, or just drawings of a sailboat. Sometimes the panel maker just couldn't finish. They'd send what they'd done, and Gert and her staff would sew the panel together as best they could. There was al-ways a last-minute push, propelled by the desire not to disappoint the stressed mourner, the dead, ourselves.

Outside the periphery, under the trees, there were little knots of people watching and waiting, and you could see more coming. It was an amazing juxtaposition of tall and short folk, of all different colors: an older couple walking slowly; a handsome young man in a T-shirt; a father with his son on his shoulders, pointing out on to the field, ex-plaining, no doubt, what was going on.

Tension was high all round, and highest as always between Mike and me. There'd been a tangle with the National Park Service, which had jurisdiction over the Ellipse and which had decided we couldn't sell our souvenir buttons on federal property. Donations might be acceptable, but the Park Service would have to check with someone higher up. We were always a thorn in their side; we were, after all, covering their well-manicured grass.

There was so much to do, but as time passed the skies lightened. We ended up, as usual, with more than enough volunteers. We all had our lists to complete, the rhythm of work took over, and the activity got us through. *Just keep on working, don't stop and think, just set the stakes, line up the canvas, correlate the panel squares, and fit this puzzle together.* And slowly the grid took shape and the bundles were placed in position, the air warmed, and it seemed as if, yes, we'd pull it off.

At 9 A.M. I began reading the names, ending with Marvin's. It's always difficult, and I was thankful that I didn't have to mention Jack, not yet at least. He'd collapsed in London during the tour and been refused help by two ambulances; when Gert had finally found him he'd been delirious, repeating, as if in a trance, "I knew you'd come, I knew you'd come." After nursing him for two months, she'd got him back to San Francisco, where he was holding on—for how much longer, we didn't know.

Mike read after me, and then came a group of families. Their voices strong or cracking, eyes dry or streaming with tears, they stepped to the microphone and read, sometimes shouting their child's name as if to hold on to this public moment as a chance to call up one last memory. *For my beloved child, my precious son . . . For my beautiful beloved son . . . We love you very much . . .* Some flung out the syllables as if in challenge to an unfair world; others spoke quietly, as if holding on to a private communication. Grief was of all degrees and tempers, and it was cathartic. Each reader's emotion, however colored, stated quite simply: this person was here.

THOUSANDS READ THE names that day for many aching hours. No one was hurried; everyone waited patiently, knowing that they too would have their turn. The slow rhythm of twelve thousand names amplified what for many of us was the strongest impression of the 1988 display: it had grown tremendously, quadrupling in number of panels from the first (1,920) to the second display (8,288). A kaleidoscopic range of emotions on a now epic scale.

Just as we never cut a speaker off, we've never edited quilts or had rules about their design. The panels contain every sort of attachment, from teddy bears to a small bag of the deceased's ashes. And very often the panel maker includes a written note on the cloth itself. You would read about a man who loved flowers and had wanted to open a flower shop, about the most mundane facts of another's life, beginning with the name of his grade school. Another would be a simple encomium: "He loved dancing"; "He had a great smile." There was unashamed sentimentality and there were quick glimpses that captured a personality in flashing epitaphs: "Is this art? No! It's Fred Abrams!"; "Stardate 1–9–97: Beam me up, Scotty."

To my mind, each expression was art, real and true. And one of the most beautiful things was joy. I remember seeing a woman dancing around a panel, pirouetting in the sun, creating a stream of ephemeral arabesques for her friend and partner in the corps de ballet. Dancers say they are most themselves when dancing, and her dance was certainly a fitting tribute.

This living, spontaneous element was nowhere recorded more powerfully than in what we call the *signature square*. If you can be proud of an accident, I am always proud of how that particular bit of Quilt ritual came about. I'd been reading about quilting and found that it was traditional among the old-time quilters to add what is called a *friendship square*. This is a sash or small square piece of the cloth where the sewers leave their names. Everyone liked the idea, and so we'd added an empty stretch of white canvas, which we'd signed with our own names and the date. It was a small thing, very much a private gesture. Gert had started something similar with the miniature panels she'd often send to panel makers, small replicas of the full panels. We didn't really think much of it until we saw that the signature square too was being read and, to our surprise, noticed that others were adding names and notes. Our always lurking fears of the Quilt's fragility kicked over into panic and we raced out to cover the signature sections—and then we read what had been written and realized we'd fallen once again into serendipity. In a twist on the old friendship squares, the people, adding their own touch, had written messages and reflections on how they felt: "Good-bye, Uncle Tom. I love you—Kim"; "May this Quilt extinguish the shadow of ignorance and fear that paralyzes so many. The Quilt lights a lamp of hope. May it shine until the deaths are no more—R.H."; "I pray that my children never see and cry over this Quilt. May there be a solution soon.—Jodie"; "Why is it only that in death we can see the value of life. I feel as if I knew you all.—A.M.P."; "I thought I would learn to better accept death but instead, found a passion for life. Do not let dreams die.—Mindy."

Leaving their own memorial filled a void for people who'd not had time to make a quilt or hadn't known of the Quilt. From the '88 display on we've always included a signature square. You'll know it by the intensity surrounding it; it's often the emotional vortex of the display.

Alongside the positive emotion in the signature square and on the panels, there was also anguish: "I have decorated this banner to honor my brother. Our parents did not want his name used publicly. The omission of his name represents the fear of oppression that AIDS victims and their families feel." And there was anger: "I hate the quilt." Sometimes deep-seated anger, as in the panel to the infamously homophobic lawyer and closeted homosexual Roy Cohn, which reads: "Bully. Coward. Victim." These were rarer but wholly legitimate, appropriate even.

And this has been the greatest conflict between me and some of my more vociferous colleagues in the gay rights movement. They want the Quilt to be angrier. Over the years they've attacked our buttons, our brochures, and the panels themselves as "AIDS kitsch." The Quilt is soft, malleable, they say, forgetting that canvas flags have historically stood for permanence and immutable power.

It stunned me then and stuns me now. I just don't get it. I've always felt that anger is a bad thing only when it is bottled up and festers into bitter cynicism and violence. Anger is released at the Quilt, it is expressed in the Quilt. Anger can be a great motivator if it's communicated in a creative way such as in the Quilt; it helps move us on with life and brings us together. The Quilt proves that on a grand scale. Here we were, in the nation's capital, proudly exhibiting thousands of irrefutable declarations of the love that dared not speak its name. And America, all of it, from every corner, was not only listening, but breaking through encrusted prejudice and joining in.

"Yes," Scott Lago said cynically, "the Quilt is very successful—a pyramid built on bones."

I was concerned with "real," not theoretical, issues. The Quilt is real. You can feel it, see people's responses. The critics denied its effectiveness by misapprehending its purpose: yes, silence does equal death, but the Quilt very eloquently says, to everyone who sees it, that we are to love each other, to care for each other, that these were real people whose lives were valued and whose memories are cherished.

At their shrillest point the detractors would transform the Quilt into a metaphor of victimization, decrying it as an outgrowth of America's fascination with the self-help movement that masked the horror of AIDS with sentimental imagery. That's confused, to say the least. AIDS is not a concept, not some sociological symptom to toy with in an intellectual game of words. AIDS was killing my friends. Call me pragmatic or idealistic, I knew that whenever my anger got me, I felt it was burning T-cells. The attacks were needlessly combative and cynical to the point of closing the nation's heart to our message. Unlike the attackers, I had faith that the American people would come together once they'd witnessed the tragedy and solve it.

I've always said I wanted my grandmother to have a place in our movement, and have kept saying it despite the fusillade of mockery that such sentiments have incited. By luck and by design, we picked every aspect of the Quilt to make it an open, nationally unifying tool, a sort of noncombat zone where all of us could focus to create a central site of healing within the epidemic, a place of dignity for a people who'd been shunned in life and erased in death. Later, as our initial hopes that we'd ignite a cure failed, we broadened the message to emphasize education as a means of dealing with the ongoing epidemic. The message we promoted was that of memory, both individual and in the collective national conscience. We tried to do things that would break down barriers to this memory. One of the most virulent perceptions we worked to change was the idea that AIDS was a gay disease. Not only was that factually wrong, but its motivating prejudice naturally enabled people to turn away from something ugly. The Quilt changed that, and I make no apologies for our efforts.

Yes, the criticism hurt. And ironically, it came most harshly from people I considered brothers and sisters in our struggle for civil rights. I remember being confronted at the 1988 display by a desperate-looking kid. He couldn't have been over twenty-one. He had an ACT-UP T-shirt on, black jeans, and Doc Marten shoes. He could have been me a decade ago. Full of fire, he began talking of how proud he was that his was the first generation that had stood up to fight. "And all you do is lay out a blanket!" he chided. It was a shocking thing to hear. I understood his frustration; the Quilt is relentlessly understated. And I also knew that he, like so many others, was blinded by his own pain and deaf to history. He didn't know of the Stonewall and White Night riots, of the postwar rise of gay organizations like the Sisters of Bilitis and the Mattachine Society, let alone of the century-old struggles in Europe and the pink triangles. "There you are on his front lawn, and every one of those presidential windows has the shades drawn," he added. Should I have opened my shirt and let him see the knife scar from when I was stabbed?

A veteran activist at thirty-two, I had to balance my own anti-authority, shout-it-in-the-streets history with the burden of memories of the last decade. It was no secret that I thought the government's lack of leadership was an atrocity. I did and do believe the Quilt is very much an accusation, bringing evidence of the disaster to the doorstep of the people responsible for it. We have never depoliticized it to that extent. We want the government to act. The political message is that human life is sacred. I told my young friend, as I've told many others, "Yes, silence equals death, but there can also be power in silence."

That evening, October 8, 1988, the night of the candlelight march, drew an unexpectedly large crowd of over fifty thousand. It was an awesome sight, thousands and thousands of flickering candles burning in the night and reflected a thousand times over in the pool. I stood with the Lincoln Memorial at my back and spoke simply:

"We stand here tonight in the shadow of monuments, great structures of stone and metal created by the American people to honor our nation's dead and to proclaim the principles of our democracy. Here we remember the soldiers of wars won and lost. Here we trace with our fingers the promises of justice and liberty etched deep by our ancestors in marble and bronze.

"Today we have borne in our arms and on our shoulders a new monument to our nation's capital. It is not made of stone or metal and was not raised by engineers. Our monument is sewn of soft fabric and thread and was created in homes across America wherever friends and families gathered together to remember their loved ones lost to AIDS.

"We bring a quilt. We bring it here today with shocked sorrow at its vastness and the speed by which its acreage redoubles. We bring it to this place, at this time, accompanied by our deepest hope: that the leaders of our nation will see the evidence of our labor and our love and that they will be moved.

"We bring a quilt. We've carried this quilt to every part of our country, and we have seen that the American people know how to defeat AIDS. We have seen that the answers exist and that tens of thousands of Americans have already stepped forward to accept their share and more of this painful struggle. We have see the compassion and skill with which the American people fight AIDS and care for people with AIDS. We have witnessed the loving dedication of volunteers, families, and friends and the extraordinary bravery of people with AIDS, themselves working beyond exhaustion. And everywhere in this land of ours we have seen death.

"In the past fifteen months over twenty thousand Americans have been killed by AIDS. Fifteen months from now our new president will deliver his first state of the union address. And on that day, America will have lost more sons and daughters to AIDS than we lost fighting in Southeast Asia—those whose names we can read today from a polished black stone wall.

"We bring a quilt. It grows day by day and night by night and yet its expanse does not begin to cover our grief, nor does its weight outweigh the heaviness within our hearts.

"For we carry with us tonight a burdensome truth that must be simply spoken: History will record that in the last quarter of the twentieth century a new and deadly virus emerged and that the one nation on earth with the resources, knowledge, and institutions to respond to the new epidemic failed to do so. History will further record that our nation's failure was the result of ignorance, prejudice, greed, and fear. Not in the heartlands of America, but in the Oval Office and the halls of Congress.

"The American people are ready and able to defeat AIDS. We know how it can be done and the people who will do it. It will take a lot of money, hard work, and national leadership. It will require us to understand there is no conflict between the scientific response and the compassionate response. No conflict between love and logic. Some will question us, asking how could that be. We will answer, How could it not?

"We bring a quilt. We hope it will help people remember. We hope it will teach our leaders to act."

CHAPTER FOURTEEN

LOVE AND CAREER

THINGS GET MIXED up when you're an activist. You get a hair-trigger debater's edge and rhinoceros skin to shrug off the attacks and fight on. And yet there's something inside that survives all the armoring, and when you least expect it, you fall in love. I could say it was Ricardo's eyes, how he'd tease me for being too serious, or how he liked that I was growing gray too early. Certainly his innocence charmed me and reminded me of what we'd fought for in the first place. But he was not innocent. Whatever we had, it was magic, shot through with the times we lived and therefore star-crossed from the first, but magic nonetheless.

I met Ricardo at a time and place where I should have been in full-throttle activist mode. I'd flown to Austin, Texas, to speak at a rights rally, one of similar rallies held across the country in state capitals following the March on Washington and the first display. Suffering from jet lag and a cold that flying had aggravated, I felt before the crowd the excitement that speaking before crowds always elicits in me, and the heat of Texas summer seemed to combine with the intensity of the march and revive me. It was going to be a physically hard, emotionally charged event—a combination I loved. And as I was looking out over the crowd, my heart racing with excitement, my speech coming together in my mind, I locked eyes with this incredibly beautiful man. Jet black hair and big, deep brown eyes looking directly into mine. Yes, there was no mistaking he was smiling at me. Time stopped. The march began and he was lost in the surging crowd. I turned to Mike Smith and said, "I'm going to marry him." Mike, always sanguine, said, "Yeah, well, you might want to get a shower and shave first."

After the march and the first speeches, everyone formed lines for the few available drinking fountains. There was a sense of anticlimax; all we wanted now in the sweltering sun was a simple drink of water. As I stood there, I noticed some jostling and turned around. There he was, standing in line just behind me. We smiled and I said, "What's your name?" "Ricardo," he said. "And you?" When I told him my name he just nodded. "I came from San Francisco with the Quilt." "What's that?" he said. At the time I thought he was being sly, making romantic banter. But there was no twinkle in this eye, just the warmth I would come to know so well, followed by a frown as he was bumped once again by the crowd. "There's too many people," he said. Then he took my hand and led me from the line and the crowds out beyond the park's edge. And we talked of nothing in particular. I can remember only the sheen of sweat on his forehead and being dazzled when he rolled his T-shirt up his torso.

Reality threatened to break the spell when an insistent voice crackled over the loudspeaker: "Will Cleve Jones please report to the speakers' platform?" Had he heard? Yes, he had, and it didn't mean anything. He was looking at me with the same trusting eyes. "Let's go," I said and took him up to my hotel room.

Afterward, while he was showering, it all crashed down on me. We'd been safe, but I'd always told anyone I was with that I was positive. And yet now I'd met someone unique, special, who seemed to be as excited as I was, and I'd kept quiet. What a fool and a hypocrite, I told myself. You tell total strangers you're HIV-positive. You announce it in classrooms and on stages to thousands of people, and you don't have the balls to tell one man. But I just couldn't look into those eyes and say, "I have a disease that will kill me." Postcrime, the best I could manage was a retreat. I decided to get his address, say a quick good-bye, and then write him a letter of apology explaining that it was such a romantic experience that I just could not bring death into it. I was sick about the whole thing.

Then the bathroom door opened and he came out wearing only a towel, tears pouring from his face. He was so heartbreakingly beautiful. "You're going to hate me," he said. "No, that's impossible, Ricardo." And then quietly, almost whispering, he said, "I am positive." We'd both been caught between the plague and love in a strange suspension of hope and fear. And I held him in my arms then, unforgettably—as I hold him in my heart now and forever.

Ricardo Eugenio Cantu came to live with me in San Francisco in a beautiful Victorian building at 32 Hancock Street, off Dolores. A one-bedroom apartment, with French doors dividing bedroom from living room, each with wide bay windows giving onto a beautiful esplanade famous for its palm trees and covey of wild green parrots.

I'd never had such a life, the comfort and routine of always knowing he'd be there when I came home, when I woke up. We were happy.

One day I came home early, and as I walked up the steps I could hear one of his favorite Mexican soap operas on the Spanish TV station floating out the windows. I opened the door and saw his suit and tie (he had quickly found work at a stockbroking firm) arranged neatly on the living-room chair as they had been early that morning. I looked over and there he was asleep in his Jockey shorts on the sofa, clutching an egg to his stomach. He kissed me hello and said he hadn't felt good all day and so stayed home from work. "What about the egg?" I asked. And then, with no sense that an egg on a stomach was unusual, he told me that his grandmother prescribed it for any sort of pain in the body.

"It draws the poison away," he explained. "Are you feeling better?" I asked him. Yes, he was, and we had dinner, watched a movie, and went to bed.

A very odd mix of old-world superstition and sophisticated tastes, he had a genius for what I can only call balance. In a time of plague so much like that of the Middle Ages, he seamlessly created a home life reflecting his Mexican-American heritage while living a completely modern San Francisco life. Once, on the bookshelf, I found a plastic bag that I suspected contained some kind of drugs, only to be told, in rather hurt tones, that it was dirt from a cemetery that a witch had given to him to ward off evil. Ricardo had all sorts of trinkets and totems to protect himself and our home and bring good luck. To this day I have a witch's cross of his, decorated with silver icons of cats and birds.

I appreciated this; in fact, it drew me to him. Yet home for me was a place where you recharged and gathered energy to go out and do whatever you were meant to be doing. I made feeble attempts to explain this—indeed, to write of it—but it was all much simpler to Ricardo: the difference between us was that I had *"el otre amante,"* another lover.

It was true. Outside the small charmed oasis of our romance, the Quilt occupied my every thought, and even in those early days of our life together, even when I was physically present, my mind was always sneaking off, thinking of the next speech, of how we could help a newly formed chapter sustain that first burst of enthusiasm, of the million and one details that made up the anchoring passion in my life.

FOLLOWING THE '88 display, the pace accelerated into the following year. In February 1989 the Quilt was nominated for a Nobel Prize by Congresswoman Nancy Pelosi after prompting by my friend Jok Church. In March, *Common Threads* was nominated for an Academy Award and we began the second North American tour. Stella set out again, and the road crew racked up I don't know how many miles to nineteen cities across the Northeast, for the first time crossing the border into Canada. And there were other projects demanding attention, such as *A Promise to Remember,* a book published by Avon Press of our collection of letters to the NAMES Project, and David Lemos's play *We Bring a Quilt.*

Each of these events spawned radio and print interviews and magazine profiles, and those in turn galvanized an increasing number of new chapters. My schedule for 1989 lists visits to sixty-three cities. On a single day in Boston I had three interviews, starting with a drive-time show in the early morning. The producer was Rocky Buono. Just after the session, he came out to the lobby to say good-bye. There were a rather prim-looking receptionist and sleepy security guard on duty. Rocky startled them both, and me, by giving me a hug and a kiss on the lips. He pulled away, still holding me by the arms. Tears were in his eyes. "My lover is dying," he said, "and my brother passed away two months ago."

I stumbled out into the cold and went on to an appointment with a reporter from the *Boston Globe.* I remember that encounter very well. My time was tight and I had been hoping to put the interview off until my next trip, if not just do a "phoner" (a telephone interview). I had called him back and asked, "Can we squeeze it in the next day?" Deaf to the fatigue in my voice, he barked out, "No, kid, we got deadlines." Oh, I was a "kid." OK. Then he asked for my schedule. Well, yes I had an hour or so after the 6 A.M. radio show . . . Surely he'd take the hint. Surely not. "Fine," he said gruffly and gave me an address not far from my hotel. This was going to be a rough one, I thought.

When I got to the coffee shop he was already there; actually, he looked liked he'd been there since the place opened in the 1920s. He was an older guy, a Ben Hecht, *Front Page* kind of newspaperman with a grizzled beard and an old tweed hat and beat-up trench coat. I was prepared for a skeptical, even aggressive encounter, and it seemed I'd been right. As I started talking about the Quilt, he just sat there like a stone. He'd look out the window, rub the steam off in a slow circle, then look down into his coffee, never sipping it. It was almost as if he were intentionally pissing me off. I thought, This guy isn't even taking notes. He'll rewrite the story when he gets back to the office, then go off for a beer with his cronies and talk about this stupid fairy blanket. I was about to confront him when he looked up from his coffee. A single tear dropped to the eggs on his plate. "My little brother," he said. "We just buried him."

And so there we were, this gruff Bostonian and I, struggling with something the quiet men of his generation rarely spoke of. He looked exhausted. "What do you want me to write?" he asked. I told him, "Just tell the truth, that's all. About your brother." Something in his eyes told me that that scared him—the tight grip on his coffee mug, how he averted his gaze out the window. Was he worried about what his friends or his church would say about his queer brother? I don't know. He was thinking very hard. Suddenly, he stood up, adjusted his hat, and walked out.

An hour later I was at another radio station taping an interview. In the middle of it, the producer, Betsey Boulard, switched off the recording machine and put her head down on the console and began to weep. She looked up a minute later and said, "I'm sorry. I can't live in the closet anymore. I'm a lesbian. I've got to come out."

This was how my days went. And in the funny world that I lived in, that all of us lived in, pain was the bridge that we met on, and that was progress.

I N   J U L Y   O F   that summer, on invitation from Jonathan Mann, I went to Montreal for the International Conference on AIDS. I was enormously proud that Mann had chosen the Quilt as a symbol of international cooperation, and extremely nervous. I was to give a speech, in French. No matter how often I speak, no matter to what group of people, my stomach gets tight and my hands tend to shake so much that turning the pages of a written speech is unthinkable. Usually I wing it, except of course if I'm speaking at the Lincoln Memorial: I couldn't bear not to be up to the mark of that monument and the many great speakers who've spoken there, so in that case I write it out and memorize every word.

Jonathan, in his signature bow tie, was his usual confident, buoyant self, and teased me for being nervous: "But you talk all the time!" Still, the words wouldn't come. As I turned on the television in my hotel room I saw that indelible shot of a lone student in front of a tank in Tienanmen Square. If I'd tried I could not have imagined a more powerful booster shot of courage. If that defenseless man could stand there, staring down a tank gun barrel, I could certainly face my speech, mangled verbs or not. China teetered on the edge of revolution, men and women were being shot and sent to prison, and I was nervous about a five-minute presentation? The humbling comparison sent my head spinning and calmed me down.

The conference was a huge event with hundreds of participants from the varied and often competing camps of the AIDS world. Though the gathering was ostensibly the equivalent of a state of the union address, a yearly report on the condition of the epidemic worldwide, the presentation of quilts from participating countries was one of the few notes of unity. The facade of a united world front had been fractured from the first. Instead of being hosted by a U.S. city, it was held in Montreal because of U.S. Customs laws outlawing the entrance of HIV-positive travelers. This schizoid situation, which would have excluded some of the best reporters and researchers, mocked the scientific facts of transmission and was mirrored in the fractious nature of the audience. On one side were hundreds of scientists and researchers presenting papers on the progress of HIV drug trials. On the opposite side were the activists, the raw street fighters whose patience with the slow pace of research had run out. Where the activists wanted, demanded, immediate access to potentially life-saving treatments, most of the scientists urged caution. A volatile combination, when so much was at stake.

For me, the best example of the conference's disjunct character was Randy Shilts's speech. His book *And the Band Played On* had just been published to great acclaim, and he was the most respected AIDS journalist of the time. Neither activist nor scientist, Randy bridged both camps with a vast depth of medical knowledge as well as an activist's sense of urgency. As the anxious audience waited to hear from this respected dean of AIDS, a hush fell over the auditorium. Instead of the usually respectful introductory words of welcome, he began with a joke: "In my travels around, people always ask me, 'Can you get AIDS from a mosquito?' And I tell them, 'Unless you have unprotected anal intercourse with a mosquito, you cannot get it.'" People started booing. It was black humor, inappropriate and desperately cynical, but the perfect note for a deeply divided conference. Someone in the back yelled out, "You're such an asshole, Randy."

It made for a difficult lead-in to my presentation. Yet, just as people are respectful of the Quilt in most presentations, they assumed a tense silence as I began. The display of international panels went much the same as always. I stood there, in the Olympic velodrome, as each country's representatives walked down from the stands with a bundle of panels. Then, with great dignity, each read the names of their homeland in French, then in English, then in the language of their country: *Allemagne,* Germany, *Deustchland* . . . It was incredibly moving to hear the roll call of so many of world's nations, so simple, and in so many accents calling up a picture of a varied yet united world. I gripped the lectern and began: "*Mesdames et messieurs, c'est avec honneur et gratitude que je vous presente ce soir un souvenir. Ce souvenir c'est une courtepointe inscrite avec le nom de mon meilleur ami Marvin Feldman, qui mourait en octobre soixante-huits.*" The word for "quilt," *courtepointe,* was very difficult to pronounce, and I stumbled over it, but overall I got through fine.

I saw Randy soon after the conference, at midnight. Many of the delegates had joined a protest march organized by Montreal's large Chinese population in support of the students in Tienanmen Square. He came over to my side and said, "Nice job, Cleve." And then, with a wink, he added, "Of course, I was setting you up." Though that particular blend of sarcasm was characteristic of Randy, it was symptomatic of many of us. Eight years into the epidemic, we were all showing signs of battle fatigue in the forcing chamber of AIDS. I hugged him and we marched on.

A T HOME IN San Francisco, Mike Smith and I were heading into a confrontation of our own. By this time our organization had developed into a pretty respectable foundation, with the orderliness and some of the efficiency that term implies. There was a head of finance, a display department, a volunteer coordinator, an office manager, a development director. As managing director, Mike was in his element, dealing with all sorts of managerial questions, from balancing the budget to sorting out job descriptions, as well as the rigorous demands of protecting our nonprofit status.

I had no patience or aptitude for the numbers side of things; that was his forte. But as executive director I felt responsibility for the entire organization, and we were always at loggerheads over the philosophical aspects of day-to-day business.

We'd always had conflicting styles, but after the L.A. display fiasco I'd begun to sense an ever stronger current of resentment. I was older, a veteran activist. Mike was a younger man chafing under my shadow. His confidence had built up as we'd made the transition from a loose-knit all-volunteer group to an organization with membership and process, and he now wanted to step up into more of a spokesman's role. We were long past the point where we could have talked it out. Whatever pointers I offered he took as patronizing.

Things had come to a cold war—glacial, actually—between us. Still, I didn't feel I had the right to fire him: Mike was the first person to dedicate his life to the project; he stayed home while I was out on the road and kept the books and figured out how we were going to pay for plane fares, for rent, for Stella. But it was clear we couldn't both run the ship.

All this came to a head in the middle of preparations for the next display. I'd scheduled some rest time for myself up at the Russian River before we went into the final push for the third display in D.C. that October. Things had got pretty hot between us the previous day when he'd made a hash of a few interviews. I felt he came across as insincere and was blurring the message, and I told him so, probably too harshly.

The expected phone call came soon after I'd unpacked my bags. "It's you or me," Mike said, then, "I'm going to resign." Much to his surprise, I said, "I accept your resignation." After a long pause, he said there'd be an uproar from the staff. I said, "Maybe," and went out for a long walk.

Mike was a whiz at paperwork, but I knew our staff and remember thinking he'd overplayed his hand. My days with Art Agnos in the California Assembly had taught me that sometimes a little absence will expose the opposition, so instead of rushing back down for a confrontation, I let things ride a little while.

After a few days I came back to the office and called the staff together for a pep talk. They were all there, Gert and Lance, Evelyn and the rest of the original crew. I started in showing more confidence than I felt. "Mike has dropped a bomb and he thinks we'll crack and we'll have to call him in," I began. "I know we don't need to do that. You guys can handle it. I'm going to step back as much as possible. I'll do the interviews and the media stuff on the road, the things I'm good at, and you do what you're good at." It worked. There was no opposition; everyone was relieved the dispute was over and was ready to get to work.

Today the tension between Mike and me is gone. We've talked about the future of the Quilt and agree on most issues, particularly on building a permanent home for the Quilt.

Ironically, Mike's departure really cemented our team at the NAMES Project. Rebeccah Lapere rallied the troops, and without Mike around pushing to follow up on the details, every department had to really tighten up; we all began to take our jobs more seriously.

Some of this was about setting policy on the ownership of the Quilt panels. Whenever someone threatened us with trouble about displaying a panel, we'd refer it to the front office, which was Mike. But now it fell on Gert, as head of Quilt production, to handle what in one case developed into a situation where our emotions were torn between principles.

Our guiding principle, then and today, is that the panels are inviolable. No matter the emotion or the demands, only the person listed in our archives as the panel maker is allowed to alter the panel in any way. We do this to protect the person memorialized and the panel maker's freedom to express his or her love. Very often, people will send us a bit of something representative to add to a panel: shamrocks, a photograph, things that recall their friend's life and personality. We will sew it on in the workshop, or if they show up at a display and want to add things, we'll cross-check their names and stand with them as they sew something on so other people don't think they have the same license. Once, at the request of the panel maker, an entire covering sheet was stitched onto a panel because a family was opposed to its display and the man's lover respected their wishes. Then, years later, the family relented and we were asked to remove the overlaying sheet.

We take this trust very seriously and come to feel a deep emotional bond with the panels and those in them. Rarely, very rarely, we make an exception. Actually, there's been only one that I know of. One night a woman called saying she wanted to come by the workshop and take back the panel she'd made for her son. Gert explained that we didn't do this and why, but the woman was crying desperately. Normally, Gert would have refused outright, but then the woman said, "I want to set my son free." If she'd said anything else Gert would not have let her have it. Soon after, her husband showed up. Gert told him that we have a rule that a panel maker can do anything he wants, so he could cut it out, but he'd have to leave a margin of it around the edge; that way, we'd be loyal, at least technically, to our rules. There was no perfect solution, only a human one.

Poor Gert. The father couldn't cut into his son's panel. Quietly, in a choked voice, he asked Gert to do it. Her hands shook as she cut out the panel. Very carefully she folded the material and handed it over, asking the father to send his wife a message: "Tell her I understand she's tormented and she thinks that this will release him, but that later on, when AIDS is over, I think she's going to be really upset that her son was not able to join in the fight." He took the panel and we never heard from them again.

A few weeks after we returned the panel to the grieving mother, it had been repaired. Gert had traced the design before giving it back, and with some of the material used in the walkways from the first display in 1987 (which is considered very precious), she re-created the large blue dolphin that had originally been there and added a little bird flying off the side as if to freedom. Exceptional as this situation was, it demonstrates how we are sometimes caught in a deeply emotional tug-of-war between the lost and the living.

We look at the Quilt as if it's made of soldiers helping to stop the epidemic. Gert especially so, to an almost religious point. Though she's as skeptical as they come, I've heard her say that if she wrapped herself in a panel, she could walk across the street in traffic and be safe.

If Mike's departure was rough, and it was, the next hammer blow was coming fast. A few weeks later, we got official notification from the National Park Service in Washington, D.C., that all our months of planning the next display had been for nothing. In their typically stiff language, they informed us that due to a superseding event the NAMES Project's application to reserve space on the Ellipse had been refused. Our old nemesis Sandra Alley, regional head of the Park Service, who'd given us so much trouble at the first and second displays over selling our buttons and brochures, had struck again.

To make matters worse, the Park Service had replaced the Quilt with a ringer: the "superseding event" was a celebration of one thousand years of Christianity by the Ukrainian Millennium Association. I was sure they were a very distinguished organization, but I wasn't about to back down.

Hundreds of hours, thousands of quilts—the survival of our organization was at stake. It was time for another staff meeting. The rumor had already spread, and everyone dragged themselves into the meeting and sat slumped in chairs or leaned against the walls as if they'd been beat, especially our media director, Danny Sauro, who was near tears. This would require a plan, which I had, as well as a bit of theater. And I got this big grin on my face and said, "I don't want anyone to get down about this. This is where it starts to get fun!" And then I told them that this was going to be an all-out campaign. Everyone was going to stop what they were doing and pull every string, call in every chit, and change this decision. I went around the room and gave everyone an assignment. We're going to get every member of Congress involved, I said. You call every chapter we've got and tell them to call their member of Congress, you guys divide up the Senate, you guys work on the House. Call every single person who's ever done anything for this Quilt and tell them the Park Service has denied us permission.

Within forty-eight hours, the tide began to turn. It worked so well that we got a complaint call from California Congressman Tom Lantos asking why his office had been "targeted." We hadn't targeted him; we'd just got on the phone with everyone we ever knew and asked for help. Senator Ted Kennedy's office said it had never received so many calls on a single issue. And, rather satisfyingly, we bombarded the Park Service so heavily that their switchboard was shut down.

In the end, we did get our reservation, thanks especially to the very well connected members of the D.C. Quilt chapter as well as the efforts of Congresswoman Nancy Pelosi, our constant champion then and to this day. But displaying the Quilt on the hallowed grounds of the nation's capital was really only half a loaf. Our goal was that the head of our nation would publicly acknowledge our battle as his and stand with us.

Since taking office the previous January, President Bush had received numerous informational mailings from us. I wrote him a formal invitation in the name of the NAMES Project, and most everyone on staff as well as hundreds of others wrote personal appeals asking this "kinder, gentler" president to make a gesture to his people. Bush's personal physician, Dr. Burton Lee, who later joined with us in the reading of names, specifically told him of the Quilt. We pulled out every stop, including a letter hand-delivered to Mrs. Bush by a close friend of hers. In preparation for President and Mrs. Bush's tour of the Quilt, we also selected the panels of two men the Bushes had known in Houston, one Mrs. Bush's hairdresser and the other someone who had catered parties for Bush's oil company.

For a brief time, we had hopes that President Bush would indeed come. Sad to say, they didn't last long. The first week in September we received notice from the White House that the president would not be able to attend because of a scheduling conflict. Later press reports confirmed that he was indeed booked that day—for elective surgery. He'd made an appointment to remove a benign cyst, a callus, from the middle finger of his right hand. Yes, that finger. Was there a not too subtle message here? I don't know. George Bush didn't usually indulge in that sort of wit. Though I remain skeptical that there was any cyst at all, his overall message was quite clear: he didn't care.

The scene that morning, October 7, 1989, our third display, was grim. It was bitterly cold, and heavy rains the night before had left the Ellipse a soggy mess. When we walked out to set the stakes for the grid, our feet sunk into the mud. We scattered straw in the puddles and laid down an extra layer of tarp to make a usable surface. Even then, looking over at the White House, some of us entertained hopes that the president would change his mind. The night before at the National Cathedral in Washington, Barbara Bush had once again been invited to attend by one of her friends who was a NAMES Project volunteer.

Due to the rains, we started an hour late, at 11 A.M. I began the reading with Jack Caster's name; I was followed by Dionne Warwick, Harvey Fierstein, Congressman Gerry Studds, and others. Just before noon it began to rain again and we stopped and quickly began gathering up the Quilt. We had practiced the emergency rain fold many times over and had it down to a science. Within a couple of minutes the twenty-five hundred volunteers had the entire Quilt refolded and secure within waterproof bags dotted across the grass. A crowd of an estimated sixty thousand stood around the edges and waited, looking up at the skies, hoping the weather forecasts were wrong and the sun would come out.

Suddenly we heard a low rumbling, and as the engine beat quickened and the roar grew louder, we began to realize what it was. We stood transfixed, all eyes turned upward toward the sound, and for a brief moment Marine 1 came into view, a dull camouflage green helicopter. There was a deepening roar of the engines, the blasting of rotors as it cruised directly over us and down again behind the trees, and then it was gone, just a low ominous idling on the south lawn of the White House.

"The President of the United States will not be with us today, but he will be overhead. Reopen the Quilt," I announced. We unfolded the quilts in under two minutes, opening the entire thing, equivalent in size to nine football fields and weighing thirteen tons, just for him. All around us security was closing in. Fire trucks moved in close on the adjacent street. Through the trees men in uniform could be seen standing ramrod stiff; men in suits with listening devices in their ears took up positions at the far corner. I suddenly felt the reality of the rumors that the president's refusal to walk the Quilt had a component of fear. Fear of us.

We aimed the speakers at the White House, and the reading began again. The names echoed against the stone walls of the executive mansion. But these were not the customarily slow and solemn voices. Friends, lovers, mothers, and fathers shouted in ringingly harsh, accusatory tones: "For my darling daughter . . ." ". . . And for all the other names that will never be heard in the house behind me," added one man. "Hear us," said another.

As the metallic throbbing quickened and grew louder, so did the readings. Then the helicopter burst into view and flew directly overhead. As if on cue, the shouting increased. People began to literally scream the names of their dead. First one, then thousands of fingers pointed upward. *Shame, shame, shame,* the chanting began. And an army of scolding fingers followed the fleeing chopper until it diminished into a small spot in the gray skies. We began the reading again, and for hours thousands of names hung in the air—a message, a warning, a sign of undying hope.

The emotional crescendo of that display was tremendous, and it was focused very personally on George Bush. Even today I know many people who've never forgiven his monumental indifference. He was president of the entire country—our father, in a sense—and he had shamed his office by ignoring the largest symbol of national grief since the Vietnam Veterans Memorial. We felt he'd abdicated the role he'd been elected to fulfill and made a starkly political calculation. Supporting the Quilt would have been translated as an accommodation to gays and interpreted as a betrayal by the Pat Robertsons and Jerry Falwells and the others who'd repeatedly described AIDS as God's judgment. The president looked at the costs and benefits, and the Quilt had come up short. Visiting the Quilt would have been religious apostasy and political stupidity. He had nothing to lose. Without support from the insurgent religious right wing, Bush could not survive. In Bush's mind we were the opposition, not in any way part of his constituency. And he was, in fact, just following the policy of his predecessor, America's avuncular Ronald Reagan.

Two years before, in June 1987, I'd joined those marching to the White House to protest the Reagan administration's inadequate response to AIDS. It had taken Reagan six years to hold a press conference

on AIDS, but nowhere in his belated speech did he recognize the majority of those dying: he never used the word *gay*. The police had been
there, too—that time, in riot gear. As we chanted, "History will recall,
Reagan did the least of all," we locked arms and laid our bodies down
on the pavement, blocking the entrance drive to the White House. Sixty-
four of us had been arrested. The D.C. police had worn long rubber
gloves to protect themselves from infection—a needless gesture from a
medical point of view, but effective for right-wing propaganda.

However, even though we were casualties of ignorance on the
streets and of electoral math in the Oval Office, much of the country
was paying attention. The mechanisms of public discourse had become
involved. Religious leaders in the Jewish, Catholic, and Protestant faiths
had toured the Quilt firsthand and spoken to their congregations of its
healing power. Every major newspaper from Miami to Minneapolis to
Seattle had extensive coverage on the medical and social impact of AIDS.
You couldn't open the *New York Times* without reading of ACT-UP's
latest "alert."

What puzzled me most was that by 1989 the Quilt was reflecting
the growing number of deaths in the heterosexual community but the
media coverage was not. Surely, I thought, even if the deaths of homosexuals could be ignored, our national leaders would be shaken from
their torpor by the pathos evident in letters from families like their own.
A biochemist in AIDS-related viral research wrote: ". . . I have dedicated my quilt square to all the 'AIDS Babies' and made it from diapers
and receiving blankets that were my own infant son's. The bottle, bibs
and toys attached were all his. He is completely healthy—for which I
am both thankful and slightly guilt-ridden. So many babies are not."
Janice Berman's family wrote, in part: "She was the kind of mother
who would share with a three-year-old the pictures in a book of Rem-
brandts, the kind of mother who would stay up late typing a term paper
for a procrastinating teenager, the kind of mother, wife and adventur-
ous spirit who would set off for a cross-country trip in a camper—with

an eight-year-old, a four-year-old, and a two-year-old (on later trips we would take the cat) . . . We miss her every day.—Karen, Robert and Ellen." One of the letters we received was also sent to the White House: "Dear Mr. President, I am writing to you today to express my outrage, my disbelief, my anger, my sadness because of the complete silence from you concerning the beautiful NAMES Project Quilt . . . The Quilt has come to Washington, D.C., for three years in a row. For those three years, there has been silence from the White House. I keep asking, Why? Why?"

The next day, at 6:30 P.M., twenty thousand of us walked from the Ellipse and then marched to totally surround the White House with a sea of candle-carrying people. Then we proceeded to the steps of the Lincoln Memorial, where I spoke:

"The time has come, Mr. President, for you to see and understand and act. The time has come for you to see us. Ten months ago you shared with us your vision of a thousand points of light. Yet when we come to our nation's capital we bring with us a thousand points of light, times ten, times ten again, and still you cannot see us.

"We appeal to you to speak with us, to learn from the painful facts of the challenges before us. Speak with us, Mr. President. Speak to the American people. Tell us of your plans to defeat AIDS as you have shared with us your plans for other wars. Tell us that your war on drugs includes rehabilitation and prevention. Tell us a cure for AIDS will be found, Mr. President, and that it will be accessible to all regardless of ability to pay and will be found in time to save those who are already infected.

"Again, we stand here seeking that appointment, and we will return, Mr. President, on World AIDS Day, when many people in many lands on every continent will stand in global solidarity against the AIDS pandemic.

"We have moved past hatred, past despair, to stand here with hearts full of love and hope. We are not here to tear down or destroy. We are here to build, to fight for our future. We are the people who every day, every hour, in every city and town in America are leading the war against an epidemic. And it is our light that will lead the way to victory, and to life."

Will you stand with us, Mr. President? It was a question I vowed to repeat as long as I was allowed to live. The naïveté of the late '70s was gone now. Much of what I'd once hoped for would not come to pass as quickly as I once believed. But what remained was the dream of acceptance and equality, what we had fought for in San Francisco, what had brought us to Washington this day, and what was written in every Quilt.

Late that night I returned to my hotel exhausted. It had been a good effort. We'd made our case peacefully and forcefully. As I undressed and prepared for bed, I began going through the routine I'd followed since my diagnosis five years before: checking my legs, my back—every part of my body—for purple blemishes. It was habit by now, like locking the doors at night. Chore done, I felt safe. But as I brushed my teeth, I saw a bit of blood on the brush. There was something inside my mouth, a roughness. And then in the hotel mirror I saw it. *Leukoplakia* is the scientific name, a patch of bacteria that looks like white moss. So now it begins, I thought. The slow dissolve. I walked over to the phone, picked it up, and put it down. It was too late to call Ricardo. I'd see him soon enough.

- -

CHAPTER FIFTEEN

HEROES AND
ANTIHEROES

R ICARDO AND I never talked much about our being HIV-positive. He felt that mentioning it was tempting fate, and I acquiesced. Yes, it was a kind of denial—I recognized that—but it was our way of protecting a small share of peace in a time of plague. Certainly it was already the language of our lives: it modified how we made love, made us strict about doctors' appointments, and then every few months we'd walk that tightrope after a blood test, wondering through the night what the report would say. The marker that we followed, as did everyone, was T-cell counts. Normal is roughly six hundred to twelve hundred. I felt comparatively rich with a five hundred, Ricardo upward from there. Rich and watchful.

While I felt the need to rush forward and fight the disease through my work, Ricardo had what I can only describe as an Aztec fatalism about AIDS. For him, all our efforts, including my work with the Quilt, were valiant but in the end futile. As long as there were no physical signs of his own sickness, he kept balance. But my minor case of leukoplakia struck a dark chord and broke through that fragile calm he'd maintained; it was terrifying to him. And then, less than a week after the display and the onset of my symptoms, the Loma Prieta earthquake struck in California and the earth itself shuddered. Cloaked in smoke, the sun a faint brightness through the skies, San Francisco was wracked with the wailing of sirens. And through it all, Ricardo was caged, helpless and isolated in a swaying high-rise, riding out the tremors and watching helplessly as the city burned in an apocalyptic landscape. Those three hours changed him. His fatalism turned to despair as he saw in the wreckage a signal of the end, the warning of his own impending death.

The signs of our separation are much clearer in retrospect: the more frequent long-distance calls to his mother and grandmother and the accumulation of the magical totems around the house, over the kitchen door, above the bed. He began to see everything through a dark prism, and bit by bit anything having to do with AIDS became taboo.

I was not a real celebrity, but I'd lived in the Castro for twenty years, and when we went out for coffee or dinner, people would stop us to say hello and tell me that they supported my work. Sometimes they would become emotional, overwhelmed by memories they associated with me and the Quilt. Whereas before Ricardo had politely slipped away when strangers greeted us on the street, now, after nightmares of the earthquake, he shunned any reminder of disease. While those encounters nourished me, for Ricardo they were painfully jarring episodes in an endless string of darkening events. With a full work schedule of his own, he couldn't come with me when I went out of town, and he began to find excuses not to come with me to the workshop. By September, he was reluctant to be seen in public with me at all, to the point of refusing to walk with me down the block for groceries. Eventually, I learned not to talk about the Quilt with him, not to see friends and associates in his presence. I understood only vaguely what was behind his withdrawal and discounted his reaction as a response to trauma, seeing his shyness and mysticism as something I had as much ability to change as my own direction.

Time passed as we slowly, then wrenchingly, moved apart, he back toward his close-knit family in Texas, me ever deeper into the Quilt. One evening as I was packing for a trip to Detroit, Ricardo gave me an ultimatum: I had to choose; it was either him or the Quilt. I told him, "Ricardo, this is my life, it's the one thing I've ever felt I was good at and right in doing." I remember him standing there, tears in his eyes. "I will die with my family," he said. "Don't leave me, Ricardo," I implored. He couldn't leave me, but of course he did. I was not his family, not when life itself was ending. And then the door closed and I heard the sharp staccato of his steps running down the pavement and then silence. If we survived this thing, we would get back together—I was sure of that then, sure enough to repeat it over and over, whenever I thought of him. Aware that the virus was within me, working as I did among the panels of others just like me, I saw little else but to move forward, both for my own survival and to continue in the role that defined my life.

EVEN AS RICARDO flew to Houston, my flight took me to Detroit and a meeting with a heroine I'd admired from childhood. I had heard about Rosa Parks as I was growing up and later when I attended Quaker meetings. She was spoken of as someone who'd followed her inner light, and pointed to as an example of how one person, even though small and alone, can change things for the better. Her quietly heroic act of civil disobedience on the bus in Montgomery had dignity—and connections to a struggle against discrimination that I identified with my own. Also, she had been born in Tuskegee, Alabama, where black soldiers had been used by the U.S. government in an experimental program to track the effects of long-term syphilis—a cruel perversion of institutional racism that, I thought, mirrored the bigotry of my own time. I wanted to meet her very much.

I was in Detroit to receive an award from the national convention for P-FLAG (Parents and Friends of Lesbians and Gays) and also to talk with members of the Detroit Quilt chapter, who contacted Mrs. Parks and set up a meeting. She agreed to see me at her church, Saint Matthew's A.M.E., and invited me to Sunday service. I walked up the steps into the narthex and asked the usher to take me over to Mrs. Parks. He turned toward the front of the church, an older woman nodded back to him, and he escorted me up the aisle. That woman was Mrs. Parks. She gently touched the space beside her, saying, "Sit here beside me." She had a quiet brilliance about her, just as I'd hoped.

I was extremely nervous and thrilled. Here I was, sitting next to the mother of the civil rights movement. I knew the story by heart. On December 1, 1955, in Montgomery, Alabama, she had refused to surrender her bus seat to a white man and was arrested for violating the city's segregation laws. A mass boycott of the Montgomery bus system ensued, led by the young Dr. Martin Luther King Jr. The nation's civil rights movement began soon after. And all of it had been set in motion because one woman decided to act on what she believed in.

And this icon, beloved and revered, believed in the Quilt. She had made panels for friends in her neighborhood. Three generations had died. A grandmother had received HIV-tainted blood in a transfusion during hip surgery; her daughter had gotten the disease through intravenous drug use and passed it on to her newborn child.

I was starstruck those first few moments and remember only Mrs. Parks remarking that the pastor had the same last name as mine—a small gesture to put me at ease. As the pastor began speaking to the congregation of the service to come, he said, "And today we have a guest speaker, a cousin of mine, Mr. Cleve Jones." The congregation laughed, and I looked at Mrs. Parks and then paled as she pointed toward the lectern. I had nothing prepared. As I stumbled forward, she whispered, "You'll do fine."

I said earlier that I'm always nervous before giving a speech. But that word doesn't begin to describe what I felt as I stood before that congregation on that Sunday morning. I was white, I was gay; I had a disease that even then was being blamed on Africa. I talked of what I knew—of how I'd just come from a city hit with an earthquake and of how, though it was a terrible ordeal, it had brought the diverse and often conflicted people of that city together. Of how after the quake we went from house to house checking on gas lines, making sure that people were safe, taking them to the hospital when necessary. We came together in that crisis, I said, and we must come together in this AIDS crisis. We never really know how people will react when bad things happen, we just hope and pray that people will respond with love and compassion. In San Francisco people came together. If we didn't overcome our fear of different kinds of people, we'd never win.

It was a straightforward parallel, but it went over well. As the service let out, it was wonderful to see the respect and love everyone had for Rosa Parks and how she responded, especially to the children. They gathered around her and hugged her before running off down the street and back home.

After church we went by chance to a restaurant I remembered from my youth, where my grandfather and grandmother had taken me for lunch. An elegant old mansion, it was now owned by an interracial gay male couple. Mrs. Parks was warm and gracious. At the time, her primary focus was on African-American youth. Still a working pioneer, she was deeply concerned about the increasingly devastating impact of AIDS on young African Americans. In this she was really alone back then among the traditional civil rights leadership. When speaking of her colleagues in the black church, she said that the African Methodist Episcopal Church was run by deacons, all in their eighties. "It's hard for them to talk about these things," she said with a bit of insightful mischief. "They haven't thought about sex in years."

I listened, and I envied Mrs. Parks her age and her perspective. She had been involved with civil rights since working for the Montgomery Voters' League in the 1930s. After her arrest, she had worked with the NAACP and other civic organizations. To have been part of such a grand movement for so many years, to watch children, grandchildren, and great-grandchildren come into the world, to watch seeds planted in another age take root and grow and reach for the future—that is what I wanted. For me and my friends to grow old and look back across the decades.

At the end of our conversation, Mrs. Parks talked of how she had maintained her spirit and humor all those years. She said that she did her best to live optimistically and with hope, looking forward to a better day. She also spoke of the still virulent racism in the country and of the resurgence of the Ku Klux Klan. She smiled and said, "Complete happiness. I haven't reached that stage yet." As we parted, I asked her what she felt, after all these years, about what she'd done. And she said she didn't feel victory, that there was so much more to do. Then she patted me on the arm and said, "You're doing a wonderful thing, young man."

What I found in Mrs. Parks was strength and clarity of vision. I realized that to know the truth you must know pain. Hope was still essential—not a wishful, fantastic hope, but a substantive faith based in resolve and a clear-eyed acceptance of the world and ourselves and others.

I HAD COME TO Mrs. Parks for inspiration. I needed it. Eight years into the epidemic I was exhausted. Many of us were. In the early days of the disease, activists all across the country had thought that we could single-handedly stop the tragedy. The driving motivation was the belief that we could as individuals make the crucial difference. Dr. Marcus Conant believed that he could halt the epidemic by sounding an early alert, by exerting the force of his personality to organize the gay and medical community. Marin Delany created Project Inform to translate medical problems for ordinary people living with AIDS. Larry Kramer had no doubt he could force a revolution down the government's throat with his plays and the fiery lectures. Randy Shilts believed in the power of journalism to tell the truth and blow the whistle on this macabre show. We were all looking for the low door in the high wall.

By 1990, finding ourselves in the middle of what seemed an unending disease, we'd realized that no amount of individual passion or willpower would work the charm we'd expected. The obituaries were still rolling in and there was no cure or vaccine in sight, no treatment that did more than slow the inexorable progress of the disease. And the nation itself was entering a long and stamina-crushing period. There was a new desperation in the air as the virus itself, which we'd confidently thought would be routed as had polio and tuberculosis, proved to have an almost mystical resistance to every medical discovery. AZT, the "gold standard" of HIV treatment, was tarnished by reports of fearsome side effects. Compound Q seemed an almost romantic answer from the ancient East for this all too modern calamity, but then it too was found to have inspired a false hope. The dialogue of AIDS, especially on the far sides of the battle, was polarized and had spiraled into a vicious hunt for blame rather than a cure. The Reverend Phelps was whipping up hatred for homosexuals, and his sentiments were echoed in a chorus of fundamentalist cant. This venom was countered by the rising shrillness of protests from the gay side—in conspiracy theories, comparisons with the Holocaust, accusations of a murderous plot.

I can't speak for my friends, but as I looked at them and how they were handling the pressures of working within a plague, they seemed to have come to a crossroads similar to mine. Marcus Conant told me during this time that it was harder and harder to watch his patients die. Like me, he avoided the memorials. Larry Kramer, whom I watched from a distance, had grown so frustrated with the bureaucracy of GMHC that he'd broken off relations with that organization to concentrate on the guerrilla tactics of his direct-action group ACT-UP. Randy Shilts, my old friend, seemed to be closing down and in on his work. He told me of a new book he was working on that had nothing to do with AIDS— one that, it turned out, would be titled *Conduct Unbecoming,* an eviscerating exposé of the military's duplicity regarding homosexuality. Each in his own way had reached a precipice and was somehow, in this desolate landscape, moving forward with a determination that I myself was beginning to lose.

With Mike Smith gone, the details of running the NAMES Project had fallen on me, and the weight was not playing to my strength. I was good at coming up with broad strokes, themes, and organizational goals, and at persuading people to embrace those goals. But administratively, I gave myself a C-minus—a generous grade, according to some, particularly those on staff who worked on the traveling displays.

Touring the Quilt was a hugely complicated process that involved everything from recruiting host committees from often conflicting AIDS service groups, each with its own regional and local identities, to writing contracts to guarantee participation and that we'd return all moneys raised to the hometown AIDS organizations, to figuring out the logistics of shipments, to arranging for people to be there, to meeting folks at dawn to get displays together. . . . Everything had to be checked and rechecked, and each of the by now over ten thousand quilts had to be catalogued and indexed. When a problem came up, the road crew was essentially on its own. If a host chapter wanted to rework the ceremony according to its own ideas, a compromise had to be worked out on the spot. When I was there in the same town, I made the decision, but often I was not.

Within the organization, insurance had to be secured; then we had to have manuals for personal procedures, hiring and policy guidelines, budgets, cash flows, grant deadlines. . . . And all those details meant endless meetings where the subject often turned to ethics and philosophy. Our staff was diverse: people came to us with their own set of beliefs, some trying to make it a spiritual organization along the lines of a traditional religion, others more in tune with New Age spirituality. And then there was the recurring argument: Was this a gay community project, or did it serve a larger population? With each new inflow of volunteers, I had to state and restate our goal of universal accessibility and participation. And then there were questions about how we raised money. If corporate contributions were appropriate, was it acceptable to put images of the Quilt on products that were to be sold?

It was very difficult navigating through the minefields of gay politics and the general hysteria that surrounded us at the time. Ideally, I would have built a convergence among all sides, shepherding the factions through disagreements toward consensus, but with a road schedule that had me out of town every other week, diplomacy often broke down into an edict. One day I was a bastard, the next a saint—which made for hurt feelings among a sensitive staff. Once Marcel Miranda, a staff member, speaking out of a frustration I did not fathom, interrupted my planning for yet another project: "You're such a goddamn dreamer!" he said. The room went silent. There was such anger in his tone, in his words. "But, Marcel," I said, "how can you say that, standing in this room, being part of this project?"

I knew that it was time to let others step in, that the day-to-day management of a large organization was a task that had outgrown my skills. And yet between the knowing and the letting go was a fierce reluctance to trust this project—my project, the legacy of my life—to someone else. It also had to do with something deeper: the fear that by giving up, I'd be giving in to the disease.

In early January, the decision was made for me. I'd gone to Marcus and learned that my T-cells had fallen, down to four hundred. The period from infection to the onset of symptoms can be as long as ten years. And in this long corridor of illness, in which progression was downward and yet unpredictable, each number had a sinister significance. Friends had contracted pneumonia with more than four hundred T-cells. At three hundred the swarm of infections often included meningitis, and things as formerly benign as diarrhea assumed drastic proportions. Then there was wasting, with its weakness and fatigue—that hollowed look at the temples, the cheekbones a sharp prominence. Below the one hundred mark the chances of Kaposi's, blindness from cytomegalovirus, or dementia from toxoplasmosis increased exponentially.

I remember sitting by the window on Hancock Street, listening to the dry rustling of wind in the palms, looking out onto a city that I felt so much a part of and that I would quite soon, I believed, be leaving. The blue of the sky, even the warmth of the afternoon sun on my skin, had a concentrated poignancy. I missed Ricardo terribly that day—how he'd always known when to let me rant and when to tell me not to take things so seriously and when to hold me and say everything would be all right. But he was thousands of miles and a world away; gone too were Jack Caster and Scott Lago and Felix Munoz and Bobbi and Frank and Paul and . . . the list was so long then, and soon I would be on it, too.

I had done my best, and now I saw that others must take over. Certainly, the process of presenting the Quilt was in good hands. After three full displays in Washington and five tours, the NAMES Project staff and the hundreds of chapter members were armed with incredible experience. Both our board and our staff were fifty-fifty male-female, fifty-fifty gay-straight, and over a third were people of color. That was an accomplishment I was proud of; it was a team that worked well and had achieved a diversity and balance that an organization of that nature at that time in San Francisco was required to have.

The solution I presented to the NAMES Project board was three-fold. First, I'd have nothing to do with day-to-day operations, but would have a role in policy, fund-raising, and special projects, and would continue as spokesman. My salary, twenty-five thousand dollars a year, would derive from honoraria paid directly to the foundation by various schools and colleges where I spoke. Second, I wanted the new administration to assure me that Gert McMullin, Evelyn Martinez, and Debra Resnick would continue to have jobs with the organization.

And finally, I wanted to see the completion of a project I'd been planning for a permanent space for the Quilt. Some months before, we had been approached by the congregation of Trinity Methodist Church with an extraordinary offer. Originally a noble redbrick structure in San Francisco at the intersection of Noe and Market, the church building had burned and the congregation didn't have the money to rebuild. Their idea, which I worked on with Trinity's pastor, Paul Dirdak, was for the church to donate the land to the NAMES Project as a site for the Quilt and a combined service center for AIDS service agencies. In exchange the church would receive a guaranteed space for weekly services.

I thought it was an incredible opportunity. We would secure the Quilt's future, and by consolidating San Francisco's many AIDS service organizations, moneys that would have been spent on administrative costs would be available for patient care.

Within three months we'd found someone who I thought was the ideal executive director. He was Latino, and so, I thought, would be sensitive to minority concerns; he was also HIV-positive, and so, again I thought, would have a sense of urgency. And he'd agreed to all of my requirements. Within a month, though, he'd violated each agreement: he'd abandoned the Trinity project, fired Evelyn, and tried to fire me.

Was the transition simple? No. It was terribly painful. There were times over the next few years when I thought the organization would fold and my dream with it. But eventually the administrative kinks were worked out. Evelyn was rehired. And for the next six years I enjoyed the freedom to plunge into the sort of activities I thought would make a difference.

CHAPTER SIXTEEN

SPEAKING OUT, PRESSING ON

I'VE ALWAYS BEEN drawn back to places in my history, the people and the memories that have formed me. I think that has helped me tremendously, creating a bridge across generations and varying backgrounds, and out of the inevitable narrowing that life and career often demands. And now, freed of executive duties, I was able to spend more time pursuing my most personal goals.

I love being on the road, and from that year forward I was increasingly accompanying Quilt displays into areas outside the highly politicized zones of the large cities and into small towns, suburbia, and rural areas. Two of the favorite people I met while traveling were Jerry and Dolores McCall. In a wonderful way, they represented the change in how America thought of AIDS, the slow but dramatic shift in perception as AIDS went from being considered a gay disease to being seen as an American disease.

Jerry, an ex-Marine, and Dolores, a housewife, lived in a small town in East Texas. They had a close relationship with their only son, yet during their visits to Jerry Jr. in Houston—for special big-city dinners and shopping trips—conversation stayed within time-honored, courteous southern paths. Their son had friends and a job, and his ideals and values reflected their own. They didn't talk much of their son being gay, and AIDS was something in the newspapers, far away.

All that changed the day they heard that their son was in the Park Plaza Hospital. Jerry Jr. had pneumocystis pneumonia, said the doctor; he had AIDS. Dolores went up to her son's room. Jerry, tight-lipped, stalked out to the Hermann Park Rose Garden. He had played by the rules all his life, upheld those rules, and now for this horror to have busted into his well-ordered life—it was wrong; every fiber in his body fought it. And with all the frustration of a man who kept his Texas-sized emotions to himself, he began viciously kicking a path through the garden. And then he stopped: "Why am I standing out here kicking a damn rosebush when my only son is up there dying?"

The McCalls never looked back. Jerry and Dolores became heroes in their own way and embody the activism that the Quilt brought to Middle America. When Jerry Jr. died in 1988, they, like thousands of other parents across the country, felt the full brunt of homophobia and ignorance, the terrible isolation of no longer belonging to their community. They saw the averted glances and heard their names mentioned by friends in low tones of disapproving pity. Instead of retreating, they made a Quilt panel not only for their son, but for each of the twenty-eight other men in the hospital AIDS ward whom they'd visited daily through the long duration of their son's stay, and even beyond his passing. When other parents would not take the ashes of Jerry Jr.'s ward mates, their own children, Jerry and Dolores stepped forward and buried them in the McCall family plot. "They're our boys" is how Jerry puts it.

Work on the panels led the McCalls to all sorts of activities with gay and lesbian groups. They worked with the local gay pride committee on floats, were regulars at sewing bees held by the Houston Quilt chapter, and overcame their natural shyness to become spokespersons for the Quilt, leading discussions in schools about what it was like to lose their son and educating kids on AIDS prevention. Along with helping themselves, the McCalls became a beacon for many of us. They seemed so American, so solid, and if they cared, we were working our way out from the darkness.

On Father's Day 1990, the McCalls were part of the volunteer staff at a large display in San Antonio. Singled out by a belligerent newscaster as a heterosexual couple at a mostly gay and lesbian event, they suddenly found themselves with a microphone in their face and the *Live at 5* camera rolling. "How does it feel on this day of all days to be a father whose son died of AIDS? And how did he get it?" challenged the newscaster. Jerry looked him in the eye with a level gaze, put his arm around Dolores, and said, "Sir, I am a veteran of the Korean War. I was in combat. I spent months in the hospital with men fighting this disease and I saw just as much courage in that AIDS ward as I saw on the battlefield. I am proud of my son and I am proud of his friends."

The clip made the television news that night and the papers the next day. And it's stories like this that brought so many families into the Quilt.

T HE McCALLS REMINDED me very much of my own parents; they too had been able to set aside old prejudices and perceptions that had once seemed an insurmountable barrier. Though they'd long since come to realize the validity of gay liberation, particularly after the murders of George Moscone and Harvey Milk, since moving to San Francisco I had yet to visit them during the summers they ritually spent at the lake house in Omena, Michigan. On a personal level, that old house retained all the raw emotion and panic that had led me as a teenager to contemplate suicide on the rocky shore. I'd stepped back from the cold waters then and forever, but an echo of despair had remained, a faint but lingering barrier to final healing. I had some family mending of my own to do.

The previous spring, I'd been invited to speak at the Grand Rapids gay pride celebration. Wanting to connect with the audience, I spoke of my summers in Omena and of the isolation I had felt there as an adolescent. Joking with the crowd, I asked, "Is anyone here today from Leelanau County?" To my surprise, hands shot up. Through those people I got in touch with a wonderful group of gay and lesbian northern Michiganers—very surprising to me, as I remembered that time and place through a lens of thinking that I was absolutely alone.

In a wonderful gesture, uniting the new and the old, my parents hosted a party on the first Saturday of August 1990, a family reunion—of relatives as well as the extended family of my gay and lesbian friends. The old house was full of music and laughter as my new friends and relatives from my youth—cousins, neighbors—came together in celebration. My dad and I built a bonfire on the same beach where I had sat in such despair those long years ago. People stayed late, and as we sat on the beach, warmed by the fire and the quiet, we watched the shooting stars and the flickering of the northern lights in the dark sky above. As I helped my father pick up the last of the party cups and empty ashtrays, I said, "We should do this more often." He nodded, "Yes, we should have done it long ago." Later, I saw the light of my parents' room go out, then a smaller light go on, and I knew my father would be reading some thick political tome into the morning. Things were changed and yet unchanged. We had talked—not a lot, not confrontationally, but enough that those secrets that had once lain so explosively beneath the surface seemed a part of the past.

The next day, as I was driving my grandmother across the peninsula to her favorite restaurant in Leland, we began reminiscing about my grandfather, and I asked, "Do you think Papa knew I was gay?"

"No. I think he understood that you were different, but I'm sure he didn't know why."

"Could he have accepted it?"

Grandma paused, then replied carefully, "Your grandfather loved you as he loved everyone in our family. But you were his first grandchild, the only son of his only son. He was frightened for you, had dreams for you, and couldn't understand your behavior."

We drove awhile longer, Grandma looking out her window at the birch forests and cherry orchards around us.

"You know," she said, "back in '72, when it looked like you might be drafted, Blythe and I talked about it and we agreed that we would help you go to Canada if that was what it took. He hated it, but he would have supported you. He would have moved us all there."

I was shocked, trying to imagine Blythe Randolph "Casey" Jones smuggling his family across the border to Ontario. We pulled into the restaurant parking lot.

"Do you still miss him, Grandma?"

"I guess I'll always miss him. It gets easier every year, but then suddenly, out of nowhere, a smell or a sound or an old song will bring it all rushing back and it hurts as if he died this morning. Somehow, you just have to keep going."

She stopped talking and looked at me while I turned off the engine and rolled up my window. She patted my arm with her old brown hand.

"But you already knew that, didn't you? You just have to keep going."

A S THE YEAR progressed, I did keep on going, particularly into the schools and among youth groups, where AIDS was rising at an alarming rate. With governmental attempts at sex education a faltering success at best, we were able with the Quilt to educate our audience through resources many communities would otherwise have no access to. Among the gay youth I met, most had no idea of the heritage the Quilt was a part of. Though they were familiar with the outlines of the civil rights struggle, they had no idea of how linked it was with our struggle—that Bayard Rustin, Martin Luther King's trusted friend and organizer, was gay or that Malcolm X and Bobby Seale and Angela Davis showed solidarity with the gay movement. They had never heard of such pioneering groups as the Mattachine Society and the Gay

Liberation Front, let alone the men and women who'd risked their lives and livelihoods by founding those organizations in the search for freedom. A zap, so they thought, was a witty term for an act of defiance, coined recently by ACT-UP. Actually, the term was at least a quarter century old, having been commonly used to describe demonstrations by the Gay Activists Alliance in the late '60s.

The Quilt was not the forum to pass on gay and lesbian history, but I, like many others, felt it was important that the history of the struggle for gay rights be rescued even as so many of its leaders were being lost to AIDS. At this time there was a terrible toll in the activist community; some of the most brilliant leaders were dying before they'd achieved their goals or had time to pass on their skills and their contacts and accumulated wisdom. Given the dramatic changes and equally startling continuities in gay experience over the past forty years, there was a sense that history must be preserved lest it be forgotten, and so repeated.

The New Pacific Academy was a summer program created by Luke Adams, Joey Van Es-Ballestreros, and me to train the next generation of gay and lesbian activists. One hundred young people—half of them men, half women, half people of color—from all over the United States attended the monthlong session at San Francisco State University. We rented a dormitory and brought in gay and lesbian leaders and activists from different fields and with varying perspectives: modern exemplars such as Roberta Achtenberg and Urvashi Vaid as well as the original pioneers who'd begun the Mattachine Society and the Daughters of Bilitis just after World War II: Morris Kight, Harry Hay, Del Martin, Phyllis Lyon.

For many of the students, meeting those heroic men and women was their first encounter with a living, breathing activist over the age of fifty— like discovering a lost race of people. Much as I had felt years ago, they were amazed that anyone so grandmotherly as Phyllis could have taken such extraordinary risks; Harry Hay in particular seemed to confound their assumptions. He's wonderfully unorthodox in thought and dress, and is famously quoted as saying, "I think we have nothing in common with heterosexuals—except what we do in bed."

Most of the storytellers were veterans of private wars: battles with customs officials to keep a bookstore open, against a corrupt and brutal police force, with spouses and courts to retain access to their children. It was amazing to see the wonder in the young kids' faces as they listened to those radical dinosaurs describing the battles lost and won—the necessity of covert meetings in the '50s and early '60s, the blossoming of street actions in the '60s, and the victories of the '70s such as the overturning of the American Psychiatric Association's designation of homosexuality as a disease and those first awe-inspiring pride marches.

Another important point was that the immense, smothering blanket of yesterday's homophobia echoed the chill of AIDS for today's youth. So many were fearful of the future. I wanted them to know that they were not the first to face seemingly insurmountable barriers and that progress could be made even in the darkest times. I wanted them to take courage from those men and women so they could to look forward with hope while taking joy in the days they were living now.

THE SAN FRANCISCO Bay area is terrifically political, a sort of fishbowl of activism. I'd swum the currents assiduously and had built the résumé of someone who has his eye on possibly running for office, putting in time on staff jobs with Harvey Milk and then Art Agnos, and later serving on various community boards, campaigns, and the Democratic Central Committee. The upcoming 1992 election for California Assembly seemed the shot I'd been waiting for and a chance to test whatever goodwill and experience I'd accrued. And I began to seriously consider running, especially as no other gay or lesbian candidate was stepping forward. There were things I wanted very much to do and felt sure of accomplishing. In particular, I wanted to bring the perspective of a gay man to a governmental body that remained wholly heterosexual. I knew the players, knew what it took to craft a bill and carry it through the political process, and thought I had what it takes to become a legislator. And, most important, others agreed.

One of my first supporters was James Hormel, the gay philanthropist whose appointment by President Clinton as ambassador to Luxembourg was so hotly debated. After floating my candidacy in the papers and receiving a reasonably positive response, I approached Jim Hormel, and he agreed to pay for a series of private polls. The results showed that I had a good chance of winning in the soon to be reshaped Eighteenth District, an area that included the Castro and was overwhelmingly gay and lesbian. Though the seat was now held by John Burton, scion of a California political dynasty, Burton's support was soft. The studies had me beating him by a comfortable margin and running neck and neck with Willie Brown, representative for the adjacent district.

But as so often happens in the game of politics, signs of opportunity that seem promising at one moment can change their tenor the next. In my case, the odds were abruptly reversed when Burton and Brown decided to swap districts. It was one thing to run against a vulnerable incumbent like Burton, and quite another to take on Willie Brown. Longtime Speaker of the Assembly Brown had power that stretched across a broad statewide base, and, more important, he trumped my own draw on local support. I'd now be running not only against the Speaker but, by the nature of the game, against his colleagues—my friends and erstwhile allies Art Agnos, Carole Migden, Nancy Pelosi, Roberta Achtenberg. All would be forced to choose between me, a relative newcomer, and a powerful seasoned veteran who controlled party patronage and committee appointments, and who had a reputation for punishing disloyalty.

Personally, the swap was a blow to my hopes, but politically I had few quarrels with Brown—certainly not on gay issues, which he'd been strongly for since 1970 when he worked to forge the fractious gay, women's, and black movements into a coalition and wrote the law decriminalizing gay sex.

Still, the idea of a maverick candidacy was unsettling to the established order, and I heard from various friends that if I ran, it would get ugly, not only because of the disorder it would create but because of another, much deeper fissure. The problem, as the pundits reported, was the pitting of two mutually supporting stalwarts of the liberal coalition against one another—gays versus blacks. The Reverend Cecil Williams, my old friend at Glide Memorial Church, laid it out plainly. "This could get bloody real fast," he said. "I don't think that's what you're trying to do." If I ran, Willie would call in the chits he'd collected over the years, bringing in Jesse Jackson, Coretta Scott King, as well as other heavy hitters—and crush me. I had neither the intention nor the stomach for that kind of internecine fight and told him so.

Willie Brown is not one to let stray threads go unknotted, so late one afternoon I found myself summoned by Cecil to a conference room at Glide Memorial Church. There was Willie in his trademark Brioni suit, smooth as always, complimenting me on my work with the Quilt, yet very much in charge of what on the surface seemed a compromise but was in reality more akin to a coach telling a team member how the game would be played. Willie wasn't so explicit as Cecil, but his meaning was clear: we respect you; we'll support you later on, but not in this Assembly race, it's too soon. Just as blacks had waited and worked for their rise to power, so now must gays earn their place in the sun. Further, the person to carry the gay banner had already been chosen. By right of succession, that was the fourth person at the meeting, my friend Carole Migden, a lesbian activist with a long history in city politics.

It was strangely anticlimactic. We all went in knowing what would happen—that my race for Assembly was over and that I would run instead for one of the six open seats on the San Francisco Board of Supervisors. Jim Hormel was more disappointed than I was. Actually, he was annoyed, and said we had bowed out prematurely. He's really extraordinary. He comes from great wealth and privilege, but he's never been blinded by his money and cares deeply about ordinary people, particularly ordinary people with AIDS and especially ordinary gays and lesbians in the fight against discrimination.

I look back on that meeting and the ensuing race with a mixture of pride and regret. On the one hand, Willie Brown's support ensured that I would benefit from the Democratic Party's overall campaign apparatus, essential both in fund-raising and in garnering the endorsements of the labor unions and the women's groups as well as the gay and lesbian clubs. There was also the underlying satisfaction of following in Harvey's footsteps. Once I declared my candidacy for supervisor, Dick Pabich, Harvey's manager, came on board my campaign and ran it expertly. If I won, many of the changes I'd envisioned when considering my run for assemblyman would be possible, foremost among them the consolidation of the city's AIDS service organizations. Following former House Speaker Tip O'Neill's dictum that all politics is local, I studied and developed positions on everything from sewage treatment to earthquake retrofitting, AIDS, drugs, child abuse, and tenancy laws, and heard firsthand the most basic concerns motivating the strongly precinct-oriented issues of San Francisco politics. I learned quite a lot over the months, getting up at six every morning, putting on a suit and tie for an average of ten meetings a day.

And, for a brief time, I did gain traction over a wide cross-section. I'd never had a car, so I campaigned as the only candidate who actually rode the bus (even then the San Francisco bus system was a mess). And I rose not only in the polls (virtually every neighborhood council endorsed me), but in the estimation of a strikingly handsome young man named Glenn. Bright, clever, and ambitious, he came up to speak to me after a speech I'd given, and I was flattered by his praise. In retrospect, I must have had something of a false glamour for Glenn, the attraction of whatever fame floats in the wake of a candidate. Later, my potential evaporated and so did he, but for a few months he offered me companionship and affection, a welcome refuge from the public life I was leading.

But for all the positive trends, as the campaign went on there were nagging problems. The least of these, at first, was my health. Despite blood tests showing a decline in my health, at the time I declared my candidacy my only symptom was leukoplakia, kept at bay by constant gargling with mouthwash. I imagined that if anyone noticed my rather antiseptic breath, they marked it down to a rigorous hygiene—a plus in the close quarters of a retail campaign. Flip, yes, and unquestionably foolhardy, but I wasn't about to let the disease stop me in my tracks, and I remember thinking, in a spasm of vainglory, that if I was going to go out anyway, I might as well do it with a bang.

The end was hardly so resounding. In the last month, my half-hearted attempts at raising money left me with inadequate resources to get my message out, and despite my efforts to patch up a long-running feud with Bob Ross, publisher of the largest local gay weekly tabloid, I was never able to win his backing. By October the pace had begun to take a toll on my health, resulting in night sweats, fatigue, and a constant battle with diarrhea, all of which I was hiding from reporters, the electorate, friends, and Glenn.

To top it off, I received a call from my mother: Dad had prostate cancer. She could barely get the words out. I could barely take them in. That night I called Carole Migden—perhaps the best decision I made that fall. I was caught in a vice: damned if I didn't finish out the race and live up to my commitments, and damned if I didn't do what my heart told me—fly immediately home to Phoenix. Carole has a rather abrasive public persona, but she was wonderful to me that evening; sensitively and very methodically, she helped me sort out priorities. Dad came first. I'd go to my father to see exactly where things stood with him, and do the minimum to keep the campaign going.

On November 6, 1992, back in San Francisco and knowing that only by the slimmest lottery ticket's chance would I win the race for supervisor, I rented a hotel room and waited. With the TV blaring coverage in one corner, I paced between there and the window, where I could look out onto city hall and, farther on, toward the Castro—packed, I knew, with people celebrating Bill Clinton's victory, carousing as if for a carnival. Television told the story—the minicams interviewing people out in the street, all the pumping Clinton/Gore signs. It was the year of the woman. It was odd not to be in the middle of it all, an also-ran.

At one o'clock I called David Binder at city hall for the vote totals. "You've lost, Cleve," he told me.

I got the highest percentage of gay votes in any precinct, but missed the cutoff by less than two thousand votes—this in a city where twelve thousand gay men had died. Though it was not a repudiation, it certainly felt like one. And yet the sadness was mixed with relief, for on the other side of my desire was the worsening illness.

Where was Glenn in all this? He was with me in the hotel that night, asleep. I woke him up and told him I'd lost, and he managed a mumbling acknowledgment before nodding back off. He'd always carefully avoided any hint of long-term commitment; I'll give him that.

A few days later, he came to the end of whatever emotional investment he could afford. We were asleep in my apartment when suddenly he woke up screaming. I got up and held him. "What's wrong, what's wrong?" I asked. He was shaking, his T-shirt drenched in sweat, eyes darting around the room, as if searching for—what? "I just had a dream, a terrible nightmare," he said. "What? Tell me!" I pleaded. Shaking his head, covering his eyes, he yelled, "No, no." I insisted, and then he choked out, "The first sign was that you'd see a flash." "Of what?" "A flash like a bomb," he said. "That's the first sign of the symptoms, of AIDS." And then he drew away from me, slowly, and we lay there separately. The universal symbol of destruction in the '60s and '70s was the mushroom cloud—the flash of nuclear detonation. The universal symbol of death and destruction for gay men in the '90s has been AIDS. He'd dreamed I'd infected him.

Nothing more was said that night. I didn't really know what to say, and the next morning Glenn was distracted and silent. Ironically, I had a doctor's appointment that morning. As I was about to leave for Dr. Conant's, Glenn offered to give me a ride. Glenn was always one to tell cab drivers which streets to take, or when he drove himself, he went surely and quickly. But this morning he puttered, hesitant. Just as we pulled up to the doctor's office, Glenn stopped and turned to me. "Even before we started going out I knew you were HIV-positive and I didn't think it would affect my relationship with you . . ." There was a long pause. He looked away. And I said, "But?" He didn't respond. Neither one of us could look at the other. We knew it was over. I got out of the car. He drove off, and I walked into Marcus's office in tears.

Marcus is many things to me: a doctor, a friend, and someone I respect at least as much for his commitment as for his learning. But the one thing I admire more than anything else is his strength. As he came into the cubicle, and saw what I admit was a self-pitying mess, he said, with that impatient look of his, "What is it? What's wrong?" Shaking, barely able to get the words past the lump in my throat, I said, "My lover had a terrible nightmare and—" Then, in a mocking tone, he interrupted, barking out, "Let me guess. He dreamed you'd infected him! Nightmare number twenty-two-B. *Next!*"

Harsh? You bet. Like a bucket of ice water. That day I would have loved a shoulder to cry on, to be allowed to feel that my suffering was unique. But he was not going to fool me with pabulum, none of that it's-going-to-be-all-right stuff. He'd known years ago, before any of us, the implications of AIDS and had no qualms about reminding me that we both knew better. Briskly, he began to go over my blood work, detailing the counts, fact by fact. Hematocrit down, gamma globulin down, red blood cells down. When he got to the cholesterol count, he began to chuckle; my level was extraordinarily high: "Too many eggs, Cleve!" He broke into a laugh, and so did I. The threat of a heart attack seemed absurdly small potatoes.

Marcus's thick auburn hair was graying now, thinning. The lines set deep around his eyes. How many times had he teased a sad sack to laughter. How many other hundreds of men had sat on that paper-topped table, feet dangling like a child's, presenting him not only insoluble medical problems, but broken hearts. I wondered how many times a day he'd had to face a dying man and what perseverance it took to get through that endless time. I think the doctors had the hardest job in those years. I can't imagine the strength it must have taken to bear the challenge of not giving in to despair as, day in and day out, they faced all those people for whom the one recurring question was, Why go on?

ONE COLD JANUARY day, sick of myself, sick of being sick, I left the city and drove north, up to the Russian River, where I'd spent so many good times. I rambled aimlessly around the country roads for a while and, without really thinking about it, started looking for a place to live. Randy Shilts had a house there, as did Marcus and my friend Dennis Peron. Passing through the little communities alongside the river, past Rio Nido, Guerneville, and Monte Rio, I found myself in Villa Grande, a collection of vaguely Victorian homes strung out under redwoods along winding lanes that curved parallel to the bending river. There were kids playing ball in the street, ladies with blue hair tending flower gardens, a dapper old gent taking a walk, an ancient Pontiac (bed for a sleeping cat) rusting in a side yard. As I was driving down the main road I saw a For Rent sign on a small raised cottage, set just off the road in the shadow of a redwood grove. It had a path off the back porch winding through the ferns and sandy soil to a wide beach and the river, where the locals sunned and swam away the lazy summer days. Three hundred dollars later, feeling a little lightheaded over the decision, the cabin was mine—a place in the woods so very much like Omena.

Sometimes I think only a city dweller really appreciates the country. Certainly, after the pavement and stone of the city so filled with loss, the greenness of the trees, the deep blue of the water, were like a tonic to me. I had never had a home or a car, and now, as they said, it was time I got my affairs in order. I quickly settled into a routine of city weekdays and country weekends.

Back in the city, I got a call from the movie director Gus Van Sant. He was in town to work on a screenplay based on Randy's book about Harvey, *The Mayor of Castro Street*, and wanted to meet me and talk about the project. I'd never met Gus before, but had loved his film *My Own Private Idaho*. I was also thrilled that he, one of a handful of out gay directors, had taken on the project.

Gus and I met for drinks at the Elephant Walk, and we hit it off right away. So well, in fact, that when he said he would need a place to stay, I volunteered my apartment and he agreed. Gus was phenomenal to be around; he'd get a bottle of whisky and a carton of Camels and sit on the living-room floor with a laptop and write like a demon. He wrote an entire book one weekend, pounding away furiously through the night. It was a kick to answer the phone and it would be Elton John or Matt Dillon. Gus asked me who I wanted to play my role in the movie and I said River Phoenix. Smiling indulgently, he said that's what he'd been thinking, but he didn't know if River was into it. One day the phone rang and it was River and he said, "Oh, you're the guy I'm going to play in the movie." "We're going to have to get together," I said. "I've got to teach you how to kiss." He just laughed and said, "Cool."

As it turned out, Gus had never met Randy, so one evening we picked up Chinese food and went to Randy's apartment on Twin Peaks. I think Gus was a little shocked at Randy's frailty. He was very sick then and hooked up to oxygen tanks and impatient with the cords. That night at dinner, Gus sat there quietly both as audience and, so we thought at the time, as future chronicler, listening to two old soldiers talking of the past with a more vivid sense of old battles than current ones. It was a peculiar night. We both felt the end was so near and that the world we'd had a part in creating was now dead. But as the evening went on the atmosphere cheered up as Randy and I remembered our glory days. Competitively, we joshed and kidded one another. With mock grandeur I declared, "I was the first one to appear on a magazine cover! *Christopher Street*!" Not one to give an inch, Randy replied,

"Yes, but under my byline. I made you, Cleve Jones! I put you on the front page of the *Examiner*!" "I gave you your greatest subjects" was my facetious reply. It was a sentimental, ghostly evening. "Somehow," Randy said, "we're still here, but that world is just gone."

Although I felt close to Randy—we'd know each other a long time—there was always a distance. He signed my copy of *The Mayor of Castro Street* with the words "To Cleve, thanks for all you've done to nurture this dream. I have more affection and respect for you than I can possibly express. Keep being yourself. Warmly, Randy M. Shilts." I loved that he used his last name; that was so typical, as was the *warmly*.

He was intensely private, so much so that in all the years I'd known him, he'd never admitted that he too was HIV-positive. I finally told him how awkward it felt knowing that all those years when he'd listened to my worries about having HIV, he'd never said he was positive too. He told me, "You know, I never directly lied to you, I just let you believe I was negative. I had to separate things."

Before he was gay, before he was my friend, he was a journalist. That was his most important identification. He made that distinction very early in the epidemic, feeling that if it were known that he was HIV-positive, his credibility as a journalist would be compromised. We all faced it as best we could, and Randy, more than any of us, submerged himself in his professional role.

In conflict with his intensely objective stance was the bitterness he felt for the ultra-activists who criticized his chronicle of the first years of AIDS, *And the Band Played On*. It was a best-seller and hugely admired by most. But Randy caught hell in some quarters for one of the chapters in the book, "AIDSpeak Spoken Here," in which he satirized political correctness—pointing out, for example, the folly of the debate over whether to use the word *victim* as opposed to *person with AIDS*. Randy was infuriated that so much time and energy had been spent on semantics—in his view, another symptom of the lunatic cruelty surrounding the disease.

The last time we talked, and this was before he had written *Conduct Unbecoming: Gays in the Military*, I told him he had achieved more than anyone else in our generation and that I couldn't believe how little satisfaction he felt. He laughed self-deprecatingly and said, "No, Cleve, I'm very happy." And I believed him.

Knowing Randy, I think he would have enjoyed his raucous funeral at Glide Memorial Church, with the Reverend Fred Phelps protesting outside, while inside were a delegation from city hall and another from the *Chronicle*, together with hundreds more paying respects. He savored the battle, and I think he would have loved that his final act had that edge.

One afternoon, Gus was on the floor of the living room, a cloud of cigarette smoke and fast typing, when I got a call from an old friend of Ricardo's in Houston, Jackson Hicks, who later became president of the NAMES Project board. Ricardo had died, he said. Something in me clicked off. I laid down the phone and went to bed, dreaming that there had been a misunderstanding, a mistaken identity. Everyone was sorry to have goofed up. Later that day, there was a knock at the door. It was UPS with a package for me. As the delivery man handed me the package, he apologized: it had rattled as he handed it over. As I opened it up, I had to dig through crumpled newspapers, first unraveling a piece of coffee cup with a fish design on it, then a broken fish fossil, then a cracked crystal fish, then a dolphin bolo tie. Ricardo was a Pisces.

Down at the bottom the box was a letter from him explaining that his doctor had said there wasn't much time left and that he should write a will. He said he'd wanted me to have these things and that I had been named the beneficiary of his life insurance but that I shouldn't expect any money: Ricardo had paid off all his credit cards and killed himself.

He had always said that when he got sick he'd end his life. He was that afraid of the suffering. And we'd argued. I wanted him to fight and promised I would fight as long as possible. I wanted that commitment between us. It was of no use; he'd visited the Hemlock Society and made his plans long before.

One of the terrible things about Ricardo's decision was that although he was clinically sick, he'd not yet had any opportunistic infections. Had he held on for just a year, there would have been hope with the new drugs. He was in fact a victim not of the disease, but of the fear of it.

Gus was always encouraging while he was around. He had so much energy, such a huge appetite for life. Just before he moved back to Portland to work on his next film, *Even Cowgirls Get the Blues,* he left me with a final thought: "How can you give in now? You lost the election and your boyfriends, but there's a lot more you can do if you stay alive." That was the problem: I didn't think I'd live.

CHAPTER SEVENTEEN

RUNNING OUT
OF TIME

From that spring on for the next year and a half, my fight with HIV settled into a pattern that would play out as a sort of grim roller-coaster ride. For a while I'd be fine and have the energy to fly around the country and speak at displays and on campuses, and then I'd careen downward in free fall, weak with diarrhea and riddled with a fatigue so debilitating that just taking a few steps out my door would leave me breathless and shaking. On those days I'd return to bed, drifting for hours as the sun came down and another day passed.

By the summer, I'd given up the apartment in the city and was living full-time in Villa Grande. Sometimes friends would come up, but often I'd just walk down the path to the river and daydream. I'd carry a stick and envision myself as an old man. I didn't know if I was on the fast track down or a slow one, just waiting, seeing what each day would bring.

Though my travel schedule was halved by this time, I see by my date book for '93 that I still managed to speak in about twenty cities that year. I'm surprised even at that number. My memory of those times is as if through a fog, though there were patches of clarity, not always pleasant. One morning, waking up in hotel room, I had absolutely no idea where I was. Reaching frantically for the phone book, I was relieved to discover the absurdly comforting fact that I was in Dallas. That untethered feeling had happened to me many times, but always before I'd enjoyed it as a game. I'd lie there with my eyes closed, not allowing myself to cheat by searching the room for visual clues, and play Where Am I? That morning, the joke lost its humor.

Most often my trips were gratifying. By this time, the NAMES Project had begun expanding its message into one of prevention and education, through two programs: the National Interfaith Program, which brings sections of the Quilt to churches, synagogues, and other places of worship; and the National High School Quilt Program, which coordinates displays in schools in all fifty states. I loved being around the students in particular—they were so fresh and said exactly what was on their minds. At Dartmouth College, in a display cohosted by neighboring high school students, I was joined by Jonathan Mann for a display and speaking session attended by ninth- through twelfth-graders. Although I'd worked with Jonathan before, it was the first time I'd shared a podium with him, and it was an intimidating moment for me; I respected him so much I always felt rather shy in his presence. He read his entire speech from notes, letter-perfect and precise. I emoted mine. Afterward, he looked at me with what I thought was a critical gaze, and then said, "You talked an hour on the fly! Without a single note. And I have to work my speeches out word for word." He was a sweet man. Dead now, too, in the Swissair crash of 1998.

The day of the display, I stood outside the auditorium watching as the big yellow buses pulled in and the kids spilled out in a field-trip mood, giggling and teasing, swinging their backpacks. After their Quilt tour they returned somber and reflective, some of them deep in earnest conversation. At one point, one of the accompanying teachers came up to me, very agitated. Someone had written what she described as "ugly graffiti" on the signature square. Too ashamed to tell me exactly what was written, she led me over to the damaged panel. "Kill All Fags" was scrawled out in black ink. Poor woman, so embarrassed and angry at the same time. She and her friends wanted to cover it, erase it—anything to expunge this, the opposite of what they were hoping to inspire. "We're so sorry." "No," I said, "let it stay so everyone can read it." I had faith in the students, in the truth. Hate and stupidity are part of this epidemic, as was the power of healing. "I think you'll be surprised at the response." Among the subsequent messages were: "What an honor to be in the presence of so much love . . ."; "I found tears in my eyes and a lump in my throat. These were real people—they will never be just names or numbers to me anymore . . ."; "Any one of you could have been any one of my friends. I won't forget . . ."

Just as the NAMES Project was filtering out beyond the urban areas, so were many of the AIDS activists changing tactics and moving from an adversarial position against the drug companies and government, bringing the two sides into something resembling a détente, if not always a comfortable alliance. Many treatment activists began accepting funding from drug companies. With the Clinton administration's avowed decision to confront the disease head-on, the FDA opened up and the process of drug research was streamlined and expanded according to many of the activists' recommendations.

My association with the AIDS industries began with a beautiful basket of fruit and flowers—the follow-up to a phone call from Stadtlander's Pharmacy. I really didn't pay much attention to the request for an interview. No, not today, maybe in a week, I said. I was too sick at the time. So much back then was "maybe later."

But the basket and get-well note were a touching gesture, and I did call back and eventually became a columnist for the company's magazine as well as a consultant. Though consultants are notoriously overrated, I do think I gave Stadtlander's a worthwhile idea. At the time I was also working on fund-raising for the twenty-fifth anniversary of the Stonewall riots. The celebration was occurring in New York simultaneously with the Gay Games, doubly guaranteeing an audience that was perfect for Stadtlander's, which was then moving into the lucrative HIV drug market. Part of my job was to give Stadtlander's publicity ideas. The two seemed a good match. What, I said, could be better than a huge rainbow flag, paid for by Stadtlander's, to be carried in the Stonewall 25 parade before an audience of millions? How big? they asked, curious but wary. I thought a mile would be sufficient.

They loved the idea, especially when I suggested that we hire Gilbert Baker, who'd designed the original rainbow flag, to be in charge of the sewing. Stadtlander's rented a house that had been Madonna's on Fire Island late that spring, and Gilbert and I had a great time there getting the thing together.

On June 26, 1994, twenty-five years after the Stonewall riots, the International March on the United Nations to Affirm the Human Rights of Lesbian and Gay People began with the unfurling of the mile-long rainbow flag. Stretching from 37th Street to 57th Street along First Avenue, the flag proceeded north to Columbus Circle, then almost a mile through Central Park to the Great Lawn. It was a glorious display, with thousands of marchers and hundreds of thousands of participants.

I love grand parades, and Stonewall 25 was a historic occasion. The size of the crowd alone proclaimed a new day far removed from that night when a routine raid on a gay bar, so typical of those times, had ignited the modern gay rights movement. But it was also a very individual moment, for in the march and the flag was a spectacular representation of the truth and the triumph of Harvey's message: come out, you are not alone, we will stand by you.

It was heartbreaking not to be able to be there. I'd collapsed the month before—the first of the little deaths that AIDS taunts you with. I'd fainted in an airport, been revived, and, though the drive is a blur, got myself to the hospital not far from Villa Grande, or at least to a chair in the emergency room. As anyone who's had pneumonia will tell you, the least physical effort is exhausting. I could barely lift my hand and whisper to a passing nurse, "My name is Cleve Jones. I'm sure I have pneumocystis pneumonia."

From then on it was a downhill slide. After batteries of tests, the reports came back as expected: blood counts dwindling so every number was highlighted as out of normal range, T-Cells down to 120. My butt had got so boney I was now used to sitting on pillows, so it wasn't a surprise when my weight came in at thirty pounds less than three months before. But no, I would not check into the hospital. After a round of intravenous antibiotics, I drove on to Villa Grande and my new home.

My parents gave me the down payment on a two-bedroom brown clapboard house just adjacent to my rental and built snug on a corner lot, with a generous side yard shaded by redwoods. In spite of the sense that this would be my final stop, I couldn't help but love that house and immediately staked my claim with a large planting of lilies descended from those my grandfather had grown in Michigan, brought to me by my sister Elizabeth.

I was handling things ably according to my lights and felt lucky in many ways. I had insurance, help when I was really bad off, and a roof over my head. It wasn't me I worried about, it was my friends and family. I was one more burden in their already overburdened lives. When my parents came to visit, they were terrified. I'd never seen such a deep sadness in my mother's eyes. She was still dealing with my father's cancer, and now she was losing her son, too. At seventy-five. When I was little, I remember seeing her bent over the bassinet patting cool water onto my feverish baby sister, how her shoulders heaved as she silently wept, wracked with worry for her tiny, frail daughter. Now, as I lay on the couch and saw her leaning over the sink washing dishes, that image of my mother in despair came back to me. She had the long figure of the dancer she had been until tuberculosis cut her down just months after joining the Martha Graham dance school. Treatment in those days was to collapse the lung daily with a long needle inserted into the lung through the back. She'd spent years in the wards as every other person died, all of them young people. She told me during this time that the epidemic reminded her of World War II. How so many young people had died and those who'd returned were changed—*damaged* was the word she used. I was determined not to put more weight on her scarred shoulders; I would not add to the burden she carried. But I did.

Gert came up after my parents left and helped me through horrible times—held my head when I vomited, cleaned up sheets I shudder to think of. My sister Elizabeth's times with me were some of the worst. After three attempts to desensitize me to the antibiotics for pneumocystis, things had gotten worse, not better. Now, along with the painful, shallow breathing and the blackouts, I had raging red welts on my chest and arms. Elizabeth was wonderfully unfazed by it all, remarkably so. In the reverse of our childhood roles, she was now the sturdy independent one, and in that new relation we began to know each other as we never had before. She was only eight when I left home, and because of our age difference and my travels, I never got to know her until I got sick and she came to look after me. I discovered that both she and her wonderfully supportive husband, John Ettinger, a jazz violinist, were much stronger than I'd thought.

Now we'd all come to peace with one another and found strength in simply setting the record straight. Elizabeth and I remembered things at such different angles, compared stories of Omena, Nana, boyfriends. We laughed a lot—the best medicine of all.

When I was alone in the house one afternoon, the fever returned and I fell into a kind of swoon. My neighbors Ben and Marigold Hill found me in a quasi-conscious state. I remember waking up to Ben holding a cup of water to my lips: "Man, you got to drink, you're burning up." My temperature was 105. They bundled me up and drove me to the hospital. My T-cells were down to 47. It was pneumocystis again, and I was diagnosed with cytomegalovirus. They wanted to put a Hickman port in my chest—an open spigot into a vein, like a high-tech poptop valve—so that I could pump in the drug Gancyclovir a couple times a day. I remember the chill those words gave me, the implicit threat. I knew about Hickman ports. No one who'd ever had one lived much longer—a couple of months, no more. I was lucky again. I called Marcus for a second opinion, and he suggested more tests—all of which cleared me. The misdiagnosis arose from one of those sickening misunderstandings that can drive you over the edge if you let them.

Slowly, I got strong enough to go home. I remember passing out from the medication one day while I was trying to garden and waking up with my face in the begonias. As I came to, I laughed. It wasn't bitter laughter, but rather a gentle appreciation of my situation: bedridden when before I'd been such a traveler—a passport and I was off. Now I spent so much time on the bathroom floor that I kept pillows and blankets near the toilet.

Physically, the hardest part was to keep things in my stomach without getting nauseated. One day as I was curled around the toilet, breathing slowly and deeply to calm my stomach, my friend Shep came in rolling a joint. "Get that out of here," I yelled. "I've got pneumonia." I'd given up pot and alcohol years before, but Shep persisted: "You've got to get a hit down, just one." I argued, shook my head: "No, no." I took one puff and stopped vomiting. A few more and my stomach eased enough for me to get up and out of the bathroom. From then on, marijuana was part of my daily regimen, soothing my nausea as well as giving me an appetite. Not only did Shep roll the joints; he cooked up four or five different flavors of food, from sweet to sour and bland and starchy, then arranged it in small portions on a large plate. I'd just pick at it, but those little bits of nourishment were crucial.

When you're very sick, life narrows to the few essential acts that must be done. Can I get this pill in my stomach and keep it down, get calories in my body? Can I ask someone to do my laundry—again? These were the sort of questions that filled my day. I didn't have anger or intense feelings of any sort, just a dogged sense of purposefulness, a narrowing of thought and consciousness to the basic tasks of survival.

As the daily markers vanished—no coffee in the morning, no lunchtime, no flight schedule, no will to check the answering machine—time took on a strangely elastic feel: hours seemed like moments, and minutes could stretch out endlessly. Snatches of conversations, certain sharp encounters, penetrated. Ben's wife, Marigold, has a deep contralto voice. I remember it's edge cutting through: "Cleve, you've changed, you've given up. You got to change back and fight." She was right. That registered somewhere. I was the one who always said, "We're going to live! We're going to beat this thing. No suicide, no giving up. We're going to live!" I believed it, and I think a lot of people believed it, too. It helped them to know that I'd been HIV-positive all those years but that I was still out there fighting it. I wanted to give them hope. Marigold reminded me of myself, my well self, before I'd adapted to this new monotonous sickbed marathon. That kept me going—the idea that if I gave up, others would feel defeated and be demoralized. And through it all, even when I was puking blood, I held on to a compulsive, logic-refusing will to know how the story ended.

There's a note in my date book for November 14, 1993: "3TC, AZT, DDC." I was starting a new a regimen. Marcus had called a few weeks before with the first good news I'd heard in a long while. There were encouraging results with a combination of drugs; Epivir or 3TC, taken together with AZT and DDC. On his recommendation, I joined an experimental research trial. I felt nothing new the first few days of the regimen. But then, about a week later, I woke up one morning—and it did seem like morning, not just another moment in bed with a little extra light. I could feel the coolness of the sheets, hear the birds out the window. To my astonishment, I had an erection. I hadn't see one of those in a year. And I was hungry. I made a huge greasy breakfast of English muffins, butter, marmalade, eggs, and bacon. And I kept it down.

I began to recover almost immediately. Within a month my toenails began to grow back, I was putting on weight, and my skin had lost that papery look. In late January my blood tests were unbelievably good.

My T-cells had gone up to a colossal 310. There was hope now, real and tangible. I could feel it in the pulse in my fingers, the sounds in my belly. And it wasn't just me. I went online and found that many others were chatting about a similar rebound. There were side effects to be dealt with, particularly for those whose drug combination included protease inhibitors. And we were in that same old price squeeze. When AZT first came out, it cost you ten thousand dollars a year—if your insurance would cover it. Now the new cocktails, as the combination was called, were ten thousand dollars plus—a month. Whether you got the new medication depended on so many factors: where you lived, what you knew, whether you had insurance. If you lived in Mississippi or the inner city, you were most likely not part of this new wave. But there were choices now, and the linchpin of the combination therapy, 3TC, was tolerated by almost everyone. After so many years of constant struggle to press forward under impossible pressures, it seemed that now there was solid medical reason to believe we had a future.

YOU'LL SEE, MY speech will really shake them up!" Larry Kramer was talking to me over lunch in the spring of 1994. He and Dr. Anthony Fauci were to be the featured speakers at an event that seemed symbolic of the new day in AIDS—the tenth anniversary celebration of Project Inform, one of the first treatment activist groups to work with the government. It was as if two generals of a bitter war had stepped out of their bunkers and made peace. As head of the AIDS division at the National Institutes of Health, the U.S. government's lead HIV doctor, Fauci had been public enemy number one for AIDS activists and come in for some of Larry's most ferocious attacks: that he was inept, an architect of genocide, a murderer. Fauci had taken it all with a military detachment. And now, at the dawn of this new phase, they were to speak on the same panel, a metaphor for the beginning of the endgame of AIDS.

Larry and I had both got involved with AIDS at about the same time. Just months after the UPI issued its first AIDS story in 1981, he'd begun Gay Men's Health Crisis and I'd begun the Kaposi's Sarcoma Education and Research Foundation. But over the years we'd met only sporadically, and the press had characterized us as opposites. Certainly our approaches were dissimilar. He spoke with passionate fervor through ACT-UP and in the op-ed section of the *New York Times*, delivering a message that was shaped in a language and form targeted to a highly literate, mainly urban society steeped in the AIDS debate.

I organized the Quilt and spoke to the PTA and in churches. I saw my audience not as the government or politicians or the experts, though reaching them was certainly the larger goal, but as a more general spectrum of people for whom AIDS was a bewildering menace so surrounded by prejudice and fear that it had gathered all the threatening aspects of a new and complicated dark age. Through the Quilt, I wanted to clear aside the social debris and reach people on a basic level, unhindered by political agenda, sexual orientation, religious affiliation, or any of the other barriers to understanding, and speak in familiar terms, from a shared background. The message was a simple, straightforward appreciation for life, a recognition of the basic humanity of us all.

If you get down to core values, Larry and I had fought for the same goal from a common set of beliefs—primarily, that America as a whole must attack the epidemic with every amount of its might. Also, we were both HIV-positive, long-term survivors. And now he and I were to get together for lunch before the Project Inform celebration, and I was looking forward to hearing what he had to say. It seemed fitting that we were to meet in the heart of the Castro at the Patio Café, where I'd first heard the news of Harvey's murder.

Larry was not what I expected. He was warm, even sentimental, admitting over the course of lunch that it was hard to sustain anger when you were in love. Larry's lover was there, with whom, as the papers said, he was happily nesting in a country home. It was a private picture at odds with the public face.

The lion was a pussycat, and I was puzzled. He'd announced his retirement many times over the years; perhaps, I thought, he'd truly decided to lay down the cudgels. Certainly if anyone deserved a rest it was him. Larry's direst warnings had come true; he'd grasped before so many the true proportions of what was to come. And now he was excited about the speech he was to give. "I can't tell you anything, but you'll see." I had no doubt he'd deliver on his promise.

He did deliver, though not as I'd expected. The speech was a harangue, delivered with his well-rehearsed Old Testament fury, dredging up all the conspiracy theories—that AIDS was a government-directed attack, that homosexuals were the victims of a murderous plot, intentional genocide as premeditated as the Holocaust. A pointless speech. It was frustrating to watch the audience get bored and wander away.

If AIDS had taught us anything, it was that we must be true to ourselves if we are to survive. The gay community was now united not only by sexuality, but also by the shared experience of a people who'd stepped out of their individual worlds and acted in noble, selfless ways countless times. And these actions were paralleled by efforts in the straight community.

Remembering the past is necessary to individual lives as well as for the community as a whole, but how it is remembered and the lessons drawn from it are equally crucial. Larry's hyperbolic characterization shut out the rest of society as nongay nonwarriors in this battle—in a sense excluding anyone not suffering the immediate torments as nonhuman.

It was the old battle all over again, a desperate claim to own the disease as an ennobling exclusion. Larry was in a strange way reconstructing the closet, a move as misguided as trying to "de-gay" a disease that in America has had the most impact on homosexuals. Larry seemed to think we had been thrown back to a decade ago. But you don't have to look for conspiracy theories, imagining evil scientists in a secret lab creating a potion to kill homosexuals. Just look at the truth of how two presidents and the Congress ignored the disease for years and you could justifiably talk about genocide. But trying to fix blame on a single source was simply inserting a gratuitous wedge of separatism.

I thought that now, even as we dealt with the ongoing epidemic, even as we buried and would continue to bury our brothers and sisters for years on forward, we must pay attention not only to the past but to the future. There were lessons to be extracted from the epidemic, about freedom, civil rights, and personal responsibility. It was not us versus them. We had learned that they are us, and they had learned that we are them—their sons and daughters, mothers and fathers.

How was the gay community to recover and move forward with memory and identity intact? That was the question we were challenged to answer. I had not lived through sickness only to wake up to life in a bunker. That was not the end of my story, nor of the stories of those I knew. Things had changed. America had turned; like a huge ship, it was steering a truer course. And in the '96 display, all of those changes and challenges came together, not in the shadow of conspiracy but in the light of the promise to come.

CHAPTER EIGHTEEN

CULMINATION
OF A DREAM

For ten days in October 1996 at the San Francisco rail yards we filled one boxcar a day, about four thousand panels at a time, for a total of forty-three tons of fabric the size of twenty-four football fields. In Washington, D.C., the coordinators were rechecking final plans for the setup: booths for information, media check-in, first aid, new-panel check-in, as well as supplies of essentials such as the twenty thousand boxes of Kleenex, twenty-one miles of walkway fabric, and thirty-six thousand tent pegs. Twelve thousand volunteers had to be trained and prepared for the three days of the display, each of which had a theme. Friday was to be Youth Day; approximately fifty thousand children and teenagers would tour the HIV education booth and help with the unfolding. Saturday was for families, friends, and lovers, some of whom would be unfolding the panels they'd made. Sunday was the Gathering of Communities, where religious and corporate teams would join forces to unfold panels and remember congregation members and co-workers lost to AIDS. It was a huge event around which twenty-five other celebrations were to occur. We were expecting a million and a half visitors—including one very important one.

Nine years after the first display, fifteen years after the epidemic came to notice in that tiny UPI clipping, 342,000 Americans had died, and still a U.S. president had not visited the Quilt. In 1992, President Clinton said to gay people, "I have a vision and you are part of it." We'd been told that things were going to change this year at the '96 display, that the president would indeed walk among the panels. But we had learned to take this administration's promises with a degree of skepticism. Now, just three weeks before the election, we were hoping that our twenty-five acres of fabric would serve as a powerful symbol of love and remembrance, and as a reminder that much had yet to be done.

I left Villa Grande at 4 A.M. on October 6 to catch a flight to Washington and what I hoped would be the culmination of my life's work. Gert, Evelyn, Michael Bongiorni, and many others of the old team would be there. Mike Smith and I had patched up our relationship and he was once again in charge of the mechanics of setting up the display. A week previously I'd received a note from Sid and Esther Feldman. It was the tenth anniversary of their son's death. They couldn't go through another memorial but thanked me for "keeping our son's name, your friend's name, alive." It was to be a week thick with memories.

My first speech, like the entire week's events, had tremendous political and personal weight. I'd been invited to speak at a Quaker school, Sidwell Friends, where Chelsea Clinton was enrolled. Once again I spoke of how the Quilt began and how its message had changed over the years, from one of alerting America to the epidemic to education and prevention. I was disappointed Chelsea was not there, but it was great to speak in a Quaker school I'd heard of since childhood. The audience gave me a standing ovation, which the headmaster informed me only two previous speakers had received. As I was leaving with the dean, a student came running up and said, "Mr. Jones. I'm the cochair of the

Sidwell Friends gay and lesbian student group and I want to thank you for being here, because every time we have an openly gay person who's treated with respect, it makes it so much easier for all of us." She was so young, pink patches blooming on her cheeks. She turned to the dean, who smiled at her. Then she put out her hand and looked me straight in the eye. It's hard to describe how moved I was. This young woman, so brave and forthright, felt such freedom on the steps of her school, in front of the dean. This was what made everything worthwhile. "No. I want to thank you," I said to her. In 1970, when I was a sophomore in high school, the idea of a gay student organization would have been inconceivable. And there she was skipping up the steps to the school doors to rejoin her friends. So much had changed.

My next speech was at the Washington Hilton Tower. The last time I'd been there was for one of the first AIDS conferences. Representatives of international AIDS research organizations had gathered to hear President Bush outline his AIDS program. Our fears were more than justified by his meager proposals. About halfway through it the catcalls began, and then the boos started. After he stormed off the platform, he must have thought his mike was off, because we heard him snarl at an aide as he left the stage, "What is this—a gay group?" It was scientists from all over the world.

Approaching the podium, I wondered if the audience would give me the same contentious response. I was speaking to the people who worked on the front lines of survival in AIDS service organizations. Many had begun their work in the days when patients were left to die in hospital corridors pinned with a note: "Dangerous Fluids—Caution." They'd created their own programs, sat with patients through the night, persevering in a time without hope, in many cases knowing that they would soon be sick themselves. They were heroes. And yet I was going to tell them to change—that they should be working now not to help people to die but to help them to live and take advantage of the significant medical advances that had been made. The response was mixed. A few people thanked me, saying I'd helped them think in a new way about their work. Others were furious. That came as no surprise.

October 11, the first day of the display, opened to a brilliant, crisp dawn. As I walked over to the Mall at about 7 A.M., I saw cars from Texas, Connecticut, one from Nevada. The sun hovered just over the horizon; the grass was still wet with dew. Volunteers dressed in white fanned out over the mile-long expanse, and you could see the clearest line down the center, absolutely straight, connecting the Washington Monument to the Capitol dome.

Our platform was set up in front of the houses of Congress. Backstage everyone was very much in control, focused. At exactly 8 A.M. I stepped up to the microphone and began reading the list of our NAMES Project volunteers, ending with Marvin Feldman.

The vice president rolled in with full ceremony—a huge black limo, with the presidential seal on the door, preceded, flanked, and followed by security cars and watched, hawklike, by men with earphones who suddenly seemed to be everywhere. It's always a shock to see a person step out of all this armoring, but the vice president's entrance was very human. Tipper had spilled coffee all over her pants. Laughing self-deprecatingly, she swept past us into the media tent to change.

It was wonderful seeing the vice president stand up to the mike, reading names in the shadow of the Washington Monument. The panels before the Gores were among the first ones. Dating back to 1987, they included one for Dr. Tom Waddell, the Olympic decathelete who started the Gay Games. One twelve-by-twelve was a giant gold lamé square created by the Sisters of Perpetual Indulgence in honor of their members and emblazoned with "Nuns of the Above." As the Gores stepped down and onto the walkways, they found the panels of a friend from Tennessee and a neighbor in Arlington. It was hard to imagine Dan and Marilyn Quayle doing any of this.

The reading continued throughout the day with Maya Angelou, Mikhail Baryshnikov, Judith Light and Jane Alexander, Harvey Fierstein and Sally Jessy Raphael, Patti Smith, and many others—all the voices projected over the sound system, some steady, some breaking with emotion, reading the continuous litany of seventy-two thousand names in forty-two thousand quilts.

It had all been so different in 1992. I just couldn't walk out on the Quilt then; it was too much, I was so sick. I couldn't face my friends' panels, the families huddled together, the solitary men bent over the panels of friends and lovers. But there was a difference this year: in all the grief and anger, there was also hope. There were people wearing shirts and buttons with messages like "Annoy them . . . survive" and "Only men, women, and children get AIDS." Three hundred activists protested outside the White House, tossing funeral urns with ashes—including my friend Joey Van Es's—over the wrought-iron fence. Police on horseback charged in, but no arrests were made. There was an enormous amount of sorrow and grief to be expressed, but you could tell that people believed we were now going to see the end of this plague. The terrible sense of despair and isolation had lifted.

As I walked around the display, I heard bits of conversation. Someone looked around saying, "This is an outdoor cathedral." Another called it a "cry for the living, not the dead." One man spoke quietly to a friend as he gently smoothed a panel: "I'm really angry, but laying this here seems to put something at rest." Just down the aisle from him was a panel decorated with a purple Barney the dinosaur, basketball hoops, and pictures of the Lion King. "It's beautiful, it helps to heal some of the grief," said a silver-haired woman, perhaps the grandmother.

At one point I came upon one of my favorite panels, made by David Kemmeries. Written on it was: "Jac Wall is my lover. Jac Wall had AIDS. Jac Wall died. I love Jac Wall. Jac Wall is a good guy. Jac Wall made me a better person. Jac Wall could beat me in wrestling. Jac Wall loves me. Jac Wall is thoughtful. Jac Wall is great in bed. Jac Wall is intelligent. I love Jac Wall. Jac Wall is with me. Jac Wall turns me on. I miss Jac Wall. Jac Wall is faithful. Jac Wall is a natural Indian. Jac Wall is young at heart.

Jac Wall looks good naked. Jac Wall improved my life. Jac Wall is my lover. Jac Wall loves. I miss Jac Wall. I will be with you soon."

It was a week of names. At the Holocaust Museum there was a documentary detailing the atrocities committed by the Nazis, illustrated with pictures and artifacts of the survivors: Jews, homosexuals, gypsies, Seventh-Day Adventists, the old, the infirm, the mentally retarded—none had been left out.

Perhaps the rawest moments took place at new-panel check-in. Over the three days of the display, 2,195 new panels came in. After handing over the panels, donors were led over to a large canvas, where they pinned their panel alongside others, to be bound with the thousands more—a symbolic moment of transfer.

By late afternoon I was steeling myself for disappointment, thinking that the president would not show up. Far down the Mall volunteers were being instructed in the folding ceremony. "Left to right, just like a book," the leader shouted. We were preparing for the day's close and there didn't seem time for all the security to be set in place. Earlier in the year, at a display at the Rose Bowl in Pasadena, California, Marsha Scott promised me that the president and first lady would attend. She had been hired as liaison to the gay community after the infamous "glove gate," that absurd day when forty-five gay elected officials from across the country were frisked by Secret Service guards wearing blue rubber gloves. When I saw her, I shrugged: "He should have been here by now—if he's coming." "He will," she said. "Hold on." I was not at all sure he would. My friend Bob Hattoy, the first openly HIV-positive person to address a political convention, the Democratic convention in 1992 (followed by my friend Mary Fisher when she spoke to the Republican convention), had also assured me that the president would come. But his influence had dimmed after leaked comments revealed his disapproval of the Clinton administration's refusal to endorse needle exchange.

What I didn't know was that even then the Secret Service was infiltrating the crowd. I got a call to come to the main booth, and as I entered, Mike Smith winked. They had already begun roping off an area, and just afterward two unmarked vans came up the Mall and drove onto the grass. Two men stood outside and the doors opened and the president and first lady got out. There were no sirens or fanfare. He'd come quietly, as a citizen. Richard Socarides, Marsha's recent replacement as liaison, briefly introduced the president and first lady to Michael and me, and then they began walking among the panels. I remember being uncertain whether I could join them because of the intense security. Everywhere you looked there was somebody with a listening device in his ear. Finally I thought, *Fuck it,* and walked right out.

As we went from panel to panel, they talked of the power of the Quilt and how despite its vastness it was so intensely personal that one needed only look at a small section to get a sense of the lives. I showed them a number of quilts we'd selected, made by people they'd known, among them Patrick Lippert, director of MTV's Rock the Vote. They also found panels of friends on their own, including one for a man the president had jogged with the morning of his inauguration. I asked the president if he knew who Harvey Milk was. "Yes, of course," he said. I told him I'd been a student intern in his office, and briefly recounted the story of how the Quilt began. And the Clintons listened. And right then a woman with a heavy New York accent called out, "Mr. President! Thank you for being the first American president to visit the Quilt." Both the president and the first lady were taken aback. "Is that true?" asked the president. "Yes," I said, "you're the first president to come here, and every single person here knows that and is grateful you are here."

He seemed stunned, as did Hillary. Perhaps it was that famous Clinton empathy, I don't know, but he seemed to realize some of the frustration we'd felt for so many years and became very human. In that vulnerability I saw an opportunity. "Mr. President?" I asked. He turned to me slowly and said, "Yes?" Then I launched into it. "I have friends who've been sick for five years and are now getting out of bed and going to work. My friends and I are all benefiting from these new drugs, but so many people can't afford them. What we need right now is to put a lot more money into research and medication funding. We need $195 million more than you requested from Congress for the AIDS Drug Assistance Program." It was not the usual Quilt conversation, but he was receptive, saying he'd talked to people at the National Institutes of Health just that previous week "and they're usually so cautious, but right now they're optimistic." "There has been a profound change," I said. "It will save this country so much money if we can speed up that research and make these drugs available." It felt like he was really listening and understanding.

By this time we'd crossed the width of the Mall. As the van idled, the Clintons posed for photographs. I must have been a little giddy, because I congratulated them on their wedding anniversary and reminded the first lady that today was also Eleanor Roosevelt's birthday. "Give her my regards," I said. She laughed, in a restrained way, possibly annoyed. She shouldn't have been. I admired the first lady's attempt to reach her spirit and emulate her example.

After they left, I cried; it was just too much. We'd come such a long way in nine years. From a time when the president wouldn't even utter the word *AIDS* to this day when the president not only walked among the panels but found friends and was moved. So many moments of joy as well as utter depression, and it took so little—thirty minutes. And I felt we'd crossed a major hurdle. The representative of the highest office in the land had stood with us. And thank God I'd kept my head long enough to lobby for federal medications subsidies, ADAP. I'd like to think that when President Clinton pushed for an increase a month later, it had to do with his response to the Quilt. I believe he heard me, heard us all.

Just as we began the closing, one of the guys from ACT-UP came over and said, "We were all ready to heckle you and the president, but we saw you wagging your finger under his nose and we thought, 'All right! Let him go!'"

THAT EVENING THE NAMES Project Foundation President, Jackson Hicks, hosted a fund-raiser for friends of the Quilt, a wonderful group of people who'd worked long and hard over many years. Usually I skip these big dinners or, if I have to make a speech, slip out the backdoor once I'm done. But this evening was a command performance and also my birthday. As I walked over to the National Building Museum, I could see some of the old friends arriving. Ann Richards and Edward Albee were to be there; and my parents had flown in for the celebration. And just as Ann's limo pulled up, another fixture on the AIDS scene showed up—the Reverend Fred Phelps and his family from Topeka, Kansas, carrying signs saying, "Filthy Fags Burn in Hell" and "Burn the Fag Blanket."

I suppose I should have been used to his antics by then, but it wasn't until I was inside that I calmed down. My mom and dad were there and so many other people I'd worked with over the years. One of the wonderful things about that night was that for the first time, I felt inside the way people perceive me from outside. My speech wasn't dramatic; I just wanted to let them know how grateful I was to be alive and to share this life with them.

I stayed until almost everyone had left. Every table was covered in roses. I grabbed a handful and a piece of birthday cake and caught a cab. My floor at the hotel was covered in roses; my room was filled with bouquets of flowers. I took off my tuxedo and went to bed.

SATURDAY, AT DUSK, a contingent of celebrities began to gather for the candlelight march in the reception tent. Martina Navratilova, Betty Buckley, Kathy Mattea, Ali MacGraw and former umpire Dave Pallone, Candace Gingrich, Army Colonel Greta Cammermeyer, playwright Edward Albee, Representative Steve

Gunderson, RuPaul, and Mikhail Baryshnikov were all in attendance. Longtime supporters of the Quilt such as Ted Danson and Mary Steenburgen were there, as well as Judith Light. Years ago, when we were planning the first tour, Judith was the only star to show up for the press conference kickoff. She's always been there for us, as have her managers, Herb Hamsher and Jonathan Stoller, as well as her husband, Robert Desiderio.

In the crush of reporters and stars, I found myself next to Donna Shalala, the Secretary of Health and Human Services. It was yet another opportunity for me, if not a pleasant one for the secretary. I warned her that my speech that evening was going to be critical of the administration's refusal to act on needle exchange. Moving away quickly, she said, "It's not just us. It's Congress, it's Congress!"

All of a sudden the crowd began dissolving. There was a rush toward the exit in a sort of celebrity onslaught as the media clamored to snap pictures of the star of the evening, Elizabeth Taylor. At the same time, the march was beginning, and things got chaotic as reporters swarmed through the crowd of people surging for the street. In the middle of it we were all lighting our candles. Somehow in the course of this, Judith Light's hair caught on fire; looking over the melee, I could see people slapping at her flaming hair. Meantime, at the head of the march was Miss Taylor, swathed in lavender silk, sailing ahead of the pack in a golf cart. I saw her turn to the media pack chasing her; she began urging her driver to speed up so the cameras would be forced to refocus on the march and the Quilt. It was all a little anarchic. We had another wryly humorous scene when protesters attempted to break up the march by barging in with posters reading: "AIDS Is God's Answer to Gays." Marchers responded by singing "Yes, Jesus Loves Me" and then skipping and singing to a play on a line from *The Wizard of Oz:* "Faggots and bull dykes and queens, oh my!"

But the levity dissipated as we turned toward the Lincoln Memorial, an estimated 150,000 people with candles marching in unison through the night. It was an incredible feeling to walk in such a huge crowd, so many thousands of people walking side by side with their candles, everyone involved for very personal reasons, from all sections of the country, all walks of life. Eventually, the huge throng encircled the reflecting pool, spilling past either end and stretching from the Lincoln Memorial to the Washington Monument, a distance of about half a mile. You could see an immense band of flickering candlelight, which was redoubled in the reflecting pool like some monumental necklace. At the head of it all was the Lincoln Monument, rising up beyond the glittering water.

The speakers that night included twelve people, from a five-year-old to Martina Navratilova. D.C. Congresswoman Eleanor Holmes Norton said, "We also light the darkness against ignorance, homophobia, and bigotry." Judith Light, quoting Dylan Thomas, spoke beautifully and with deep emotion: "Let none of us lose our determination. 'Do not go gentle into that good night. Old age should burn and rave at close of day. Rage, rage against the dying of the light.'" Then Chaka Khan and the singing group Tony Rich Project sang "Amazing Grace," followed by performances by Kathy Mattea and Teddy Pendergrass.

While I was waiting backstage, Elizabeth Taylor's assistant came running over and asked me to speak with her. She was nervous, he explained. The fracas at the beginning had upset her. He brought me into her trailer, and I was shocked. Her eyes darted around; she was trembling, evidently terrified. I was so touched, and found her very human and still very beautiful. "These people love you," I reassured her. "Not just because you're a movie star but because you were the first movie star to stand up for AIDS, the first famous person to go public about how you'd been touched by the epidemic." That seemed to help, but then I told her that since the airport was nearby it was almost inevitable that her speech would be interrupted. "Jets above me! Loud noises, all that?" she said. Trying to be as calming as possible, I gave her a tip: as the inevitable plane went over, she should just stop talking and wave at it; everyone in the audience would understand, and no one would feel awkward. Sure enough, just after she began speaking, I heard the drone of a jet overhead and she looked up and, exactly as instructed, paused, waved at the airplane, and waited until it passed. (A few months later Gus Van Sant commented, "Cleve, you directed Elizabeth Taylor!")

She continued her speech with amazing control and urgency: "The Quilt has taught us much about how elegantly life can be lived and how quickly it can be lost. This Quilt invites us step into the private space of people's lives, where we can share in timeless, personal moments. In order to go forward we must go back, we must acknowledge the grief and the love, confront the collective pain, to achieve a hard-won sense of peace. Then and only then can we focus our energy and anger at the real enemy, the virus itself. The Quilt shows us that although we are all different, we are all the same."

She then ended the program. I'll never forget the hushed silence when the candles twinkled in the reflecting pool for one last moment as, lighting a huge torch, she asked everyone to extinguish their candle and call out aloud the name of someone they loved and remembered. "Tonight we unite all our energies into one pure and solid flame," she said. And then all 150,000 of us began singing "Amazing Grace," thousands of voices in the darkness before that monumental statue of Abraham Lincoln, golden with the light and reflected in the pool. It was an overwhelming moment.

The weekend was such a culmination of things for me. I'd always dreamed, hoped, imagined, prayed that I would live long enough to see us reach that point. And for me it all came together that weekend. The quilt that I had envisioned had accomplished what I'd dreamed of so long ago. Our organization had made the display happen and showed the world what America could do. The president participated and we finally had real, solid, rational reason to believe that the epidemic would come to an end. And to have it all happen on my birthday—a day I never expected to see—wonderful!

THE NEXT DAY, Sunday, was just amazing. I walked the length of the display I don't know how many times. At the Capitol end of the display were the early panels, most of them overtly political and angry. Many of the names were first names only, often spelled out in materials simple as a sheet. They were stark and spoke of sudden, alarming loss and frustration. As the years progressed, the panels became more a reflection of the person's life, with photos and letters attached, as well as mementos from a collection or hobby.

Each told a story. Brian Chamberlain died five days before his eleventh birthday. His panel shows a photograph of a child beneath cartoon characters; the inscription reads: "The bravest Ninja Turtle of them all." One man told me he saw himself in several of the panels: "It's like looking in a mirror." The panel for New York's lesbian and gay community center is made up of small squares: 510 names, each embroidered beautifully within an individual frame.

It was an awesome sight: hundreds of people kneeling at particular panels, hundreds of hugs being exchanged. The enormity of lives lost was palpable, but the Quilt, in its monumentality, as colorful as a rainbow, surrounded by masses of people, now gave the message of hope.

I saw so many familiar faces. Paul Hill and Joni Justin were there coordinating the readers as they had in previous displays. All of the living original staff members were there, except where was Gert? I got up and said, "We will end this display as we began it, with the names of our own." As I read the long list of Quilt volunteers and staff who'd died, I began to hear the faint chimes of Tibetan bells. It was Gert, of course, out there on the Quilt, ringing the bells she'd been given by Jack Caster, calling up his name and so many others. They were all there. As I stepped aside, Paul took the microphone and said, "This concludes the display of the AIDS Memorial Quilt. Please don't make us come back."

EPILOGUE

I JOINED THE GAY liberation movement in 1972, when
I was seventeen years old. There were no openly gay or
lesbian elected officials then, no openly gay or lesbian characters on
television, and participants in the Stonewall Day marches rarely numbered more than a few hundred. Homosexuality was illegal in almost
every state, and the bars that provided the only opportunity for gay
people to meet were harassed continually by the police. Even cities with
reputations for tolerance, like San Francisco, still ruthlessly suppressed
their homosexual citizenry. Like other veterans of those early days of
gay liberation, I am very proud of the extraordinary progress that has
been made during the past quarter century by our people and our movement.

When the AIDS epidemic began and my friends began to die, I wondered how we could possibly survive the horror of this new lethal
enemy. It seemed possible to me that our movement would be destroyed,
our few advances rolled back, and that an even deeper, more hateful homophobia would find roots and fertile soil in our country and elsewhere. Many of us feared that our brothers and sisters would return to

those closets so recently abandoned, that our tiny new community would vanish. The staggering financial cost of caring for the sick threatened to bankrupt the few community organizations we had created. Gay culture was on the verge of being wiped out and gay sexuality would be equated forever with death. Those were not irrational fears in 1982.

Instead, the opposite happened. As the virus spread among us and our friends sickened and died, gay people throughout the world dedicated their lives to the fight against AIDS. For us, the struggle against the virus was inseparable from the struggle for justice. In the face of appalling loss, our community united and, with the support of large numbers of heterosexual allies, launched the global campaign to stop HIV. In the process of organizing to fight AIDS, we discovered skills, strengths, and resources we never knew we possessed.

I am amazed by the power, diversity, and beauty of the community we have created, a community that is flourishing today in every part of the country despite continuing losses from AIDS. We have built large organizations to fight AIDS while electing hundreds of openly gay, lesbian, and bisexual public officials across the country. We have cared for the sick while fighting for custody of our children and the right to marry, hold jobs, and serve in the military. We have raised the money to fund AIDS research, education, and care while simultaneously creating film festivals, newspapers, churches, community centers, synagogues, resorts, civil rights organizations, campaign funds, theaters, youth programs, addiction services, historical societies, marching bands, political clubs, magazines, television shows, choruses, sports leagues, publishing companies, senior support groups, and thousands of other community-based organizations and businesses nationwide.

While still affected by the racial and sexual divisions of the larger society, our community has also shown a remarkable commitment to inclusion and diversity. We have worked hard to unlearn the language of racism and sexism. Women and people of color are now among the leaders of our local communities and national movement. In recent years, we have come to understand more about transgendered people, and begun to welcome the letter "T" to the alphabet soup of our organizations' names. We have begun to bridge the destructive chasms between the generations and to address the special needs of our youth and senior citizens, two groups of people that still often remain cut off from the benefits of our growing acceptance.

We have also joined our heterosexual friends and neighbors as openly queer men and women in the Democratic and Republican parties, in environmental and civil rights organizations, in labor unions and chambers of commerce, in schools and professional associations and neighborhood clubs.

These achievements are extraordinary. That they were accomplished in such a short period of time, during years in which tens of thousands of us were killed, is certainly the greatest possible testament to the power and solidarity of our united community.

I've been so lucky to have been a part of this movement and survived. The Quilt has been in thousands of schools and, through the National Interfaith Program, has forged new bonds and understanding with religions of all kinds. Internationally, we've had wonderful breakthroughs. Last year a quilt chapter was founded in Guam. And the Euro-Quilt toured Russia, appearing in St. Petersburg and Moscow in the spring of 1999. In 2000, the South African Memorial Quilt will be displayed in cities and towns from Johannesburg to Cape Town.

Last year, I was in Topeka, Kansas, where I gave a speech to a group of about three hundred people who were brave enough to walk into the hotel convention room through a barrier of the local hate mongers—the Reverend Phelps again with a dozen or so supporters holding up placards saying "AIDS is a message from God" and "Queers will burn in hell."

Phelps's hate, anyone's hate, always shakes me up, and I wondered how those I was to address were reacting. I stood in the lobby checking faces. Most of the people were midwestern looking, with more women in dresses, more men in suits, than on the coasts. Yes, they had a concentrated look, which could have been interpreted as armor against Phelps's attacks, but mostly they ignored him. And held on to bundled quilts. If they were bent or turning as they came in, it was only against the Kansas wind.

Curiously, it was other people, attending to other business at the hotel, who took offense. Two men in particular, standing near me in the lobby, scowled at Phelps and his cohort of protesters. "What are they doing here? Let's go look at the schedule . . ." Both men had on suits and ties and the sort of neat blow-dried hair that might be featured on a TV commercial. They were typical of a certain kind of American that so many in the gay movement dismiss. They looked at the hotel's events list and remarked, nonplussed, "Oh, the Topeka AIDS Network is here. That must be it." And then, in the shorthand of midwestern men, "We lost my wife's cousin, you know." A shrug and they walked away.

To me, that little shrug was huge. It was a dramatic statement of how far the Quilt's message has come and how deeply it is appreciated. The talk of divine retribution, the fearful, hateful bullshit singling out gays as a sign of the End, was dismissed in a small, eloquent gesture. The Quilt does its work.

In June 1999 I traveled to the Black Hills in South Dakota to attend a health conference and met a number of Lakota Sioux from the Cheyenne River Indian reservations. I met the Iron Lightning family, the Jumping Coyotes family, and members of a group of young students and alumni of the Takini School, established for the survivors of the Wounded Knee massacre and their descendants. One of the students in this isolated school in South Dakota had been killed by AIDS, and the other young people had made a beautiful panel for him, decorated with extraordinary beadwork and woven horsehair. Once again I was amazed at the Quilt's extraordinary ability to reach across vast geographic and human distances and to always achieve the same result, to convey the same love and power. That's what the Quilt is all about— the connection between all these different people united in one particular challenge through a message that transcends AIDS and sexual orientation, and teaches us to understand that all lives are sacred, all lives are valued.

My hope is that one day AIDS will be over and we will have to look upon all its different aspects: how it drew a country together from across cultural, ethnic, and religious divisions, and how it was, like the Holocaust, a crucible of definition. I think the Quilt will have a role in this discussion and a place in our history as memory is preserved and recreated in this symbol of our natural desire for community.

Since 1994 I have remained relatively healthy. I've had side effects from the miracle drugs—bowel problems, wasting, multiple hernias—and am now being told I'm a borderline diabetic. All these problems are minimal compared with those of many others. There are stretches when I'm feeling fine. I still have dreams of people from my past—bizarre, vivid dreams where friends who've been dead for years walk into my bedroom. I raise my head, and I can see them sitting on the bed and feel them move and notice every detail—the pores on Scott's nose, Ricardo's eyelashes. Sometimes I'll be walking down the street and I'll see someone I haven't seen in years and my heart leaps and I think, *There's Billy! Where's he been?* I start to run and hug him and say Goddamn its good to see you and then I remember. Billy's been dead for ten years. It's not Billy. And I question whether the pain, the struggle, the hate, the murders, and the disease could possibly have any redeeming value.

But there are more times when an old activist is doing the job he was born to do. Moments like when the old woman from Kentucky handed me the quilt she'd made for her son and went home to clean out his room. I felt so humble and proud at that moment that we in San Francisco, mainly young and white and gay, had found a symbol that touched this woman alone with her grief in the hills of Appalachia. She and her son, through the Quilt, were joined with all of us, men, women, and children, all across the planet who in the course of fighting this disease have come to understand what a tiny planet we inhabit and how irrevocably our lives are linked.

- -

THE NAMES

PROJECT AIDS

MEMORIAL QUILT:

1987–2000

REMEMBERING INDIVIDUALS,
CELEBRATING LIVES,
AND FIGHTING AIDS

1987

FEBRUARY

Cleve Jones and Joseph Durant make the first two fabric memorials for individuals who died of AIDS. Approximately the dimensions of a human grave (three feet by six feet), the panels commemorate Marvin Feldman and Ed Mock. They are the beginning of what will become the AIDS Memorial Quilt. Jones first had the idea for the project in November 1985 when the number of San Franciscans dead from AIDS reached one thousand.

MARCH

The *Wall Street Journal* reports that "AIDS has been cruel to Greenwich Village and its homosexuals. Young men these days get around with the help of canes or walkers. Wartime metaphors spring to people's lips."

MAY

A group of San Franciscans first meet to organize a memorial project to commemorate friends, lovers, and family members killed by AIDS. Led by gay activists Cleve Jones and Mike Smith, they use the idea of the traditional American folk art of quilting.

President Reagan mentions the word *AIDS* publicly for the first time, six years into the epidemic.

By year's end, the number of Americans who have been diagnosed with AIDS is 49,743; of those, 27,909 have died.

JUNE

NAMES Project workshop opens at 2362 Market Street in San Francisco's Castro neighborhood.

First public showing of the AIDS Memorial Quilt takes place at San Francisco City Hall. Forty Quilt sections are hung from the balcony of the mayor's office. AZT, the first drug that fights HIV, is approved by the Food and Drug Administration this month.

OCTOBER

The first display of the entire NAMES Project Memorial Quilt takes place on the National Mall in Washington, D.C. Some

1,920 memorial panels are exhibited during the March on Washington for Lesbian and Gay Rights. Attendance is estimated at 650,000.

NOVEMBER

The NAMES Project is incorporated.

DECEMBER

The Quilt is displayed in Moscone Convention Center in San Francisco as a fund-raiser for the upcoming national tour. Some 85,000 people visit over four days, with lines up to four hours long to enter the hall.

At year's end, the AIDS Memorial Quilt comprises 1,920 individual panels.

1988

JANUARY

NAMES Project receives nonprofit status from the U.S. Internal Revenue Service.

MARCH-JULY

NAMES Project volunteers take the Quilt on a twenty-one-city national tour. Lasting four months, the tour raises $500,000 for hundreds of local AIDS service organizations. Stops include Los Angeles, Phoenix, San Diego, New York, Houston, Dallas, Baltimore, Chicago, Cleveland, Detroit, Kansas City, Minneapolis, Denver, Atlanta, Provincetown, Philadelphia, Portland, New Orleans, and Boston.

MAY

In Atlanta, the first meeting of people to form future NAMES Project chapters takes place, resulting in chapters in Boston, St. Louis, New York, Atlanta, Houston and Dallas. Simon and Schuster publishes *The Quilt: Stories from the NAMES Project*.

OCTOBER

Second display of the entire Quilt in Washington, D.C., takes place on the Ellipse. Some 8,288 panels are exhibited, four times the number of the original display one year before.

One year after the March on Washington for Lesbian and Gay Rights, ACT-UP members from across the country rally in a "takeover" of the Federal Drug Administration building in D.C.

DECEMBER

First World AIDS Day is commemorated. NAMES Project participates with a number of Quilt displays around the world, including Geneva, Switzerland; London, United Kingdom; Tel Aviv, Israel; Oslo, Norway; Paris, France; San Francisco, U.S.A.; and Sydney, Australia.

At year's end, the AIDS Memorial Quilt comprises 8,288 individual panels.

1989

FEBRUARY

The AIDS Memorial Quilt is nominated for a Nobel Peace Prize by San Francisco Congresswoman Nancy Pelosi.

MARCH

Second North American tour of the Quilt opens in Salt Lake City, Utah; bringing the Quilt to nineteen cities in the United States and Canada, among them Cincinnati and Columbus, Ohio; Tampa and Miami, Florida; Birmingham, Alabama; Austin, Texas; Oklahoma City, Oklahoma; Philadelphia, Pennsylvania; Rochester, New York; Portland, Maine; and in Canada: Halifax, Toronto, Montreal, Vancouver. October. Third display of the entire Quilt in Washington, D.C., takes place, once again on the Ellipse.

JULY

A Promise to Remember, a collection of letters to the NAMES Project written by people who have made panels, is published by Avon.

DECEMBER

NAMES Project marks World AIDS Day with Quilt showings in Rome, Italy; Washington, D.C., New York, Houston, New Orleans, Miami, Los Angeles, Seattle, San Francisco.

At year's end, the AIDS Memorial Quilt comprises 10,088 individual panels.

1990

MARCH

Common Threads: Stories from the Quilt wins the Academy Award as the best feature-length documentary film of 1989.

JULY

Larry Kramer, author and activist, calls for a "Manhattan Project" to battle AIDS.

OCTOBER

Quilt displays of five thousand panels each take place simultaneously in five cities: Houston, Atlanta, Chicago, Los Angeles, and Washington, D.C. A total of 100,000 people visited the Quilt at these showings.

Ryan White, a symbol of AIDS discrimination, dies at age eighteen.

DECEMBER

At year's end, the AIDS Memorial Quilt comprises some 12,200 individual panels.

1991

FEBRUARY–MARCH

Over two hundred Quilt panels tour Ireland and Northern Ireland. Stops include County Cork, Galway, Dublin, Londonderry, and Belfast.

Mother's Voices, a group founded by five mothers who had lost a child to AIDS, is founded by Suzanne Benzer, calling themselves "ACT-UP in sheep's clothing because as mothers they were able to appeal to heterosexual politicians on the basis of their shared family values."

Ryan White funds become available; the first large federal funding of AIDS care distributed to states under the CARE Act funding for primary medical care, food, housing, and medications.

Basketball star "Magic" Johnson announces he is HIV-positive.

DECEMBER

Kimberly Bergalis dies of AIDS at the age of twenty-three.

At year's end, the AIDS Memorial Quilt comprises 14,900 individual panels.

1992

APRIL

Arthur Ashe, the former United States Open and Wimbledon tennis champion and a pioneer in sports and social issues, says that he contracted AIDS.

Magic Johnson resigns from the National Commission on AIDS, contending in a letter to President Bush that the administration had "utterly ignored" the commission's recommendations and "dropped the ball" on AIDS.

OCTOBER

Fourth display of the entire Quilt in Washington, D.C. For three days, 20,064 panels are shown on the grounds of the Washington Monument. More than 600,000 people visit the Quilt.

The International Olympic Committee moved to quell controversy by ruling that athletes with HIV, the virus that causes AIDS, are eligible to compete and opened another by again suggesting the use of blood tests to detect banned substances.

DECEMBER

At year's end, the AIDS Memorial Quilt comprises 20,800 individual panels.

1993

JANUARY

NAMES Project D.C. area chapters marches with Quilt panels in President Clinton's inaugural parade.

APRIL

Signature Squares representing each U.S. city that the Quilt has visited are displayed on the National Mall during the March on Washington for Lesbian and Gay Rights. As the one million marchers file past, new panels are turned in and pinned over the signature squares. By day's end, more new panels have been added in one day than were in the first display in 1987 (1,920 panels).

JUNE

The international AIDS conference in Berlin is described by the *New York Times* as "one of the bleakest moments in the fight against the disease since the AIDS virus was first recognized."

OCTOBER

The NIH Revitalization Act of 1993 incorporates many of the reforms suggested by activists groups such as TAG and Project Inform. The *New England Journal of Medicine* reports: "Because AIDS activists have demonstrated the degree of influence that a well-organized, highly motivated advocacy group can have, we can be certain that the empowerment of patients will be a major part of the American social landscape."

A study by the federal government finds that "Giving Addicts Clean Needles Cuts Spread of AIDS."

NOVEMBER

The World Health Organization finds that outside the United States and Western Europe, the overwhelming majority of HIV infections are transmitted through heterosexual sex.

DECEMBER

At year's end, the AIDS Memorial Quilt comprises 25,200 individual panels.

1994

JANUARY

NAMES Project begins to photograph and archive the entire AIDS Memorial Quilt as part of its archiving process and in order to display them on its Web site at www.aidsquilt.org.

To help stop the spread of HIV among America's youth, the NAMES Project Foundation begins the pilot phase of National High School Quilt Program, a project that enhances HIV prevention curricula in classrooms around the country.

The San Francisco public health department finds that nearly two-thirds of the estimated 75,000 gay men in San Francisco at the start of the epidemic in 1981 had been diagnosed with or died from AIDS.

SEPTEMBER

Black women are nearly fifteen times more likely than white women to have AIDS, while black men are five times more likely than white men to have the disease, the Centers for Disease Control and Prevention announces.

Quilt displays occur at thirty-four colleges and universities across the nation, including University of Wisconsin; University

of Alabama; Merrimac College, Massachusetts; Stetson
University of Florida.; Pennsylvania State University; University
of Rhode Island; Ohio State; Indiana State; University of
Wyoming; University of Illinois, University of Arkansas;
Notre Dame, Indiana; Marin College, California; Morris
College, New Jersey; Goucher College, Maryland.

DECEMBER

In this year alone, forty NAMES Project chapters around
the United States sponsored nearly eight hundred displays;
sections of the Quilt are viewed by an estimated 800,000
people.

At year's end, the AIDS Memorial Quilt comprises 28,270
individual panels.

1995

JANUARY

NAMES Project Foundation begins the National Interfaith Program, which brings sections of the Quilt to churches, synagogues,
and other places of worship and to spiritual communities around
the country.

JUNE

NAMES Project displays seven hundred Quilt panels from
thirty-five countries in San Francisco as part of events commemorating the fiftieth anniversary of the founding of the United
Nations.

The Twelfth International AIDS Candlelight Memorial and
Mobilization is observed in 250 cities in forty-five nations.

International displays include Montreal, Canada; Taipei, Taiwan; Chiang Mai, Thailand; and Barcelona, Spain.

DECEMBER

AIDS Memorial Quilt goes online with launch of NAMES Project Foundation's World Wide Web site (http://www.aidsquilt.org). Each month, the site receives some 200,000 hits, and is seen by approximately fifteen thousand new visitors.

The *New York Times* changes its policy against allowing obituaries to use the word *lover* in a death notice.

At year's end, the AIDS Memorial Quilt comprises 31,600 individual panels.

1996

JANUARY–SEPTEMBER

Sections of the Quilt are shown in Saks Fifth Avenue stores in sixty locations around the United States, including New York City's flagship store, Boca Raton, Las Vegas, San Francisco, White Plains, Pittsburgh, and Cincinnati.

SEPTEMBER

Simon and Schuster releases the book *Always Remember,* a retrospective of memorial panels created by and for a spectrum of international fashion designers. NAMES Project Foundation reaches out to millions of people around the country with launch of its America Online site (keyword: NAMES Project).

OCTOBER

Fifth display of the entire NAMES Project Memorial Quilt in Washington, D.C. More than 40,000 panels cover the National

Mall from the Washington Monument to the grounds of the U.S. Capitol. President and Mrs. Clinton, Vice President and Mrs. Gore, and 1.2 million others visit the display in the largest AIDS awareness event in history.

Despite its vast size, the Quilt still represented only about one in eight Americans who have died of AIDS.

DECEMBER

NAMES Project Foundation observes World AIDS Day (December 1) with nearly two hundred Quilt displays around the world and the first online display of the Quilt on the NAMES Project Foundation's America Online site (keyword: NAMES Project).

This year the number of panels received by the NAMES Project reaches a high of 4,904. (The number of panels received falls in subsequent years as the new therapies save lives: 1,194 in 1997; 1,036 in 1998; 657 in 1999.)

At year's end, the AIDS Memorial Quilt comprises 41,000 individual panels.

1997

JANUARY

NAMES Project partners with the Until There's A Cure Foundation to hold displays of the Quilt in three high schools in every state in 1997.

FEBRUARY

Federal Centers for Disease Control and Prevention announce a 12 percent drop nationwide in the number of AIDS deaths occurring in the first half of 1996, the first decline in the AIDS death toll noted since the epidemic began sixteen years ago. The NAMES Project partners with the AIDS education and advocacy group The Balm In Gilead to bring sections of the Quilt to African-American churches around the country.

Observing Black History Month, the NAMES Project Foundation holds an online Quilt display on its World Wide Web site that features panels made for African Americans who have died from AIDS.

MARCH

Observing National Women's History Month, the NAMES Project Foundation presents a month-long online Quilt display on its World Wide Web site featuring panels made for women who have died from AIDS.

DECEMBER

The AIDS Memorial Quilt currently comprises 42,194 individual panels. Since the epidemic began in 1981, more than 580,000 Americans have been diagnosed with AIDS; of those, 343,000 have died.

International displays include Quilt showings at member chapters in Ho Chi Minh City, Vietnam, and Havana, Cuba. Other major displays include Fort Worth, Fort Lauderdale, Miami, Atlanta, Houston, San Antonio, and Seattle.

1998

Expansion takes place at international level, with new affiliates in Europe and Africa and Asia. Introduction of on-site HIV-test counseling and prevention awareness.

APRIL

The NAMES Project board of directors passes a resolution to build a center for the Quilt in the Washington, D.C., area and institutes planning seminars for Quilt chapters on preserving and conserving Quilt panels.

DECEMBER

Seventy percent of the entire Quilt is sent around the United States for displays in forty-eight states commemorating World AIDS Day.

Five students accompany the Quilt for a Hong Kong Quilt exchange highlighting prevention and education for chapter affiliate Teen AIDS Hong Kong.

At the end of this year, the Quilt weighs over fifty tons. Over the course of this year, all these panels were moved in and out of the warehouse and to displays, more than ever done before at any one time with exceptions of full displays in D.C.

At year's end, the AIDS Memorial Quilt comprises 43,229 individual panels.

1999

The City of San Francisco officially recognizes original home of the NAMES Project at 2362 Market Street as a historic site, with a brass plaque and a bench.

OCTOBER

The Historically Black Colleges and Universities Tour begins with keynote speaker Coretta Scott King. The national Quilt tour will include large displays of the Quilt together with HIV prevention education programs, on-site testing and counseling, treatment information, and referrals to local service providers. It is partnered with the United Negro College Fund, the National Association for Equal Opportunity in Higher Education, the National Council of Negro Women, the National Quilting Association, as well as national sororities and fraternities and local AIDS service providers.

San Francisco Bay Area Quilt Display first display in San Francisco in nearly ten years, bringing it home, making it real. At the Concourse Exhibition Center, first display on the Internet at www.aidsquilt.org.

DECEMBER

World AIDS Day Display at the Parliament of World Religions in Cape Town, South Africa, is part of a broader effort in South Africa to spread awareness, encourage Quilt-making and promote HIV prevention education and outreach in a country where over 14 percent of the country's 32 million people are infected with HIV. Working with Archbishop Tutu's office, the Harvard AIDS Institute, the NAACP, and other organizations and individuals in South Africa and the United States, volunteers from NAMES Project Chapters throughout the United States will work with their South African counterparts to organize Quilt-making and Quilt displays in townships and rural areas across South Africa.

At year's end, the AIDS Memorial Quilt comprises 44,429 individual panels.

2000

SPRING

The Historically Black Colleges and Universities Tour, funded in part by a grant from The Ford Foundation, continues on campuses in the southeastern United States, including Morehouse College,

Morehouse School of Medicine, Spelman College, Morris Brown College, The Interdenominational Theological Center, and Clark Atlanta University. The tour will also include World AIDS Day displays at Howard University in Washington, Hampton University, as well as campuses in Alabama, Arkansas, Florida, Louisiana, Mississippi, Missouri, North Carolina, Tennessee, and Texas. In all, the program expects to reach over 240,000 young African Americans on HBCU campuses and in surrounding communities.

APRIL

Quilt display at the Millennium March on Washington (April 30); volunteers from across the nation will organize to display sections of the Quilt at the march, the sixth display in D.C.

Over fifty national chapters and thirty-seven international affiliates and growing. Durbin South Africa International AIDS Conference Quilt display.

DECEMBER

The AIDS Memorial Quilt is the image presented on World AIDS Day in hundreds of quilt displays in museums, churches, and schools around the world, commemorating the people who've died from AIDS and those who continue the fight.

At year's end, the AIDS Memorial Quilt continues to grow.

- -

HOW TO MAKE
A QUILT PANEL

WHAT IS A PANEL MAKER?

A panel maker is someone who has made a panel for the AIDS Memorial Quilt. Anyone can be a panel maker: panels are made by family members, friends, lovers, co-workers, and others, working in groups or individually. They are young and old; rich and poor; gay, straight, and bisexual. They are as diverse as those affected by the epidemic, as richly unique as each panel in the Quilt itself. All it takes is fabric, a little imagination, and the desire to remember and pay tribute to a special person who has died of AIDS.

HOW TO MAKE A PANEL FOR
THE AIDS MEMORIAL QUILT

All kinds of people have made panels for the Quilt, in a variety of colors, fabrics, and styles. You don't have to be an artist or a sewing expert to create a moving personal tribute. It doesn't matter if you use paint or fine needlework; any remembrance is appropriate. You may choose to create a panel privately as a personal memorial to someone you've loved, but we encourage you to follow the traditions of old-fashioned sewing and quilting bees by including friends, family, and co-workers in the process.

To create a panel for the Quilt, just follow these steps:

1. Design the panel.

Include the name of the friend or loved one you are remembering. Feel free to include additional information such as the dates of birth and death, and a hometown. Please limit each panel to one individual.

2. Choose your materials.

Remember that the Quilt is folded and unfolded many times, so durability is crucial. Since glue deteriorates with time, it is best to sew things to the panel.

A medium-weight, nonstretch fabric such as a cotton duck or poplin works best.

Your design can be vertical or horizontal, but the finished, hemmed panel must be three feet by six feet (90 cm x 180 cm)—no more and no less! When you cut the fabric, leave an extra two to three inches on each side for a hem. If you can't hem it yourself, we'll do it for you. Batting for the panels is not necessary, but backing is recommended. Backing helps to keep panels clean when they are laid out on the ground. It also helps the fabric retain its shape.

3. Create the panel.

To construct your panel, you might want to use some of the following techniques:

APPLIQUÉ Sew fabric, letters, and small mementos onto the background fabric. Do not rely on glue; it won't last.

PAINT Brush on textile paint or colorfast dye, or use an indelible ink pen. Please don't use "puffy" paint; it's too sticky.

STENCIL Trace your design onto the fabric with a pencil, lift the stencil, then use a brush to apply textile paint or indelible markers.

COLLAGE Make sure that whatever materials you add to the panel won't tear the fabric (avoid glass and sequins for this reason), and be sure to avoid very bulky objects.

PHOTOS The best way to include photos or letters is to photocopy them onto iron-on transfers, iron them onto 100 percent cotton fabric, and sew that fabric to the panel. You may also put the photo in clear plastic vinyl and sew it to the panel (off-center so it avoids the fold).

4. Write a letter.

Please take the time to write a one- or two-page letter about the person you've remembered. The letter might include your relationship to him/her, how he or she would like to be remembered, and a favorite memory. If possible, please send us a photograph of the person along with the letter for our archives.

If you are able, please include a donation to help pay for the cost of adding your panel to the Quilt. The NAMES Project Foundation depends on the support of panel makers to preserve the Quilt and keep it on display. A gift of any amount is welcome. Gifts of $250 or more will be acknowledged in our annual report.

5. Turn it in.

Once your panel is completed, there are several ways to turn it in to the NAMES Project so that it becomes a part of the AIDS Memorial Quilt. You can send it to the NAMES Project Foundation. Be sure to send it by registered mail or with a carrier that will track your package, such as UPS or Federal Express. You can bring it to a Quilt display;

please be sure to contact the local display host for information on the procedure they are using for collecting new panels. Or you can bring it to one of our local chapters, where your panel will stay in the community for up to three months, being used for education and outreach, and then will be sent to the Foundation to be sewn into the Quilt.

Important: Be sure to fill out the panel maker information card and include it with your panel. This information helps us to stay in touch with you and keep you up to date on your panel and the Quilt.

HOW YOUR PANEL BECOMES PART OF THE QUILT

After your panel arrives at our main offices in San Francisco, it is carefully logged and examined for durability. Sometimes a panel may require hemming to adjust for size, reinforcement, or minor repairs. Next, it is sorted geographically by region. When eight panels from the same region are collected, they are sewn together to form a twelve-foot square. This is the basic building block of the Quilt and is known as a twelve-by-twelve.

Once sewn, each twelve-by-twelve is edged in canvas and given a number, making it possible to keep track of that block. All the panel, panel maker, and numerical information is then stored in our huge Quilt database. Once this happens, you are sent information on the block number your panel is in as well as how to request your panel for displays of the Quilt and a current display schedule.

The entire process, from receiving your panel to incorporating it into a twelve-by-twelve in the AIDS Memorial Quilt, takes between three and four months.

The NAMES Project Foundation
310 Townsend Street, Suite 310
San Francisco, CA 94107
tel.: 415.882.5500
fax: 415.882.6200

FACTS ABOUT
THE AIDS MEMORIAL
QUILT

QUILTING AS A TRADITION

Many cultures around the world have traditions of fabric arts. The AIDS Memorial Quilt is based upon the American tradition of quilting. In the past, neighbors and relatives would gather in groups to sew old scraps of fabric together to make blankets. These blankets, called *quilts,* were beautiful works of art that also provided warmth and comfort.

Working together made people feel part of a community, giving them the chance to tell stories, trade gossip, sing songs, and enjoy each other's company as they sewed. Today, as people gather together to make panels for the AIDS Memorial Quilt, this tradition gives comfort in a time of grief.

SOME OF THE MATERIALS USED IN THE QUILT

Included in the Quilt are, among other things, afghans, Barbie dolls, bubble wrap, burlap, buttons, car keys, carpet, Champagne glasses, condoms, corduroy, corsets, cowboy boots, cremation ashes, credit cards, curtains, dresses, feather boas, first-place ribbons, fishnet hose, flags, fur, gloves, hats, human hair, jeans, jewelry, jockstraps, lace, lamé, leather, Legos, love letters, Mardi Gras masks, merit badges, mink, motorcycle jackets, needlepoint, paintings, pearls, photographs, pins, plastic, quartz crystals, racing silks, records, rhinestones, sequins, shirts, silk flowers, studs, stuffed animals, suede, taffeta, tennis shoes, vinyl, and wedding rings.

FACTS ABOUT THE NATIONAL HIGH SCHOOL QUILT PROGRAM

In the two-semester pilot phase of the program, over eighty-five thousand high school students saw the Quilt in their schools. Since 1994, over 470 schools in towns all over the United States have participated in the program, including Ketchikan, Alaska; Montgomery, Alabama; Walla Walla, Washington; Hiram, Maine; Mediapolis, Iowa; Seth, West Virginia; Thibodaux, Louisiana; Miami, Florida; Hartford, Connecticut; Bronx, New York; Memphis, Tennessee; Tuba City, Arizona; Spearfish, South Dakota; Austin, Texas; Cambridge, Massachusetts; Corydon, Indiana; and Meriden, New Hampshire.

The NAMES Project Foundation is represented across the United States by over fifty chapters, which together form one of the largest grassroots volunteer organizations in the country. Each of these chapters is a partner with the Foundation, working in its community to increase awareness of AIDS, encourage HIV-prevention education, inspire local action, facilitate panel making, raise money for local AIDS organizations, and help bring an end to the AIDS epidemic.

Organizations in more than thirty-five countries, from Argentina and Ireland to Thailand and Zambia, have adapted the idea of the Quilt to their own cultural traditions and use the Quilt in their work against HIV and AIDS. Through their efforts, they have created a rich, multicultural tapestry of the lives cut short by the global pandemic.

QUILT FACTS

Number of visitors to the Quilt: 12,542,000

Number of panels in the Quilt: over 44,400

Number of names on the Quilt: over 80,466

Equivalent number of football fields: 16 not including the walkway between sections; 25 with the walkway

Miles of fabric: 48.75, if all of the three-by-six panels were laid end to end—a distance greater than that between Providence, Rhode Island, and Boston, Massachusetts

Total weight: 53 tons

Volunteer hours (as of fiscal year 1997): 1,229,540

NAMES Project chapters: 53

International affiliates: 38

Countries contributing panels: 35. They are Argentina, Aruba, Australia, Belgium, Brazil, Canada, Chile, the Dominican Republic, England, France, Germany, Guatemala, Hong Kong, Ireland, Israel, Italy, Japan, Mexico, the Netherlands, New Zealand, Northern Ireland, Norway, the Philippines, Poland, Romania, Russia, South Africa, Spain, Suriname, Sweden, Switzerland, Taiwan, Uganda, the United States (including all fifty states, Guam, and Puerto Rico), and Zambia.

ACKNOWLEDGMENTS

O OVER THE YEARS, I have been privileged to know and work with thousands of extraordinary women and men. Many people and events of great importance to my life do not appear within these pages. Likewise, it would be impossible for me to list here the names of all those who have enriched my life with their friendship or inspired me by their work. I sincerely hope that no one will feel slighted by their omission.

This book would not have been completed without the persistent encouragement of Bob Young, who first suggested that I collaborate with his partner, Jeff Dawson. I am equally grateful to Jeff for his patience, skill, and dedication as he transcribed, edited, and transformed hundreds of hours of taped interviews to create the book you hold in your hands.

I want to especially thank the men, women, and children who created the Quilt—NAMES Project National Office and Chapter volunteers, staff, board members, sponsors, contributors, and, most important, the tens of thousands who created and contributed Quilt panels, entrusting us with the names of their children, parents, spouses, lovers, family members, and friends.

Mike Smith was the first person to embrace my vision of the Quilt. As cofounder of the NAMES Project, Mike deserves enormous credit for his role in charting our course for those first, most difficult years.

The first Quilt volunteers, those who took a dream and made it real, included: Gert McMullin, Jack Caster, Debra Resnik, Evelyn Martinez, Ron Cordova, Joey Van-Es Ballestreros, Scott Lago, Sandy O'Rourke, Danny Sauro, Lance Henderson, Larkin Mayo, Garth Wall, Nancy Katz, Jeannette Koijane, Marcus Faigle, Jeff Bosacki, Jeff Thur, Lisa Heft, Paul Hill, Joanie Juster, Danny Linden, Michael Bongiorni, Beth and Russ Milham, Rebecca Lapere, Leslie Ewing, Rick Solomon, Tom Panagiotaros, Nancy Blanford, Christopher Priestly, Rod Shelnutt, Jenx Jenkins, Stephen Pullis, Geoffrey Wooley, Libby Denebeim, Kim Corsaro, David Thompson, David Gere, Jimmy Vinson, Norman Polse, Gerard Donelan, Sky Renfrew, Shadow Morten, Jeff Kuball, Jim Poche, Ron Grey, Terry Blankenship, Cliff Lowe, Rob Pettipas, Dan Carmell, Christopher McKenna, Ron Henderson, Steve Newberger, Jok Church, Michael Bento, Rob Morse, Cindy Ruskin, Pat Cool, Billy Kempf, Sharon Tracy, Charles Sublett, Max Navalta, Michael and Ford Merrill, Steve Abeyta, Jerry and Dolores McCall, Wes Cronk, James Bryson, Miller Griffith, Greg Stull, Mirielle Key, Bonnie Ulmer, Elaine Mack and the Mack family, Jackson Hicks, David L. Jackson, Geppitto Apadaca, Ben Carlson, Brian Potts, Nikos Kaflakis, Brad Shearer, Paul Sporer, Doug Frank, David Kaplan, Marty Kahn, Bina Frank, Ma Jaya Bhagavatti, Derrick Jaganath Edmundson, Frank Palmieri, Cathy Robinson, Richard Rosenkranz, Gurga Mayee Mitchell, Brad Gammel, Chandra Davi Kantor, Lucy Horn, Kumari Mullin, Troy Garber, Suzanne Gautier, Jerry Suarez, Rob Epstein, Jeffrey Freidman, Linda Guinee, Phil Seigal, Keith Wetmore, Rachel Krevans, Barbara Cymrot, Dafna Wu, Deborah Zemke, Jan Mauro, Julia Sawabini, Trish Drew, Dale Melsness, Michael Cover, Tim from Boston, Rick Solomon, Steve Sams, Roberto Esteves, Sally Gearhardt, Michael Berg, Richard Hutson, James Goodfellow, Charles Thompson, Carolyn Reidy,

Michael Barrett, Claudio Schnier, Leah Sample, Harry Ray, Clarissa Crabtree, Lynn Penny, Deborah Steckroth, and many others.

Also present and past NAMES Project staff members: Rachel Brewer, Thom Weyand, Skeeter Buck, Heather Reisz, Fred Tse, Stephen Mackay, Tisa Bryant, Gene Yuson, Alexandre Petrakis, David Lemos, Lori Davis, Jaime Cortez, Ragene Brown, George Renz, Gary Pinley, Claire Banajeree, Philisha Montgomery, Kathleen Dederian, Eric Christiansen, Susan Hall, Tonisa Clardy, Michael Frederickson, Martha Fitzgerald, Ifeoma Udon, Linda Hunter, Leonard Riley, Giselle Ibanez, David Lueck, Scott Croft, Michael Carr, Michael Mack, Judith Federico, Miguel Gualip, Judy Blake, Mikal Gilmore, Nasus Aransu, David Varella, Ferdinand Dollero, Aishe Berger, Georgette Brisson, Kate Carpenter, Juan-Carlos Castano, Fred Dolaway, Tai Kam, Kelly Lee, Dr. Tim Wolfred, Greg Lugliani, Mike Moreno, Judy Noddin, David Ortman, G. Scott Osten, Doris Owyang, Laura Perez, James Robertson, Karen Rouse, Tim Speese, Scott Williams, Sue Martin, Lance Henderson, Sue Baelon, Cathy Johnson, Danny Linden, Lisa Catapano, Jim Fox, Pam Nishikawa, Blaine Cunningham, Corey Mees, Susan Fleming, Anne Garwood, Julie Doherty, Marcel Miranda, Mike McCormack, Alphonso Ortiz, Mike Brown, Paul Margolis, Lisa Wade, Scott Miller, Ken Borg, Paula Harris, Brian Holland, Rhett Stecklein, Christina Sundley, Tom Herndon, Marsha Bratcher, Kimberly Webster Moore, Dimitri Mosheyannis, and my good friend Eric Hallquist.

I want to also thank my family: my parents, Austin and Marion; my sister and brother-in-law, Elizabeth and John Ettinger; my grandparents; my aunts and uncles; and all my cousins, second cousins, and other kin from the Jones, Rupert, Evans, Mulligan, and Hatton branches of our family. Also the families of my friends Marvin Feldman and Scott Rempel.

During my own struggle with HIV disease, I have relied on the advice and care of many medical professionals and activists. Among them I am particularly endebted to Dr. Marcus Conant, Dr. Donald

ACKNOWLEDGMENTS

Northfelt, Dr. Marge Poscher, Dr. Monica Minguillon, Dr. Steven Hubbard, Dr. Paul Volberding, Dr. David Ho, Dr. Marty Markowitz, Dr. Richard Bland, Terry Winters, R.N., pharmacist Sabahat Imran, Jonathon Mann, *AIDS Treatment News* publisher John James, Foundation for AIDS and Immune Research founder Linda Grinberg, and Project Inform founder Martin Delaney.

I am deeply grateful to Andy Ilves, Executive Director of the NAMES Project Foundation; and Edward Gatta, President of the NAMES Project Foundation Board of Directors; as well as the current members of the Board of Directors and staff for their continuing efforts in the fight against AIDS.

I am inspired every day by Deborah Scheer and her son, Dillon McDevitt.

And finally, Damon Lance Jacobs, for reasons he knows well.

Cleve Jones

S PECIAL THANKS TO the inspiration of this book and so much more, Cleve Jones. I'd also like to thank the extraordinary gatekeepers of the NAMES Project Gert McMullin and Michael Bongiorni for their immense help; Dave and Marsha Pelzer for their unwavering enthusiasm and support for this project; Brian Tart for his invaluable professional advice; my friends Bo Hewitt, Bill and Carolyn Dowd; my parents, Janice and Gerald; my brothers, Joel and John; and my illustrious editor, David Hennessy.

And lastly, in memoriam for all they gave in their too brief time: Jamie Burks, Steve Straub, Billy Garbe, Vincent Leone, Buddy Powell, Brant Dame, Mauricio Arana, Bobby Bowers, Jason Wigley, Del Jewell, Stephen Jamail. I miss you all.

This book is dedicated to Bob Young and Sport and Duker.

Jeff Dawson

INDEX